THE 5 PRACTICES OF HIGHLY RESILIENT PEOPLE

THE 5 PRACTICES OF HIGHLY RESILIENT PEOPLE

WHY SOME FLOURISH WHEN OTHERS FOLD

TARYN MARIE STEJSKAL, PhD

NEW YORK

Cover design by Terri Sirma

Cover image: Ginkgo leaf © ilonitta/Shutterstock

Hachette Go, an imprint of Hachette Books
Hachette Book Group
1290 Avenue of the Americas
New York, NY 10104
HachetteGo.com
Facebook.com/HachetteGo
Instagram.com/HachetteGo

First Edition: April 2023

Hachette Books is a division of Hachette Book Group, Inc.

Library of Congress Cataloging-in-Publication Data has been applied for.

ISBNs: 978-0-306-83161-4 (hardcover); 978-0-306-83163-8 (ebook)

Printed in the United States of America

LSC-C

Printing 3, 2024

For the people who helped me understand resilience: mothers in rural Maryland, survivors of neurological injuries and their family members, along with every person I had the honor to interview. Thank you for trusting me and teaching me.

For all of us, remember to rest, because rest is important. Then, keep going.

CONTENTS

INTRODUCTION

Resilience—The Essence of Being Human

With the significant challenges we've all encountered during the past several years, the need for and power of resilience has become an immense point of interest. Many of us are tired of talking about the pandemic, and although its impact continues, our day-to-day experiences are compounded by significant social change, political division, gun violence and mass shootings, unpredictable and extreme weather, an enhanced need for support for mental health and well-being, and general unrest.

Have you felt an increase in feelings like uneasiness, stress, strain, or sadness? I certainly have. The good news is, if you have, you're not alone. There has been an uptick in emotions that feel negative, gloomy, and pessimistic. Many people think it's directly related to the pandemic, but it isn't. The pandemic accelerated this trend, but it's not solely responsible for our feelings of frustration, unhappiness, and worry. The experience of emotions that feel negative have been on the rise for over a decade. Long before the pandemic showed up.

It's no surprise so many feel this way. We are all searching for guidance about how to adjust to so much change and uncertainty, to keep functioning. We ask ourselves and others, "How do I make sense of this? How do I process everything that is happening when it all seems so overwhelming? How do I lead my people? How do I parent my children? How do we create a sense of normalcy when nothing feels normal? What does 'normal' mean, anyway? How do I sustain myself when life so often feels unsustainable?"

Being resilient is more important now than ever.

Resilience is much more than enduring adversity and returning to life as it was "before." Many aspects of human development are additive tools, such as shifting our mind-set or learning breathing techniques. Yet, resilience is a multiplier. People that demonstrate greater resilience enhance themselves and those around them, their families, teams, and communities. When you increase your resilience, you multiply the development and growth of those around you by role modeling how to solve problems, navigate challenges, and reemerge after setbacks, and through your actions, you teach others how to do that same.

Resilience is not a special skill you need to acquire. Resilience isn't something you go out and find, because by virtue of facing challenge, resilience has already found you. You're already resilient. Think about it. You've survived every loss, hardship, disappointment, and rejection you've ever faced. And you're still here. How? Because resilience has been the fabric of your human existence, your essence since your conception. This book won't teach you to be resilient; it'll teach you the key practices that will allow you to harness and amplify your resilience to an even greater degree.

Some people tell me that they dream of a day when they will never have to be resilient again. They feel exhausted by the efforts required to be resilient. I, too, have reached the edge of my mental, physical, and emotional capacity. But not because of resilience. The experience of facing a continual onslaught of challenge, change, and complexity is stressful. The circumstances of processing war, significant changes in governmental laws and access to health care, along with addressing persisting inequities and social justice, to name a few, are overwhelming, to say the least. It's not resilience's fault that we feel this way. Resilience isn't exhausting or excruciating. Resilience is the treatment for what ails you, not the problem. Challenge isn't going away. So, you're likely going to get to demonstrate your resilience for years to come. The Five Practices of Highly Resilient People is the playbook that allows you to tap into your resilience to a greater degree, the skills that guard against stress, exhaustion, and burnout. These practices and tools aren't detractors that derail your ability to cope. Quite the opposite. Resilience promotes a more positive mind-set and enhances your mental health.

My desire to understand the commonalities that allow us to effectively face challenge, which would lead to The Five Practices of Highly Resilient People two decades later, began while I was in graduate school, and later, as a neuropsychology fellow. After I completed my fellowship, my inquiry continued in private practice, then as a management consultant, along with my experience in corporate leadership development at Nike and Cigna, and today as the chief resilience officer at Resilience Leadership Institute (RLI). My goal was, and still is, to help people effectively address challenges so that they can emerge from adversity empowered and better for their experience.

Maybe you're dealing with the aftereffects of abuse or violence, grieving the loss of a loved one, or looking to rebuild trust and connection in important relationships. Perhaps you're in the throes of burnout, stress, or exhaustion, or realizing you need support for your mental health. Maybe you desire to enhance your confidence and self-esteem, accept yourself, and finally feel worthy.

No matter what your challenges and goals are, my goal is to help you see adversity as an opportunity for growth and expansion. It is often assumed that hard times, such as job loss, illness, or traumatic events, diminish our ability to function, yet while they may slow us down or stop us temporarily, the slowing down or stopping is an important aspect of our healing and resilience process. Challenge is simply a well-disguised occasion for growth. I wrote this book not to teach you to ignore or minimize your experience, but instead to give you the manual to be present with your difficulty and move through tough times, not around or above them. To offer you a blueprint for emerging from adversity enhanced, rather than diminished, with more humility, openness, empathy, wisdom, and joy.

The Five Practices of Highly Resilient People are the five behaviors that we can all choose, anytime we face challenge, change, and complexity, to create a more positive and productive outcome. Through learning and adopting The Five Practices, your problems will become pathways to a better life. How do I know? Because I have lived it. Now, I am here to help show you the way.

Over the years, I have worked with many high-achieving clients, executives, athletes, and public figures. You may be surprised to learn that those at the top of their game have not been free of challenge. Most have faced more difficulty than you would imagine. So, how do people face truckloads of challenge and still rise? People come to me, not to rescue them from their challenges, but to teach them how to effectively address them. They are not trying to engineer challenge out of their life. Why? Because they understand that challenge is the common fiber that knits together our strength, resolve, and confidence. Think of a time you faced a circumstance that you thought would end you. A time when you thought there was no way you'd make it. Somehow, you did. Looking back now, do you feel more or less confident for having gone through these times in your life? If you're like many people I've interviewed, you feel more confident because you surprised yourself and realized just how much you can take, right? Exactly.

THE DOCTOR IS IN

If we could travel back in time, to my middle school days, you would see me racing home from school to complete my homework before attending swim practice. Then, in the evenings, I knew my friends would be calling me for support to talk through things like how to tell another classmate that they liked them as more than a friend, break up with a boyfriend or girlfriend, or be more confident in themselves.

This was a time before cell phones. My parents, unable to make outbound calls or receive an inbound call during the evening hours between seven and nine because I was always on their phone, decided to give me my own phone and line in my bedroom. They agreed to allow me this privilege, which had the added benefit of giving them their phone line back, provided I maintained my grades.

To be honest, I've never fit in with my peers. Middle school was no different. I've always been mature for my age, and I was interested in politics and the environment, things that other kids just weren't into yet. To be clear, I was never cool. Looking back, I've reflected on how, at that young age, I already knew what to say to console my friends. My knowledge and maturity were, in part, born of my own early struggles. These challenges not only gifted me with wisdom beyond my years, but they also put me on a career path to be in service of others. I learned empathy for others by first learning to offer compassion to myself, learning that it was better to give myself grace during my own difficulties than to beat myself up mentally.

The first of my personal challenges, undiagnosed dyslexia, a learning disability, emerged in elementary school, making learning to read, reading comprehension, and spelling extremely difficult for me, landing me in the lowest reading group. Eventually, I was diagnosed with dyslexia, but not until the age of thirty-seven, long after I had concluded my formal education. For a long time, like many with an undiagnosed learning disability, I didn't feel confident in my ability to learn and believed I wasn't very intelligent.

Despite teaching myself strategies to memorize words, dyslexia proved to be a relatively minor hurdle compared to a monstrous threat that arose in my early teens, which I will go into in greater depth in the pages to follow. I mention it now to share with you that the material in this book is based on my academic and professional research with hundreds of people, and reinforced by my own deeply personal, life-changing, and formative experiences with challenge.

My focus on resilience has not been from the perspective of someone in an ivory tower or as an observer of other people's challenges alone. I have received professional training as a clinician and a doctoral-level researcher. I have also been a client, attending therapy to support my mental health and personal growth. Since I have lived many trials and tests personally, I've learned as much in the university classroom as I have as a student of my own life. In many cases, I have been where you have been, or where you are now.

My interest in resilience sprang from both my own struggles, and as I pursued my advanced education, I went deeper to understand the science and psychology of resilience. I've always been fascinated by people's stories of facing challenge, seemingly impossible circumstances, and how they prevailed in the end. My desire was to learn beyond what I had experienced, so that I could help you move beyond your own challenges and offer you comfort as well as tools. Observing how deeply powerful The Five Practices have been in my life and in the lives of hundreds of thousands of people, I felt compelled to make them widely accessible, not simply narrowly available through my coaching and consulting work, and to share them broadly with you.

FINDING RESILIENCE

In graduate school, I was involved in learning about two seemingly unrelated groups of people that amplified my interest in resilience and its powerful positive impact on our lives: mothers in rural Maryland grappling with financial sustainability; and survivors of neurological (brain or spine) injuries and their family members.

As a young graduate student, I felt privileged to be invited into these people's lives to both listen and learn about their experience, so that together, we could create better services to support them. At the University of Maryland, College Park, our extension department had identified twenty Maryland mothers who were living in rural areas with their families and facing financial or food instability. I was part of the team that analyzed the mothers' in-depth qualitative interviews conducted annually over a three-year period to better understand how they were navigating the demands of daily living on a reduced income in rural areas. The goal was to learn about their experience so we could create better social services to enhance the support they were receiving.

We found that, for these women, access to reliable transportation was the single greatest component that helped them enhance their resilience and effectively address adversity. In the rural areas where they lived, grocery stores, medical care, and workplaces were often many miles apart, with no options for public transportation to bridge the gap. One woman described how she and her husband set aside $50 a week until they could purchase a vehicle. I felt elated when I read about the sense of freedom she felt when they were finally able to have their own vehicle:

> It felt so good to get the kids . . . the feeling of me, my husband, and all four of my kids getting into our van, this weekend. We shut the door, we started down the road, and I know this is going to sound stupid, but all I could do was cry. We have waited years to do this and we're just now doing it. . . . And I smiled all the way.

She smiled ALL THE WAY! When I read those lines, I smiled, too, picturing her in that car! I was struck by the importance of transportation and how access to a van made a significant difference for her and her family. I could feel her joy as I read her words, and when we wrote an article with our findings, we highlighted transportation as a resource that enhanced resilience. I didn't know it yet, but her experience would not just inspire me, her words would be instructive on my journey to understand human resilience.

It was a few years later that I took a position as a neuropsychology fellow at Virginia Commonwealth University (VCU) Medical Center on a grant from the National Institute of Disability and Rehabilitation Research (NIDRR). While working with people who had sustained brain and spinal cord injuries, along with assisting their family members, transportation once again emerged as a key factor in promoting resilience.

When a person sustains a neuropsychological injury, they and their family members experience considerable emotional trauma, along with the physical trauma of the injury. As the family members of the person who sustained the injury gathered in the intensive care unit (ICU) or in the emergency room (ER), they shared with me that what they most wanted to know in that moment was what would happen to their injured family member.

Yet, when we followed patients and their families after they were discharged to our outpatient clinic for months, and oftentimes years, to come, we realized something troubling. Our patients' rehabilitation prognoses, essentially the doctor's belief about what would happen to the person that sustained the injury, were often wrong.

Back then, we based a person's prognosis on three things:

1. The person's age,
2. Where the injury occurred in the person's body or brain, and
3. The severity of the injury.

Months and even years later, I noticed patients were doing better than their prognosis or not as well as we thought, but rarely were we accurately predicting the patient's rehabilitation outcome. At a time when families most needed our predictions to be correct, we were often inaccurate. We wondered: *What if there was more to our patients' rehabilitation than the three simple factors upon which we based our predictions? What if there were other factors that could assist us in more accurately predicting our patients' rehabilitation?*

This led my colleagues and me to look more closely at the factors that would account for the differences in rehabilitation outcomes we observed in our outpatient clinic. Our inquiry was one of the first-ever studies on resilience and neurological injury.

We found a host of additional factors that contributed to the quality of a person's rehabilitation beyond the narrow information doctors were initially considering at the patient's bedside. The research allowed us to give patients and family members a more accurate picture of the road to rehabilitation. The single most important factor that influenced patients' rehabilitation was as surprising as it was simple.

Like the mothers in Maryland years before, patients who had access to reliable transportation after injury had more positive rehabilitation outcomes. Reliable transportation was, statistically speaking, the difference between living independently after a neurological injury and living in an assisted care facility. As a result of our findings, we created programs that subsidized transportation. As these were the days before Uber and Lyft, patients were now able to access their therapies and rehabilitation services, making a profound difference in their recovery of functioning.

Now, you may be asking yourself, "What do these two groups of people have to do with me and the power of resilience?" I wish I could tell you that I made that connection overnight. I didn't. It took me many years to understand the link that existed just outside of my awareness. These seemingly diverse people had one thing in common: In both cases, having access to reliable transportation was transformational. While transportation is something many of us take for granted, it allowed these people to harness and enhance their resilience, and in doing so, heal, grow, and develop beyond what was initially believed to be possible for them.

During periods when I continued to deal with my own personal and professional challenges, I found myself reflecting on the experiences of the Maryland mothers and survivors of neurological injury, wondering: *If reliable transportation was the common thread that made a significant, positive difference for these two very different groups of people, knowing that challenge is an inevitable part of life, is there a factor or factors, like transportation, that have the power to transform us all?*

The Five Practices of Highly Resilient People is our transportation, demonstrating in thousands of cases to be the differentiator between what allows us to harness our resilience, transporting us to transformation. When facing difficulty, The Five Practices is the playbook that differentiates between those that flourish and those that fold. Given that challenge is the fabric of our human existence, The Five Practices is your blueprint to support you in facing challenge, knowing that challenge is unquestionably an inevitable part of your human experience.

Building on what I learned with the Maryland mothers and the survivors of neurological injury over two decades, I have been conducting interviews to further my understanding of the productive and positive behaviors people engage in when they face challenges. I continued with my own research while working in private practice, as a management consultant, and later as an executive in leadership development at Cigna and Nike. I still conduct interviews and research to this day. Over the years, I have asked hundreds of people to reflect on their personal and professional lives and answer this question: "Think about a time when you faced a significant challenge: Looking back, how did you effectively address this challenge?"

Once they completed their initial answer, I asked them to consider additional factors that may have supported them when they faced adversity. These factors might include their personal strengths, mind-sets, support systems, environment, and personal skill sets, such as having specific knowledge or unique abilities.

I asked them to reflect on additional factors that may have supported them to prompt additional ideas, experiences, or perspectives so they could consider all resources that helped them effectively address challenge. I do this because we often take our gifts, strengths, and circumstances for granted. I once heard someone say that if you asked a fish to describe its environment, water might be the last thing it noticed. I find that our natural strengths and skills often come so naturally to us that they go unrecognized, like water to a fish.

In my initial series of interviews on this topic, I talked with a racially diverse group of 150 male and female participants ranging in age from twenty-five to seventy-one. New questions emerged from the data collected. Over the years, I've interviewed several hundred more people, and in addition, I have reviewed thousands of newspaper and magazine articles, along with blogs, social media posts, stories, podcasts, and interviews as well as academic journals and books on resilience.

Over time, through these research interviews and observations, alongside reflections from my own life, five universal practices emerged from the data as a result of my inquiry.

When we face challenge, we often say, "What can I *do*?" Knowing that action is a natural response for many of us, I wanted to learn what *behaviors* people engage in when faced with challenges, to provide a unique contribution to the existing understanding of resilience. The five universal practices that I found worked time and time again are:

1. Vulnerability
2. Productive Perseverance
3. Connection
4. Grati-osity
5. Possibility

Now that I understand the power of The Five Practices, they are at the core of the work I do, and I have presented them in keynote addresses and motivational speeches on stages across the globe. I incorporate them into workshops, training classes, and retreats, as well as my executive coaching and mentoring programs. As a result, hundreds of thousands of people have already engaged with their power.

This book, then, presents the results of my ongoing professional and personal research: The Five Practices of Highly Resilient People, a guide to generating positive and productive outcomes when faced with life's inevitable challenges, changes, and complexity, The Three C's. In the pages that follow, together, we will explore The Five Practices and how you, too, can apply them when faced with your unique difficulties.

THE 5 PRACTICES OF HIGHLY RESILIENT PEOPLE

PART I

RESILIENCE FINDS YOU

1
Challenge Cultivates Resilience

As you know, in addition to my research, I've examined my own life experiences to better understand resilience. I've used myself as my own research instrument to ask myself, as The Five Practices were emerging, How does what I am learning fit or not fit with my own circumstances? Like many other people, I had a series of traumatic experiences when I was younger that were part of shaping me into the person I am today. In complete integrity, I still grapple with the trauma at times. As with all life experiences, they become a part of us, and my experience with trauma will always be a part of me. For years, I pushed what happened outside of my consciousness for fear that if I brought my experience to the surface, people would look at me differently. I felt ashamed, as though I'd been damaged in some way by what happened to me. The post-traumatic growth from trauma has been to transmute an experience that left me feeling broken into something beautiful by sharing my resilience story in service of lighting a path for others' healing, growth, and resilience.

If you may be triggered by the trauma of stalking, assault, and abuse, please know this is coming, and read on with this warning or skip to the section entitled "Embracing Adversity" on page 10. Come back and read this story if or when you are ready.

As a fourteen-year-old freshman in high school in October 1993, I was dressing for school early in the morning, in my first-floor bedroom of our family home in Ann Arbor, Michigan. The window that looked out onto the driveway was open a crack, to let in the fresh fall air, and just a small portion of the window was not covered by the shade. As I prepared to leave the room, I was listening to music, and when I went to turn off my stereo, I saw the outline of someone's face at the bottom of my window. As I stared into the shadows, with the light from my bedroom only illuminating his nose and chin, he stood up and there we were, facing each other, just feet apart, on opposite sides of the window, with just a screen, wood, glass, and a shade between us.

I had not gotten a good enough look at him to make out his features. In my confusion, disbelief, and fear, I searched my fourteen-year-old mind for an explanation that would make sense of what was happening. As I spun through my memories like a Rolodex, I recalled a time when my father had hidden outside to scare my mother and me. Perhaps this was just my dad outside playing a trick on me.

"Dad?" I ventured, tentatively.

"Take off your clothes; you're beautiful," a voice said from the other side of the window.

Definitely NOT Dad!

Terrified, I sprinted from my room, screaming for my parents.

My parents called the police, and when they arrived, the officer who took the report concluded that this was nothing to be concerned about. Probably just someone passing through the neighborhood. A fluke.

About ten months later, in June 1994, my parents were out of town. Since that incident, I'd always kept that window on the driveway shut tight with the shade all the way down. But this was a hot summer evening, and I'd opened my other bedroom window, the one that faced the backyard, to allow air to circulate through the screen.

I'd gone shopping at the mall earlier that day with girlfriends, and I tried on my new clothes, including a new bathing suit, in front of the mirror. When I removed my clothes, I heard his voice coming from the open window in my room.

"I've been waiting a long time for this," he said.

I knew that voice. It was etched in my mind.

In that moment, my life changed forever as three truths emerged:

1. I was naked in front of a man for the first time.
2. My childhood bedroom, which should have been one of the safest places for me, had become profoundly unsafe.
3. This was not a fluke.

I felt the room closing in around me. Everything got small, tight, and compact, the way I feel when I watch a horror movie. My mind did the calculations. There was only a wire screen between us. *Should I run? Scream? Get dressed first?*

Fear paralyzed me. I couldn't decide what to do, much less even move.

Finally, after what seemed like forever, I screamed for help.... The sound came out of my mouth, but no one came. My parents were out of town. They'd left my brother and me in the care of a young couple who had small children of their own. They were upstairs putting their kids to bed and couldn't hear me over the commotion of the nighttime routine.

"No one is coming to help you," he said through the screen.

I knew he was right. Then, I remembered I had the phone in my bedroom. If I was going to get help, I was going to need to get it myself. I reached for the receiver and dialed 911.

The man was still outside my window when the 911 operator picked up. But I don't remember what happened next. My memory of that moment is clouded black, inaccessible to me. Time stood still, and the next thing I remember is hearing the police sirens getting louder as they approached our home. Later, I would understand why I lost time in between my 911 call and the police's arrival. I'd gone into traumatic shock. This is the body's natural defense mechanism when our brain is unable to process overwhelming emotions. People often freeze or dissociate, disconnecting from reality to protect our psyche.

The babysitters came downstairs and found me huddled behind my bedroom door, still naked, shivering in fear. They covered me up as a police officer searched my room. No sign of entry. The window screen was intact.

Another police report was taken and filed, but this time it wasn't written off as a fluke, or just some creepy guy passing through the neighborhood. This was someone targeting me, watching me, stalking me. That seemed obvious. Even so, my parents seemed strangely passive, as if they didn't really believe me, or didn't want to believe me. Now, as a parent myself, I imagine it was too horrific for them to believe. Maybe it was easier for them to deny the truth of what was happening for as long as they could, without the perspective of hindsight we have today, rather than confront the trauma and danger that had found its way to our home. My parents did install a light with a motion sensor outside my windows. Looking back now, having the wisdom of knowing what happened next, I know they wished they would have done more.

I've resisted using the word *stalker*. That word has become sensationalized. I tried on other descriptions, like "peeping Tom," but those seemed too innocent. "Prowler" sounded like someone wandering around in the yard. I experienced him as a stalker. Someone who watched me unbeknownst to me, waiting for a moment when I was alone to strike.

Time passed again, and the following winter of 1995, he appeared again. The ground was coated in snow. My parents had gone out for the evening, and my brother was at a friend's house. I was home alone waiting for friends to pick me up. I saw the motion-sensor light flip on in the backyard. We'd recently gotten a chow chow mix puppy from the Humane Society, and her ears pricked up. Looking out the window, I saw someone standing on our back deck in the dark. His movements looked agitated and staggering. I walked closer to the sliding glass windows in our sunroom and we faced each other for a long moment. He was wearing a hat, and I couldn't make out his face. Without warning, he picked up a plastic chair, patio furniture we hadn't brought in for the winter, and threw it at the sliding glass doors that stood between us.

I screamed. The puppy barked.

He threw another plastic chair against the glass. Then another. He was trying to shatter the glass and break into the house. I knew I didn't have much time.

I ran to the phone and called 911. When the police arrived, they surveyed the backyard strewn with patio furniture and footprints. Out of an abundance of caution, they tried to match the tread on the bottom of the shoes to a pair of shoes in our home, but nothing matched. I heard one of the officers say to another that if the man had found any of the large rocks my mother used to landscape the garden under the camouflage of snow, he would have had no trouble shattering the glass. I understood that his behavior was escalating, and this time, I had narrowly escaped a home invasion, let alone being attacked or even killed.

More time passed before I was aware of his presence again. I wondered if he'd gone away for a while or become so stealthy that I was not conscious when he was near. My final encounter with this man, that I am aware of, occurred the following summer of 1996, before my senior year of high school. My parents lived across the street from a park, and I was babysitting three neighborhood kids, along with one of their friends.

The three kids lived in a house just behind ours, and when the evening sky turned to twilight, we cut through my parents' backyard to take them home instead of walking around the block. As I unlocked the door to the house and held it open for the children to walk inside, I saw a man standing on the lawn. He didn't appear to be much older than me but looked disheveled and intoxicated by the way his body swayed back and forth.

Without warning, he began advancing quickly toward us, and I pushed the last child into the house and then followed them in, slamming the door and locking it behind me. Their home was a renovated farmhouse with large windows six or so feet off the ground, and to my horror, I noticed some of them were open. Trying not to frighten the children, I rushed around locking the other doors, and enlisting their help, telling them, as calmly as I could, "Let's close all the windows, kids."

Then, I turned off the lights so he couldn't see us inside, gathered the kids in an interior room, and dialed 911. When they heard me talking to the operator, they became frightened. I felt terrible that they were scared. I felt guilty, too, as though it was my fault this was happening to them. I'd dealt with this before, and rather than going into shock, I now knew how to think quickly and act decisively.

Someone knocked loudly on the back door.

The police hadn't yet arrived but were en route. "What should I do?" I asked the 911 operator.

"Are you expecting anyone?" she asked.

The little girl who was over on a playdate said, "It might be my dad. He's coming to get me."

"You have to go to the door then," the 911 operator told me.

You can imagine how I felt about that. To say that I was terrified to leave the room and walk through the dark house toward the knocking on the door is an understatement.

I handed the phone to the oldest child and told them I'd be right back, willing myself to follow the operator's instructions. Just as I arrived at the back door, the knocking stopped. After a couple of seconds, I pushed the curtain aside and peeked out the window. There was no one there. I exhaled and began walking back to the kids when I heard someone knocking, this time on the front door. I walked through the dark house to the front door.

This time, when I looked out the window, I recognized the girl's father from the neighborhood, and I let him inside. "Were you just knocking on the back door too?" I asked.

"No, was there someone there?" he wanted to know. "Why are all the lights off?" he inquired.

"Come inside, and I'll tell you," I said.

I didn't want to tell him the stalker story. It was the first time I remember willfully hiding my story out of embarrassment, but certainly not my last. I felt ashamed and damaged, like there must be something wrong with me to have the stalker target me. Now, because of me, he was targeting me with children in my care and frightening them! *What had I done to attract his attention? Had I done something wrong?* I was just coming into womanhood and maturing physically, mentally, and emotionally. This unwanted attention was not only terrifying, degrading, and traumatic, it was confusing. Young girls are supposed to want to be attractive, but all I wanted was to disappear, to hide away from being noticed, so this weirdo would leave me alone.

To spare the kids' father the details, I kept it on a high level. As I heard the police sirens in the distance on their way to the house, I told him there had been a suspicious-looking man in the yard who'd made a move for the front door when we returned from the park. The father was concerned and thanked me for acting so quickly to protect the children. Then, I went home my own house. I didn't know it yet, but thankfully, that would be the last time I'd see the strange man.

I graduated from high school in the summer of 1997 and moved into the dorms at the University of Michigan that fall. Although it was only a few miles away, on campus, I felt more at ease that I was no longer in my parents' home where I had experienced the stalker. For a while, aside from nightmares, uneasiness, and being afraid of the dark, I rarely thought about what happened. I was grateful to leave that experience behind. Or so I thought.

The following year, my mother called me early one morning. The blaring ring had disturbed my roommates, who were still asleep, so I took the receiver into the hallway, with the coiled cord winding out the door behind me. Before I could chastise my mother for the hour of her call, she began to recount the news. She told me that a single mother in our neighborhood had been raped and severely beaten. Still half asleep, I didn't process the urgency of her call, until I heard her say, "We think this could be that man who came to your window." Then, I understood.

News accounts said the attacker had entered the woman's home in the early morning hours while she was sleeping. He beat her badly after raping her, and she told police that she was sure he intended to kill her. She never got a good look at his face.

Police found no sign of forced entry to the house, even though the woman said she always locked the doors at night. During the investigation, she told detectives that she'd been remodeling her home and had hired carpenters and a painter. She had given them keys to the house so they could come in when she wasn't home.

The detectives obtained blood samples from two of the contractors and sent them to the crime laboratory to be compared with semen taken from the woman after the attack. These were early days of DNA testing, and two full months passed before the test results returned. They matched the DNA of the painter she'd hired. The painter she'd hired lived with his parents, across the park from where I played as a child and with the children I'd been babysitting that evening, just four houses away from my parents' home.

He was found guilty on the rape charge and sentenced to fifteen to forty years in prison. There was never any investigation into whether the painter had been stalking me all those years. He was going to prison on a much more serious charge, so if it was him, I reasoned, he would now spend many years behind bars. I'd soon learn that I, too, would spend time in captivity: I had developed post-traumatic stress disorder (PTSD), a diagnosis that would cage me in fear, nightmares, and anxiety for twenty years. I experienced severe survivor guilt, imagining that I could have suffered a fate similar to my neighbor's, enduring a brutal rape and attack.

EMBRACING ADVERSITY

Given that the title of this chapter is "Challenge Cultivates Resilience," you may be wondering how these nightmare encounters I shared in the prior section, which haunted me for most of my teen and many of my adult years, could make me *more* resilient. The definition of resilience that has emerged for me after interviewing hundreds of people and reviewing thousands of pieces of data no longer endorses unhelpful myths of resilience like "bouncing back" or "quickly recovering from adversity." The new definition of resilience I have uncovered is:

> Resilience is the ability to effectively address challenge, change, and complexity in a manner that allows us to be enhanced by the experience, not diminished.

I've learned that through resilience, it is in adversity that we discover our strengths, talents, and wisdom, either for the first time or we are reminded of their existence within us. Resilience isn't about quickly recovering or avoiding challenge, it's about facing the challenge that comes our way and figuring out how to effectively deal with it for our ultimate growth and benefit. Rather than thinking about challenge from a victim mentality, as in "Why is this happening to me?," we get to adopt the mentality of a warrior and a learner and reframe the question to see what we can learn from it. To adopt this mind-set, we can instead ask ourselves, "Why is this happening for me?" Therefore, the experience of challenge, by creating an environment that, though difficult, provides fertile ground to cultivate our resilience.

BEING RESILIENT DOESN'T ALWAYS MEAN *FEELING* GOOD

Facing challenges like the loss of a job, or a troubling medical diagnosis, call for resilience. You will likely feel out of balance, anxious, and unmotivated in moments like these. This is natural. Many of us imagine that being resilient should feel good. Being resilient and feeling resilient are not the same thing. Being resilient doesn't always feel resilient, let alone feel good. This is an important distinction. Resilience is a workout for our psyche. We don't always feel like exercising. Some workouts are hard and grueling. We sweat and gasp for breath. Yet, no one is ever mad about having worked out.

Facing challenge, even when you're demonstrating resilience, like an intense workout, doesn't feel awesome. Adversity never feels good. Often, it's in hindsight that we can appreciate our resilience more when the difficulties are closer to resolved or behind us to some degree. Hard things are hard because they're hard. When we're wrestling with something, if it was simple, we would have figured it out already.

Demonstrating resilience in the face of dyslexia and trauma has never felt good in the moment. It felt more like a street brawl. Most days, I felt like I was just barely making it. I held on to hope and fought on, believing that eventually I could get better. It's not until years later that I feel good now, in looking back, seeing that I demonstrated significant resilience.

As you learn and practice The Five Practices, you'll become more adept at navigating challenge. Yet, initially, even when you are practicing these techniques and doing your very best you can in the moment, you still may not feel good, let alone resilient. But you are. Remember, in those moments, that barely making it is still making it. Gasping for breath is still breathing, and fighting on, even though you feel depleted, means having the courage to keep showing up for the challenging times.

Just because you don't feel good in the moment doesn't mean you're not doing well. Applying The Five Practices often doesn't feel good because of the magnitude and importance of what you're facing in the moment. Typically, it's not until you look back on your experience that you can fully appreciate your own strength and how you've grown.

REFRAMING CHALLENGE

Writer and poet Maya Angelou, who faced many challenges in her life, said, "I can be changed by what happens to me. But I refuse to be reduced by it." That is a powerful statement and guide for treating adversity as a gift, an opportunity to emerge stronger than before. So often, we view challenge as something to be avoided, an experience that requires us to backtrack or blocks our ability to move forward. Recently, a CEO said to me in our coaching session, "Why does this have to be this hard? I feel like I have been a good enough human to deserve an easier path without so much pain and difficulty." I said, "You are absolutely right about everything you just said. But unfortunately, it doesn't work like that." This CEO has founded a technology and cryptocurrency company. With the volatility in the marketplace, he has navigated through several "hundred-year floods" in the last six months.

I went on to share with him the principles of challenge that I'm sharing with you. Here are some new ways to think about challenge in your own life:

- *Challenge can't (and shouldn't) be entirely avoided by careful planning.* Many believe that, with careful preparation and planning, they can strategically engineer challenge out of their lives, they will avoid adversity, and the path will be made clear. Sounds good, right? Contrary to popular belief, this isn't how it works. Without challenge, we miss out on instrumental experiences that are some of our greatest teachers in this life.
- *Challenge happens (even) to good people.* The irony is that many good people point to challenge as crucial moments that softened their sharp edges and made them into the good person they are today. Stuff happens. Bad things happen, even to good people. The key is to learn how to find the opportunities for growth within those challenges. A life without obstacles is like a potter without a wheel to form the clay. The challenge is the potter, forming us on the wheel, and we are the clay. The obstacles do not detract from our development, they are essential elements in our formation, our learning and growth.
- *When challenges arise, it doesn't mean you are on the wrong path.* A common misconception is that the detours, roadblocks, and potholes placed in your path only show up when you are off course. Life isn't a golf course, a perfectly manicured lawn that only gets

bumpy when you're off the fairway. Challenges arise without reason. You may be doing exactly what you were meant to do *even* when a loss occurs or a storm arrives. Do not think of challenge as a punishment or a signal that you're going the wrong way.

- *The more important the work, often, the greater the challenge.* Do you want to do big things in this world? Even when your heart is big and your intentions are pure, challenge will still be a constant companion. Challenge both readies us for what is to come and is a test, a life checkpoint to see if we're ready to be granted the next level of responsibility, the new relationship, or the expanded influence we desire. Following our life purpose and calling will inevitably bring challenge as the crucible to see if we're ready to lead the change we envision.
- *Think of challenge as an invitation.* Ask yourself: "Is this worth it? Do I want to keep going in this direction?" Elizabeth Gilbert, author of *Big Magic*, described rejection letters from editors of her early writing as an invitation that asked her, "Well, Liz, do you want to keep creating things?" Gilbert says her answer was always yes, and she went on to write many books, including the runaway best seller *Eat, Pray, Love.*
- *Challenge means it's this or something better.* When you don't give up, when you are unwavering in the face of difficulties, you will find opportunities to elevate your life. The way may not appear right away. It's through determination that you prove your mettle and possibly open the door to something even better than you had imagined.
- *Resilience doesn't prevent challenge; it gives you a toolkit to navigate the inevitable obstacles and setbacks.* Resilience won't inoculate you against challenge. Resilience gives you the tools to have the confidence to show up amid challenge and effectively address the issues at hand, rather than ignoring them or giving up, generating more strength and wisdom.

- *Challenges are rarely unilaterally positive or negative.* A new baby is a joyous occasion to celebrate a new life and comes with lost sleep and strain as all family members adjust to a new structure and routine. Similarly, a tragic loss may be deeply upsetting and unbalancing, but with time, many people can find goodness, even gratitude, that emerges from the tragedy, such as bringing them closer to friends and family, and a deeper appreciation for what it means to be alive.
- *Challenge is not something shameful.* There is no reason to feel guilty or victimized when challenge emerges in your life. It was easy for me to feel that I had done something wrong to bring the challenge of the stalker on myself. Blaming ourselves is never productive. Many people think they need a perfect track record, experiences unblemished by challenge, to be worthy. However, challenge doesn't detract from our worth and value. Challenge provides the moments in which we learn just how much we are worth.
- *Challenge is the comma, not the period at the end of the sentence.* When challenge shows up in our lives, so often, we think challenge is the last word on our dreams and desires. We say to ourselves, "Uh-oh, here comes challenge, I guess I'm not gonna get that promotion." Challenge itself is never the final word. Instead of seeing challenge as the final say, the period at the end of the sentence, view challenge as the comma in the middle of the sentence, asking us how we'd like to write the rest of our story.

Your challenges are part of your life story. You may not welcome them at first. You may not want to fight through them, to change, or to grow. You may cling to the status quo and simply ignore the moments when life gets hard. Many people deny their most challenging experiences, hiding from the experiences themselves, or hiding the challenging experiences from the world. They wall off the hurt to numb the pain. They mentally shut down to avoid feeling the discomfort. You can try that. I tried that. I can tell you from experience that it didn't work. Challenge and the emotions that accompany challenge don't go away when we ignore them. Your feelings get processed in your body, and find a way to surface, no matter how deep down we try to exile them.

Most of us resist change until it becomes impossible to ignore it any longer. You may need time to step back and see the issues clearly. My healing from the stalker encounters took decades. As humans, we can't engineer challenge out of our lives. Since challenge plays a key role in your formation and growth, you don't want to shut challenge out of your life. The good news is that challenge is not the end of your story. Remember, challenge is not the period at the end of the sentence; it's the comma in the middle. When challenge shows up in your life, it's not the final word. No matter how bad challenge feels, in my experiences, there is never a drop of pain that is wasted in our formation and growth. Ask yourself, just as Elizabeth Gilbert did, "Do I want to keep going?" Whether the answer is yes or no, The Five Practices will guide you to effectively navigate these critical times in your life.

2

The Five Myths and Truths of Resilient People

Before I take you too far on your journey to greater resilience, I want to dispel some common myths about resilience that can not only trip us up, but can also block our ability to recognize and access our resilience.

Myth #1: Resilience is about bouncing back.
Truth: Resilient people bounce *forward*, not back.

Challenge fundamentally and forever changes us. What I mean by that is our neurons are constantly growing and changing, firing, and rewiring into networks that are mirroring our external experiences. This is called neuroplasticity. Given that our neurons are constantly reorganizing, reshaping, and restructuring themselves to best serve us, why do we still subscribe to the belief that resilience is about being unchanged by our experience and returning to a prior state? Any experience we have changes us down to the neurons, to the cellular level. Allowing us to be changed by our experiences is a hallmark of our human resilience, not a weakness. Think about the challenges you have experienced. Did you ever go back to the way you were before that experience? No, right?

When I was treating individuals, couples, and families dealing with a brain injury, I was careful to always use the word *rehabilitation* rather than *recovery* in referring to the path ahead. This was because there is no going back to "normal" after a traumatic brain injury (TBI). TBIs change the person with the injury and their family members fundamentally and forever. Bouncing forward for my patients and their families meant facing realities and building a new life. "We keep going, we keep getting better and better, but no one goes back to the way they were," they'd tell me.

I once treated a brilliant woman who sustained a brain injury and was no longer able to work, write, or live independently. "I just want my brain back," she told me. She was frustrated that she had lost her intellect and independence in the car accident.

Bouncing forward means you may leave some parts of yourself behind. You will likely go through a range of feelings from frustration to fear, even to feeling a sense of freedom. Letting go of former aspects of yourself frees you to build new experiences and create a different life that honors all the adversity you faced and the strength you summoned to face it. The aspects of your life that you leave behind may be difficult to let go of because they may very well be things you enjoyed and liked, so you miss them. You may mourn the people, experiences, and elements of yourself that you've lost or let go.

Bouncing forward is for all of us, not just those that have experienced brain injury. Many of us have asked ourselves in the last few years, When will life return to normal? Bouncing forward, rather than backward, instructs us to not go rushing back to the way things were, but instead allow ourselves to be changed for the better. There is a prevalent belief that to be resilient, we must be unchanged by our circumstances, going back to the way we were, rather than forging a new path. The belief that we should be unmoved, unfaltering, blocks our ability to recognize our resilience, thinking that if we'd been resilient, we should somehow be unaffected.

Many people get tripped up by this myth. They ask me, "Dr. Taryn, I feel like I was resilient, but I haven't gone back to the way I was before the challenge. Why not?" The answer is: because we're human, not Teflon. Knowing that the myth of resilience is that we bounce back, and the truth of resilience is that we bounce forward, you are armed with the knowledge that after challenge, you're not meant to go back to a prior state, you're meant to be fundamentally and forever changed by your experiences, down to the cellular level, and bounce forward.

Myth #2: Resilience is about waiting for time to heal our wounds.
Truth: Resilience is an active process, not passive.

We often hear phrases in the English language like "Time heals all wounds." This belief is so pervasive, a similar expression exists in Spanish: *"El tiempo lo cura todo."* These common sayings suggest that healing is a passive process, rather than an active engagement in your personal, emotional, physical, mental, and spiritual evolution. While time does lessen the sting of wounds, losses, and grief, resilience is not about merely waiting passively for time to pass. To effectively face challenge and harness resilience, along with the lessons of your experience, you get to show up and be present as an engaged participant.

Resilient people take an active approach to facing challenge.

Resilience is not a Netflix series where we sit on the couch and watch our lives play out. You get to play a leading role in your healing and in your becoming the person you want to become. It's not so much that "time heals all wounds"; rather, in Andy Warhol's words, "Time changes things, but you have to change them yourself." Warhol's perspective wisely highlights that the experience of facing challenge and cultivating resilience is active, not passive. Challenge, change, and complexity (The Three C's) happen to us. Resilience is a choice. You choose to show up and take control of what is within your power to influence. This is the true meaning of being empowered.

Resilience isn't about waiting for things to happen to you; it's about making things happen. It isn't about waiting for the law of attraction to kick in; it's about being a force of nature. It's not about waiting to be inspired; it's about being the genesis of your own inspiration. It's writing your own story, instead of passively defaulting to a story written for you.

While we know what is in our control, our mind-set, actions, and words, we may not always exercise this control. When we say, "You made me angry," we're not taking an active role in being responsible for our emotions. Although we know what is within our control and what is not, I've noticed that many people spend only about one-third of their time and energy focused on what is within their control and as much as two-thirds of their time on things that are outside their control. This means that 66 percent of our time and energy or more is focused on things we can't control or influence. Take stock of how much time and energy you spend on things that are within your control. Imagine what it would be like if you spent even 30 percent more time actively engaging with the aspects of your life you can control. Taking an active role in facing your challenges as well as your healing and growth means that rather than being an observer in your life, you become the driving force in creating the life you would like to live by focusing on the aspects of your life you can change and influence.

Myth #3: We are born with a set amount of resilience.
Truth: Resilience is dynamic, not fixed or finite.

Sometimes people ask me if resilient leaders are born or made. My answer is, "Both!" Many people think of resilience as something we have or don't. As you know, we are all resilient because resilience is the very essence of being human. You were born resilient, and you didn't receive only a fixed amount of resilience. Rather than being finite, resilience is yours for the growing. In facing every letdown, failure, and misstep to date, you have strengthened your resilience in the process.

You may also notice that your resilience has been strengthened over time. This is the dynamic nature of resilience, that fact that we see resilience continue to grow and evolve over the course of our life span. Perhaps you've noticed that something that was challenging for you at one time is now a challenge you face with much greater ease.

It is through the experience of The Three C's that resilience is primarily formed. While those sunny days when everything is going off without a hitch feel great, it is the thunderstorms and the hurricanes that blow into our lives that dramatically enhance our resilience because the storms teach us so much more about ourselves and life than the sunshine ever could. It is also having experienced those storms that make us more grateful for the sunny days. Knowing just how dark the skies can get, how unforgiving the storms of challenge can be, allows us to appreciate the warmth and brilliance of the sunshine on the good days.

Resilience both brings us new capabilities and reminds us of the talents that have been unknown or unused. In fact, the word *silience* means the unnoticed capabilities that have always existed within us. If some of the precious jewels of our own skills are buried below the surface, *re-silience* means to unearth these hidden resources in moments of challenge, bringing greater awareness to our aptitude and potential.

When you are willing to show up and effectively address challenges, rather than ignoring them, the resilience you can generate is limitless. There is no cap or quota for how much resilience you can have. For many people, the amount of resilience they develop is directly related to the magnitude of The Three C's they experience.

Myth #4: Resilience is about ignoring our internal selves.
Truth: Resilience is about connecting deeply to our internal selves.

There is a myth that resilience is synonymous with ignoring our internal selves. When preparing to speak to organizations, people caution me by saying, "Please don't tell our people to put their head down and just keep going. That's not what we need to hear right now." Hustle culture has done a number on us, making many of us believe that the recipe for success is a 24/7 all-on work life and no days off.

Resilience is still being used as a reason for people to ignore their burnout, stress level, or exhaustion in favor of "pushing through." The constant expectation of productivity is not only detrimental to our health, happiness, and relationships, it is toxic and damaging. Continually pushing past our limits for the sake of production, numbing our inner needs and desires in favor of creating deliverables, will ultimately derail our mental and physical health, not to mention our relationships, along with our organizations as people become disillusioned at scale. In fact, it's already happening.

All burnout, exhaustion, and overwhelm comes, first and foremost, from ignoring our internal selves, continuing to grind, even when we feel ground down. The genesis of burnout is when we cut our sleep short, skip our workouts, stop eating the foods that we know nourish our body, and allow the pleasurable experiences that make our days engaging to be crowded out.

So, why don't we take a break? Unfortunately, there is a degree of heroism that has been associated with burning the midnight oil. Self-care, rather than being celebrated as a critical buffer for burnout, is still experienced by many as guilt inducing. One of my clients told me that he can't work out at lunchtime because he is afraid others won't think he is working hard enough. We look around at everyone else and think, they're doing fine, so why should I take a break? Self-comparison isn't helpful to self-care because other people have different needs than you do. Just because people act like they are okay, doesn't mean they are.

Resilience is about learning how to recharge, not simply to persevere. Rather than quieting the internal signals that tell you're tired and depleted, to start being more resilient, you must listen to those voices within you and stop. Burnout and exhaustion are not just resilience detractors, they are the exact opposite of resilience.

To invest in your resilience, you must invest in your recovery. Recovery doesn't only mean rest; it means time away from work, not just physically, but emotionally and mentally too. Often we physically leave our office but continue to worry and wonder about work while we're away from the office. To connect deeply to your internal self, to listen to what your body and mind need to recover, you'll need to switch off your screens and take time to disconnect.

Myth #5: Optimism makes us more resilient.
Truth: Being a realist (and an optimist) creates greater resilience.

In his well-known interview with Admiral Jim Stockdale, who was held prisoner by the Vietcong during the Vietnam War, Jim Collins wanted to know if resilience was fueled by optimism. Collins asked Stockdale, of the prisoners of war he encountered, who fared the worst over the course of the eight years he was held captive? "Oh, that's easy. It was optimists. I think they all died of broken hearts," he said.

While painting a picture of the bright vision ahead is important, so too is—paraphrasing Stockdale—confronting the brutal reality of today. Optimism can amplify resilience to a point, but an unwillingness to also be a realist, to confront the clear and present challenges of the moment, can leave even well-meaning people sounding disconnected and tone deaf. After one of my client's product launches failed epically, he suggested that he rally his team by glossing over the failure and focusing on the vision for the road ahead. Remembering Stockdale, I cautioned him about this approach. The Stockdale Paradox suggests that the most resilient people both acknowledge the reality of today, no matter how brutal, and demonstrate optimism by holding fast to the hope of the imagined future.

Toxic positivity is when we focus exclusively on what is going well and ignore the pressing reality of the current moment. Rather than focusing all his energy on the future, I suggested my client spend equal time with his team on a retrospective, unpacking the lessons of the failed product launch and applying those lessons to the imagined future ahead. The myth of resilience is that the most resilient people are optimists. The truth of resilience is that optimism, balanced with realism, is the most potent path toward greater resilience.

3
Your Reverse Bucket List

What's on your bucket list? Mine is mostly focused on travel. I have a long list of pleasurable places I want to visit across the globe: Cinque Terra, Croatia, Cambodia, Cuba . . . to name a few. No, they don't all start with the letter "C"!

Traditionally, bucket lists are focused on positive things and experiences. Yet, when I enjoyed my bucket list experiences, I noticed that these pleasurable moments didn't compare to the amount of learning and growth that occurred in the difficult times, times I'd hoped to avoid.

The reverse bucket list is about taking stock of the times we faced pain, rather than pleasure, and recognizing just how much adversity has already taught us. Often, it is through the reverse bucket list exercise that people can really see how challenge has already formed and shaped them for the better.

Here are three of my own reverse bucket list items that have shaped me into the person I am today:

- *Reverse Bucket List Item #1: Lose Something You Love*
- *Reverse Bucket List Item #2: Face a Health Diagnosis*
- *Reverse Bucket List Item #3: Do the Thing(s) That Scare You*

Before you look at my reverse bucket list items, spend five minutes reflecting on your own reverse bucket list moments by reading the following questions and writing down your answers:

- What challenge or challenges that you have faced significantly formed you into the person you are today?
- How have those challenges shaped you in positive ways and for the better?

REVERSE BUCKET LIST ITEM #1: LOSE SOMETHING YOU LOVE

Early in my career, I founded my private practice, and as I began working with more companies and people in leadership, I felt drawn to make the leap from clinician to the corporate world. I found a boutique consulting firm in the city where I was living, and after signing several executive coaching clients, I got the idea to approach the firm about coming on board to work with them so I could learn more about the management consulting industry, bringing my client contracts with me.

As I scrolled through the firm's website, looking at the employees' bright smiles, vibrant faces, and impressive bios, along with the colorful workspace they'd curated, I dreamed of what it would be like to work with such incredible people. This is exactly where I wanted to belong, and if I could work there, I imagined, it would be a tremendous career opportunity for learning and growth.

I didn't know anyone at the firm, so I scoured my relationships to find a mutual connection to request an introduction. After nearly a year of networking, followed by interviews (I got an interview!) to land this position, I was beyond thrilled when I was hired. I put all my energy into learning the business and delivering exceptional client work. Although my first son was a young baby, I worked late and missed family time some evenings. I rationalized my late nights by telling myself that I'd worked hard to make this opportunity a reality, after all it took over a year to be hired by the firm, and I wanted to learn and contribute as much as I could. Unfortunately, when the firm lost several key clients and fell on tighter financial times, they couldn't afford to keep me on board. Since I was the most recently hired consultant and had the least experience, my position was eliminated.

I'd been working since I was fourteen years old. Now, I felt adrift without a job to define my identity or career goals to occupy my time. I felt embarrassed by job loss. I'd spent more time networking for the role than being employed at the firm. Which made me feel foolish for believing that I could dream of a bigger career. Losing a job I loved brought me face-to-face with my fear that I didn't have what it took to be a management consultant. I had hoped to avoid this reverse bucket list experience of unanticipated and unwanted loss. I worried incessantly that I would never work in my chosen profession again. Old insecurities arose, and I felt consumed by self-doubt. For many days, I lay on my couch and cried, alternately anxious and inconsolable.

Looking back, I allowed myself to value the prestige of the job and firm more than my own worth. Eventually, I realized that there were benefits in this bucket of unanticipated loss. Once I grieved the loss, I took the time to reflect on what I truly wanted from my career. The experience sharpened my determination, rather than dulling my desire to pursue a business career in the field of leadership development.

Two months later, I landed a new job in a consulting firm that came with a promotion in title and responsibility, not to mention global opportunities that were not available at my prior consulting firm. The time for reflection allowed me to articulate my strengths and prepare for this new assignment. This time, I projected my worth from within myself, and I didn't attach my value to my work, title, or salary. Losing something I loved taught me that even if I lost my job, I wouldn't lose my identity, and I would still retain my self-worth.

REVERSE BUCKET LIST ITEM #2: FACE A HEALTH DIAGNOSIS

I began swimming competitively when I was eight years old. My parents wondered whether I knew what I was getting myself into with practices several times a week year-round. I loved the discipline of the sport, how I could let my mind run while I swam from one end of the pool to the other. By the age of twelve, I was a state champion, placing in the individual 200 freestyle event, the longest sprint, requiring strength, speed, and stamina.

Heartened by my early success, I dreamed of swimming in college. Maybe even the Olympics. My grandfather missed competing on the Olympic diving team by just one-tenth of one point. I dreamed that I could achieve his dream and become the first Olympian in our family.

While practicing in high school, I noticed that my arms and hands tingled when I swam. Initially, it felt like the pinpricks you feel when your foot "falls asleep." Then, my arms and hands went numb altogether.

For the first time in nearly a decade, I couldn't finish a workout when I'd been one of the strongest swimmers on the team. I couldn't explain to my coach or my parents why I'd lost control of my arms while my teammates paddled effortlessly through the water around me.

After months of doctor visits, physical therapy, and meetings with specialists, I finally received a diagnosis of thoracic outlet syndrome (TOS). The tingling and numbness were brought on by a congenital defect in the structure of my shoulders that blocked blood flow to my arms and hands. When I raised my arm straight in the air, my pulse would literally disappear.

Unfortunately, as for my grandfather, my Olympic dreams were not meant to be. I was fortunate that the condition wasn't life threatening. Receiving this health diagnosis, and once again ticking a reverse bucket item of my (unwanted) list, taught me two important lessons:

1. Sometimes you must go slow to go fast; and
2. Every ending is a new beginning.

Sometimes You Must Go Slow to Go Fast

Despite my deep disappointment at the prospect of giving up my beloved sport, I decided to complete my final season of my senior year with my teammates. Rather than continuing to train with the varsity team as I had every year prior, I trained with the junior varsity team to trim the distance I was swimming given the limitations of my TOS diagnosis. As my teammates got better around me, I felt awkward and self-conscious backtracking in my speed and swimming ability for my senior year. Cutting back my yardage during training ended up having a benefit that no one expected. During finals, I swam faster than I ever had with my TOS diagnosis at the most debilitating it had ever been. I learned that cutting back and going slow is sometimes necessary to go faster.

Every Ending Is a New Beginning

Being on the swim team was demanding and time-consuming. When I arrived on the University of Michigan's campus, I had time for the extracurricular activities that I had not had time to enjoy in a decade. I joined a sorority, studied abroad in Italy, and volunteered at the local hospital. My own health concerns made me more empathetic to the patients with whom I volunteered, and seeing the serious health concerns of many patients gave me more gratitude for my health, even my shoulders. I learned that sometimes doors must close so that other doors can open. By closing the door on my swimming career and letting go of those dreams, I got to open new doors and opportunities that would not have been available to me otherwise.

REVERSE BUCKET LIST ITEM #3: DO THE THING(S) THAT SCARE YOU

When I began publishing my writing online on LinkedIn, I was ambivalent, torn between feeling a strong calling to share my insights, while also feeling afraid about what others would think.

I worried that if people really knew me, they wouldn't like me, let alone love me, and they might leave, ending our personal or professional relationship. Spoiler alert: I later learned my fear surrounding my vulnerability associated with sharing my writing is a normal experience for nearly every human, but I didn't know this yet!

Despite my fear, I reluctantly forged ahead, my heart filled with desire, at odds with my head that was filled with dread. When I hit the key to upload my first article online, I waited with trepidation for what would happen next. *Would my boss call and ask what I was thinking? Would I lose my job? Would people laugh at my perspectives or belief that I thought I had something meaningful to share?*

I am delighted to report, as I write this book no less, that none of those things happened. Instead, I watched as the "likes" and supportive comments accumulated with each new article. People related to my writing, thanked me for expressing my thoughts, and said they resonated with my perspectives.

Each time I uploaded an article, the process became a little less frightening. I shared a piece of myself with the world, and as a result, developed a deeper, more authentic voice. Doing a thing that scared me taught me that my life could expand beyond my imagination when I had the courage to push past my fears.

A question people often ask me is: "When will I ever stop feeling scared?" My answer—the truth that I have uncovered by continually ticking the facing fears reverse bucket list item—is that if you constantly push the envelope of your comfort zone, you will probably never stop feeling afraid. With each new challenge you confront, new fears will emerge. Remember that fear is just an emotion, one that serves a purpose and helps you survive. Fear won't kill you, even though it can feel so strong you swear you'll die of fright. You won't. Know that fear will be a constant companion and learn to make friends with the monsters under your bed instead of allowing them to paralyze you. Just as the periods of darkness in my life have allowed me to have greater appreciation for the lighter experiences, spending time with fear has expanded my experience of joy.

Today, rather than attempting to eradicate fear, I embrace fear as a constant companion. Many people tell me, "I just need to demolish my fear and limiting beliefs, and then I can write my book, apply for that promotion, share with people the truth about who I am, start my new company, etc." It doesn't work like this. The formula for facing fear is not "When fear is gone, then I will do _____." You face fear by staring it straight in the face, acknowledging its presence, and then doing the thing that frightens you anyway. If you wait for fear to disappear, you'll be waiting your whole life, because fear never truly goes away. Instead, learn to live with fear and shelve limiting beliefs enough to step into the elements of your life that are unfamiliar, and ultimately, will be deeply rewarding.

PART II

YOUR RESILIENT LIFE—THE FIVE PRACTICES OF HIGHLY RESILIENT PEOPLE

4
The Practice of Vulnerability

Vulnerability!

Wait, what?

When I introduce The Practice of Vulnerability, people often have two questions:

1. *Is it true that vulnerability creates, not detracts from, resilience?*
2. *Does this mean enhancing my vulnerability will also increase my resilience?*

The answers are, *yes* and *yes*.

Let me explain how The Practice of Vulnerability promotes resilience.

How would you complete the following sentence?

"People would think I was crazy if they knew..."

Your answer is your resilience story. Resilience stories are the stories we often don't want to tell, but most need to be told. Everyone has at least one resilience story. When you have the courage to share your resilience story, three powerful things occur:

- You deepen your own resilience and others learn from your experience.
- You face your fear of being vulnerable and role model vulnerability for others.
- You encourage others to demonstrate vulnerability and create a climate where vulnerability is accepted and encouraged.

When I was diagnosed with PTSD, I vowed to myself that I would tell no one. As a therapist, I'd encourage my clients to share their stories with me to aid in their healing, and I sought my own therapy. However, for years, I did the opposite. In the world of my professional life and with many people in my personal life, I was determined not to talk about my experience with the stalker or my diagnosis, as I didn't want to change people's perception of me.

My fear of vulnerability and being viewed differently if people had known this story is understandable, and of course, human, but also self-defeating. You may know the feeling. After all, nearly all of us felt vulnerable during the pandemic. Even though it was a universal experience with the spread of COVID-19 around the globe, we worried that our experience would be unique. That we'd be the only ones who felt a certain way or faced a certain challenge.

When the world shut down, many of us were isolated. We didn't go into offices. We stayed home and had our groceries and our meals delivered, or we picked them up curbside. As we adjusted to the new circumstances, during our online interactions, we often talked about our concerns about the pandemic and its impact. We dared to be vulnerable. And what happened? Our coworkers, friends, and family related to our concerns and shared their own. As a result, we felt less alone. We bonded. A new sense of community formed. We were vulnerable with one another, and this vulnerability enhanced our resilience.

THE RESILIENT PRACTICE OF VULNERABILITY

Resilient Vulnerability is the ability to navigate the paradox of both possessing personal strength and being open to sharing our challenges. While the polarity of these two elements might sound impossible to reconcile, The Practice of Vulnerability is a foundational practice of resilience. If you're like many people, you were brought up to think that resilience is about toughness. However, the people who are most resilient allow themselves to be softened by their experiences, not hardened.

To be vulnerable is to allow your "inside self" (your internal thoughts, feelings, and experiences) to match your "outside self" (the person you show to the world). This mirroring of the inside and outside self is called congruence. Vulnerability, then, is the lifelong practice of allowing our inside and outside selves to be in harmony with one another as much as possible.

Vulnerability is a key element in resilience because the more congruent we are as people, the more we can function in moments of challenge without burning up a lot of energy to navigate and manage two separate personas—the inside and outside selves. The most resilient people share their experiences, challenges, changes, and complexities with the people in their lives who support them in these tender moments.

Being vulnerable enough to share your experiences is an advantage in the moments when you face challenge and are brave enough to share your feelings about your experiences to the outside world. When you let people know what you are going through, they are more likely to offer support, information, and resources to you.

Vulnerability is also a basis for your human connections, the cornerstone of authenticity and empathy. You cannot be either authentic or empathetic if you are not willing to first be vulnerable enough to be open with others about your own thoughts and feelings. That is why The Practice of Vulnerability serves as the foundation for many of the other practices. With practice, vulnerability allows you to shine forth from within, to share your feelings and express yourself with less fear of being shamed or rejected.

THE VULNERABILITY CHECKLIST

Some of the behaviors associated with The Practice of Vulnerability are surprising to many people. The Vulnerability Checklist is a resource that you can use to note which behaviors associated with The Practice of Vulnerability you're already demonstrating as well as determine new ways you might like to be more vulnerable to enhance your resilience. If you are already engaging in some of these aspects of demonstrating your vulnerability, you can also ask yourself what you might like to do more of.

VULNERABILITY CHECKLIST

- ☐ BE PRESENT.
- ☐ LISTEN.
- ☐ ALLOW OTHERS' EXPERIENCES AND CHOICES TO BE DIFFERENT FROM YOUR OWN.
- ☐ ACCEPT MORE, JUDGE LESS.
- ☐ ACKNOWLEDGE PEOPLE AS THEIR WHOLE SELVES.
- ☐ RECOGNIZE YOU ARE NOT ALONE.
- ☐ DON'T ALLOW FEAR TO KEEP YOU SILENT.
- ☐ BE BRAVE ENOUGH TO TELL YOUR STORY.
- ☐ REMEMBER THAT YOU ARE NOT YOUR PAST.

THE VULNERABILITY BIAS

So, if we know vulnerability is good for us, why aren't we all running around living our best, most fabulous vulnerable lives? If we *know* that vulnerability enhances resilience and amplifies human connection, why are so few of us *being* vulnerable? I wanted to understand the disconnect between knowing and being vulnerable.

I termed the answer I uncovered in my research The Vulnerability Bias to explain why sharing our most resilient stories is so often difficult. Even though we think more of others for sharing their resilience stories, The

Vulnerability Bias leads us to believe that people will think less of us if we share our own resilience story.

This bias in our mind capitalizes on a persistent belief that sharing our resilience stories and being vulnerable are signs of weakness, when quite the opposite is true. Most of us are drawn to the strength and honesty of those who are brave enough to share their resilience stories.

The Vulnerability Bias is a powerful prohibition that tells us that if we are truly vulnerable, allowing ourselves to be seen and known, then there will be three negative outcomes, which I call The Three L's:

1. People won't *Like* us.
2. They won't *Love* us.
3. They might *Leave* us.

Fear of The Three L's keeps you locked in your Vulnerability Cage because you fear repercussions for being vulnerable. Yet, when you gather the courage to share your resilience story, you will find that The Three L's are simply a faulty fear-based bias. Most people discover that, contrary to The Vulnerability Bias, their openness and willingness to be vulnerable deepens their connection to others.

VULNERABILITY AND THE INTEGRATION OF SELF

(Sexual assault trigger warning—if you need to, skip to the section "How I Became My Own Case Study" on page 38.)

Vulnerability is about full integration of all parts of yourself by aligning your internal thoughts, feelings, and experience with the version of yourself that you show to the world. To do that, you must love and accept yourself. Ahem, all of yourself. Now, you may have aspects of yourself that you don't like, or love, whether it is something physical or something you have done in the past, or perhaps something you feel guilty about, like a bad decision or a failure.

I was working with a coaching client on practicing her vulnerability when she stopped me as I talked about being unhappy with certain parts of ourselves.

"What do you mean?" she asked.

"Sometimes we tend to wall off or hide things we don't like about ourselves or our lives," I said.

I could see that this struck her. In our next session, she told me that she'd been sexually assaulted in high school, an experience she had disowned, never discussed, and gone on to pretend never happened. Naturally, it had been traumatic for her, and when she finally allowed herself to be vulnerable and verbalize what had happened, she was able to release all the pent-up emotions she didn't even recognize she was still carrying years later.

After giving voice to this traumatic event, this client freed herself of the insomnia, anxiety, and claustrophobia she had dealt with since being assaulted; she had not before connected that those concerns were related to her disowned and unprocessed trauma.

While she had walled off this memory from her day-to-day consciousness, her pain and torment still lingered in her subconscious. Bringing this memory to the surface took a great deal of courage. For years, she had carried this experience in her body and psyche, creating debilitating mental-health concerns. Below the surface, unacknowledged, dormant, she couldn't heal what had happened to her, but when she could voice it and feel it, she could heal it.

HOW I BECAME MY OWN CASE STUDY

While at Cigna, and in a short period of time, I'd been promoted multiple times with successively greater scopes of responsibility. Now, I was leading global leadership development. I feared that if my colleagues knew about my PTSD diagnosis and experience with the stalker, it would hurt my reputation and harm my career path.

My feelings began to change when I uncovered the powerful connection between vulnerability as a practice to enhance our resilience. I thought: *Isn't this story of the stalker and my PTSD one of my most meaningful resilience stories? If this is the story I most don't want to tell, is this the story I most need to tell?*

Even with my understanding of the power of vulnerability and The Vulnerability Bias, I was still hesitant to share my resilience story. There are several symptoms that commonly accompany a diagnosis of PTSD that gave me pause. The first was hypervigilance. At that time, when I still met the diagnosis for PTSD, when I was in circumstances that reminded me of the experience with the stalker, like being home alone, I would be on edge and every little sound would make me jump. The second symptom was auditory and visional hallucinations. When I was home alone and on edge, sometimes I would hear things that weren't there like footsteps on the stairs, or I would think I saw someone in the room out of the corner of my eye, when it was really just a coatrack. I'd also have difficulty falling asleep and staying asleep, as well as nightmares. I had learned to cope with these symptoms, but I wasn't sure I wanted other people to know about them. I was petrified that people would think I was "crazy," rather than understanding my symptoms as a normal and natural response to having been exposed to trauma.

I had never liked calling attention to myself or standing out from the crowd. I'd always been self-conscious about being tall for my age, and now at five foot eleven inches, I don't exactly blend in. Yet, I was learning from my resilience research interviews that the most resilient practice I could engage in was vulnerability. That meant doing the exact opposite of what I wanted to do. It meant allowing my inside self to match the outside self I showed to the world. If I was going to help others and confirm the accuracy of my research, I knew that I needed to share my story and, in effect, become my own case study.

The thought of sharing the story that I'd vowed to hide was frightening. On the other hand, I felt that I owed it to myself, not to mention all the people I had interviewed, to find out the truth about The Practice of Vulnerability and The Vulnerability Bias. I engaged in what my colleague Susan Cain calls "a year of speaking dangerously." Susan, the best-selling author of *Quiet* and *Bittersweet*, is an introvert. She shared with me how she'd faced her fears of public speaking, and she encouraged me to do the same.

I decided I would learn something either way and make it a win-win. If I shared my resilience story and The Three L's occurred—people wouldn't like me, wouldn't love me, and they might leave, as I'd feared—I would know my research was incorrect, and I would go back to keeping my experiences a secret. But if I shared my resilience story, and The Three L's didn't occur, then I would know my research was accurate. I would be my own case study, confirming that vulnerability does enhance resilience, and The Vulnerability Bias is only a lie we tell ourselves.

When I presented my research on resilience at human resources conferences, and I spoke about The Practice of Vulnerability, I decided to share my story from the stage with my colleagues, other heads of leadership development and professionals in the fields of talent management, talent strategy, and human resources. I would tell the story I most didn't want to tell, but that most needed to be told.

Can you guess what happened? The Vulnerability Bias did not come true: no one stopped liking me, no one stopped loving me, and no one left or abandoned me. In fact, quite the opposite occurred. Sharing my resilience story brought people closer to me and me to them. When I had the courage to share my resilience story, people liked and loved me more. Rather than people leaving, new opportunities emerged for speaking engagements and Cigna invited me to speak at town halls to our teams about the power of vulnerability and The Five Practices.

BECOMING REAL

Becoming real is a lot like the story of the *Velveteen Rabbit*. Being unreal and invulnerable looks sparklingly flawless, like a new toy. Becoming real, as the Velveteen Rabbit did, is having the courage to have our shiny facade stripped away, and for people to see the imperfections that exist beneath the veil. Why does it feel so difficult to know how to be real, to determine how much to share about yourself in your personal and professional life?

My research demonstrates that the most resilient people are those who integrate themselves holistically, who allow their inside self to match the outside self they share with the world. Many people I have interviewed, when considering what and how to share their resilience story, run through mental arithmetic where they think that if they told people "a" thing, those people would think "b" thing about them, and sharing "b" thing will create "c" outcome. Because they've already worked out the computation and concluded that vulnerability will not yield a positive result, they've taught themselves not to share "a" thing to avoid "c" outcome, which in their mind, equals safety. Rather than breaking out of our Vulnerability Cage, we've learned to stay quiet. The price of our perceived safety is that we never give people a chance to truly know, see, and understand us. And we are robbed of the ability to be authentic to ourselves.

Using this simple arithmetic to vet our professional and personal interactions, we think we are offering a kindness by keeping things nice and clean for people—not making them uncomfortable by perhaps sharing too much. We reason that if people don't know the gooey details of our lives, of our humanness, they won't have to worry about us. Or support us. Or help us. Or be burdened by us. And, conveniently, we won't have to rely on them either.

Rather than overshare, many of us tend to undershare our resilience stories. Often, we are all about listening to others' resilience stories, meeting the needs of others, and taking care of others. We're willing to give a great deal, but we don't ask for our own needs, wants, or desires to be considered, let alone met, in return.

This usually continues for some time.

For me, things changed when I was heading up global leadership development at Cigna and I received feedback on my performance. All was good *except*, I was told, I came across as too polished. *Too polished?* In my tidy world, there was no such thing as too many coats of lacquer. Didn't everyone want me to walk around with a flawless veneer? Apparently, they did not. There was a variable I hadn't accounted for in my slick formula: r = relatability.

LIVING OUT LOUD

Without my neat calculus, I felt confused about how and when to take up more relational space in my relationships. *What did people want to know about me? How would I know when my pendulum swung far enough in the opposite direction toward authenticity and vulnerability when every personal detail felt raw and exposed? What if I went too far, and—gasp!—overshared?* As Hermann Hesse said, "Everything becomes a little different as soon as it is spoken out loud." There is, without question, both a risk and reward attached to being vulnerable and allowing ourselves to be more fully known by others.

This may mean that you are too much for some people.

Or not enough.

Or perceived as too complex or messy.

Those are not your people.

Rather than staying silent and hiding my inner self beneath an immaculate coat of varnish, I began finding my voice.

While at Cigna, I was invited to moderate a live discussion with our CEO for hundreds of employees around the globe. Instead of greeting the attendees with an idyllic smile when they approached me before I went onstage, while my heart pounded out of my chest from nerves, I told them I needed to rehearse and then I took time to breathe and focus before taking the stage.

Our employees later commented that I always seemed so pulled together, and they benefited from seeing that I got nervous too. They related to my imperfection more than they did when I was trying to create a false perfect exterior. They said to themselves, She's human after all!

When I wasn't holding myself to an excessively high standard, others felt less pressure to appear faultless too. Rather than keeping a medical concern to himself, one of my clients decided to engage his vulnerability and confide in a colleague. When his travel schedule got hectic, the colleague reminded him to make a clinic appointment to care for himself.

This colleague also found a couple mistakes in my client's recent report and helped him by editing his work before a meeting with the board. They've become a real part of each other's lives because he had the courage to step out in his vulnerability with his health diagnosis. Subscribing to the "shoulds"—who we think we should be, or think others want us to be—doesn't allow us to be seen, known, understood, or loved.

"Shoulds" almost always indicate that shame, disappointment, or a belief that we are lacking is present, because the word *should* indicates a discrepancy between what is and how we believe things ought to be. When his clients used the word *should*, the late Albert Ellis, a pioneering psychotherapist who founded rational emotive behavior therapy, would say, "You're 'shoulding' all over yourself." Be mindful of when you hear yourself using the word *should*, because this often indicates that you're being hard on yourself or believing that something is wrong with your experience, when in truth, you are right where you're meant to be.

Becoming more real, sharing vulnerably, and showing up authentically allows others to take a vested interest in you, to develop yourself in the ways you so generously give to others. The awkward moments that have transpired between my clients and their colleagues, rather than being cringy, have given them a good chuckle and have deepened their relationships.

VULNERABILITY IN SERVICE OF WHAT?

True vulnerability can be difficult to identify and express. Anytime I consider taking the courageous step of being vulnerable, I ask myself, "What is my vulnerability serving?" This simple question can help you distinguish between sharing to create lasting bonds and enduring human connections, versus sharing from a place within yourself that is seeking attention or desires to have your ego stroked.

PERFORMATIVE VERSUS GENUINE VULNERABILITY

If you watch reality television shows, you've certainly noticed that nearly every contestant seems to have a backstory involving a grueling challenge. Many times, these stories are touching, yet sometimes, they are too much information (TMI) and seem contrived to win sympathetic votes. Reality television is virtually founded on people's performative vulnerability. I am not saying that many stories are not heartfelt and genuine, but a lot of them aren't. That's okay. It's entertainment. In contrast, vulnerability is not TMI or oversharing or "putting it all out there" on a reality TV show, with your friends, or even in a team meeting.

I explored this with my colleague Michael Bungay Stanier, a.k.a. MBS, author of the best-selling book *The Coaching Habit* and a guest on my podcast *Flourish or Fold: Stories of Resilience*. During the podcast episode, we talked about people who express their vulnerability as a performative art versus those who are truly wading through the muddiness of their psyche. My conversation with MBS really got me thinking about how to distinguish our motivations for vulnerability. I developed the concept of performative versus genuine vulnerability to help distinguish when vulnerability comes from a place within that is focused on elevating ourselves, *performative vulnerability*, versus from a place within ourselves that seeks authentic connection, *genuine vulnerability*.

Performative vulnerability is posturing, sometimes attention seeking or even, at times, manipulative. It's a way of saying "look at me" that is more of a transaction than an interaction. Performative vulnerability is about telling people a story to manage their impressions of you. It's about feeding our personal ego by seeking recognition, gaining followers, or wanting to be seen in a certain light, rather than seeking personal connection.

Genuine vulnerability is focused on enhancing human connection and is greater and more meaningful than impression management or bolstering reputations. Genuine vulnerability is an attempt to be authentic and understood, to have the courage to be seen and known as our authentic selves, to give people a peek at our humanity with the desire to bring others closer to us.

A great example of this is my work with my coaching client Cassandra (not her real name). As a high-potential leader and an executive, she wrestled with expressing genuine versus performative vulnerability after she was promoted into an unfamiliar but exciting operational position—from marketing, where she had spent her career—at the company where she worked. She was both excited about the new challenge and terrified that she would let her new team down.

When we discussed how she would introduce herself to her new team, she said, "I'm just going to go in there and tell them that I have no idea what I'm doing." I paused for a long moment knowing her approach would compromise her credibility and introduce doubt into the minds of her new team members.

"How does that approach serve you?" I asked her.

At first, Cassandra was thoughtful, then said with a laugh, "Well, hopefully they will take pity on me and have really low expectations for me."

That is a great example of performative vulnerability. Cassandra was talking about lowering expectations because of her fear of failure. I suggested a different approach involving genuine vulnerability.

We decided that, instead, Cassandra would share her genuine vulnerability with her new team, not to lower expectations, but to create deeper connections with those she would be leading. When she met with her team, she said, "I'm so excited to be working with all of you, and I am truly delighted to be learning operations. I have deep tenure in marketing and there are a lot of transferrable skills to operations. And I would be lying if I said I didn't also feel nervous about taking this role. I have a lot to learn, and I looking forward to learning from all of you."

Cassandra's genuine vulnerability allowed her to showcase her experience and leadership strengths while also being honest about her fear and her desire to learn. This balanced approach, in service of creating a space of authenticity and genuine connection with her new team, allowed them to see her as both competent and honest, as well as authentic because she was able to be genuinely vulnerable in service of creating a connection.

AUTHENTICITY AND EMPATHY

The Practice of Vulnerability is the cornerstone of both authenticity and empathy. We cannot share ourselves authentically if we do not, first, share aspects of ourselves vulnerably. Similarly, we cannot connect with others empathetically without first connecting with vulnerable aspects of ourselves.

Both authenticity and empathy require that we connect with ourselves vulnerably to offer listening and deep understanding to others, based on our lived experience. One of my favorite stories from my colleagues at Nike was how shoe designer Tinker Hatfield Jr. leaned on his natural tendency toward empathy to create a shoe that then–NBA star Michael Jordan never wanted. A shoe that went on to become one of the best-selling and most iconic sneakers of all time!

The Nike Shoe Designer Who Kept Air Jordan from Flying Away

Nike's most high-profile athlete endorser, Michael Jordan, the NBA Rookie of the Year in 1983, was coming up for his contract renegotiation with the company in 1987, and there were whispers that the Chicago Bulls' rising star was considering other shoe brands. Peter Moore, Nike's creative director and lead shoe designer, called Hatfield into in his office and said: "You do it. Design Michael Jordan's next basketball shoe."

Hatfield was panic-stricken. He had never worked on an Air Jordan design. He had never met Jordan and had no idea what he wanted in his next Nike shoe. Hatfield spent a few days hanging out with the famous athlete who was already a fan favorite and had just won his first of seven scoring titles but had yet to win the first of his six NBA Championship titles with the Bulls.

The shoe designer wanted to get to know Jordan as a person to better understand his sense of style. He observed Jordan buying fine suits and plush leather shoes, noting that Jordan's flair for fashion hadn't been reflected in the previous two Air Jordan sneaker designs.

When Jordan talked about the elements of performance and style, Hatfield listened and envisioned his design. He listened with empathy to the person, to Jordan's humanity, not the celebrity athlete. The shoe designer had majored in architecture, and he believed that you can't design a house without knowing the people who will live there. He wisely applied this same principle to designing Jordan's next shoe.

Jordan wanted a mid-top. The original Jordan and Jordan II were high-tops; mid-tops were not as popular at the time. Some even disparaged them as the shoe version of capri pants. Yet, Jordan shared his desire for a lighter, less restrictive shoe. Hatfield observed Jordan's penchant for Italian dress shoes and imagined making a shoe that would have the fine materials, soft suede and buttery leather, that Jordan gravitated toward. Hatfield also found inspiration in a photo of Jordan leaping in the air to dunk a basketball with his legs splayed out to the sides, arm extending toward the basket, to create his design for Air Jordan III.

When Hatfield and Nike founder Phil Knight went to meet with Jordan to show him the design, Jordan was still on the golf course. As the hours ticked by, Hatfield and Knight thought this was not a good sign. There were reports that Jordan was on the verge of signing with another shoe company, and when he finally did show up for the meeting, he seemed disinterested.

Once again, tapping into his empathy and connection with Jordan, Hatfield sensed the athlete's mood and did not try to sell Jordan on his design. Instead, he asked him again about his vision for his playing shoes. Once Jordan completed his description, Hatfield pulled the cover off the Air Jordan III mid-top sneaker that had been sitting, hidden, under a piece of fabric on the table. I imagine that Jordan picked up the shoe, turning it over in his hands, feeling the smooth, stylish suede. He saw that the Nike swoosh had been moved to the back of the shoe and in its place was his silhouette performing his signature dunk. Hatfield had listened to Jordan with empathy, had done his research, and had put Jordan's image front and center, and Jordan could see that his vision had become a reality.

Today, the Air Jordan brand has an estimated value of $10 billion, and Michael Jordan has earned more than $1.5 billion in their endorsement deal. Years after creating his first Air Jordan, Hatfield asked Jordan why he stayed with Nike. Jordan said the two factors that swayed his decision were the advice of his father, who told him to stay the course, and his own gut feeling that Hatfield had put his own ego aside, listened to him, and taken the time to know him as a person while designing a shoe that reflected his tastes and desires.

If Hatfield hadn't been able to connect to elements of his own vulnerability, he couldn't have connected to Jordan's authentic style and personality to create the iconic Air Jordan III. Today, Jordan is a successful businessman said to be worth more than $2 billion, and Hatfield is Nike's vice president of design and special projects. Both men are legends in their respective fields, though I've never heard my colleague referred to as "Air Hatfield."

HOW TO SHARE YOUR RESILIENCE STORY

My 2022 TED Talk entitled *How Resilience Breaks Us Out of Our Vulnerability Cage* has been viewed by more than one million people. The number one question people ask me is: How can I effectively share my resilience story to expand my own vulnerability *and resilience*.

Here are the steps to follow to share your resilience story.

First, recognize the power of YOUR story! The most important story any of us will tell is our own resilience story. It is your choice to tell your resilience story, what resilience story you share, and with whom. Telling your resilience story gets to be your conscious choice, and telling your resilience story, while feeling vulnerable, is entirely within your control. Key questions to ask yourself when preparing your resilience story to share with others are:

What is the purpose of sharing my resilience story?

It is important to be aware of the greater purpose of sharing your resilience story. Simply sharing anything and everything about our lives is not vulnerability. Without a clear understanding about why we are sharing a resilience story, it is easy to get caught up in performative vulnerability instead of genuine vulnerability.

We get to ask ourselves:

What is my intention in sharing this story?
What is sharing this resilience story in service of?
How is sharing this story in service of supporting the development and growth of others?
Is my desire to share this story genuine or performative?
What do I hope to accomplish or what change do I hope to effect by sharing this story?
How will sharing this story create more genuine connection with other humans?

By asking yourself these important questions, you determine the true nature of your motivations and become more conscious of the reasons you're choosing to share your resilience story. If you ask yourself why you're sharing a resilience story, and the answer you hear is that you want people to like you or see you as smarter, wealthier, more successful, and so on, this story is likely being driven by performative vulnerability, not genuine vulnerability. I would suggest sharing a different resilience story that truly showcases your genuine vulnerability, to deepen your connections with other humans. Once you've determined if a particular resilience story is being driven by genuine versus performative vulnerability, ask yourself these series of questions about the content of the story you are considering sharing:

What is the story I have told myself about this experience?
Does it support the highest aspects of the person I am and am becoming?
How might I (re)tell my resilience story, so the narrative is empowering and highlights my strengths as a person, in leadership and life?

This series of questions is important because in sharing your resilience story, you have an opportunity to rewrite your resilience story to become your resilience narrative.

Your narrative is the conscious story you tell yourself and others about the events that occurred. Your story is what has happened to you. It is a set of events that you can recount. When you craft your resilience story, you have an opportunity to look at the element of story (the events that happened to you) and the element of narrative (the meaning that you make of the experiences, the identity that you formed based upon them) and to question your existing narrative/identity.

You may begin to realize that you don't have to feel afraid or angry about what has happened to you anymore; you can craft a new narrative around your experience that is more positive and more holistic.

Rather than your resilience stories making you bitter, how can you rewrite their narrative, so they make you better? When you embrace vulnerability by sharing your resilience story, you help others to do the same by role modeling vulnerability.

Who is likely to be able to empathize and accept you in the sharing of your story?

Are there people who you believe will have the ability to be empathetic and accepting of your experience?

Who may have a similar story and be able to relate to your resilience story?

Are there people who may have had a similar experience, and rather than feeling triggered or retraumatized by your story, will be able to relate?

Be the listener you'd like to have listen to you.

If you share in a group, you might make it part of other people sharing their stories as well, to create a stronger connection within the group. Be sure to really listen to what other people have to say about themselves, rather than, if you're feeling nervous about sharing your story, being distracted by what you have to say.

Who has earned the right to hear your resilience story?

When sharing your resilience story, especially for the first few times, it's imperative to choose people who you believe will have the ability to receive your story and respond thoughtfully and supportively. Although today I share my story publicly, the first times, it was of critical importance that I felt heard and believed, and that the recipient of my story could empathize with my experience.

Fortunately, the people with whom I confided gave me the gifts of being seen, known, and heard. I could see that they thought more of me for the experience I shared, not less of me, as The Vulnerability Bias would have me believe. If your story is not received in a way that allows you to feel supported, do not let this experience silence you and keep you from sharing your resilience story.

The degree to which people can support us is a measure of their capacity to hear hard things, NOT a measure of our worthiness.

Often, when we tell our resilience stories and they are not received in the way we would like, we believe this is measure of our worthiness, when it is actually a measure of the listener's emotional capacity. If the listener does not have the capacity to hear your resilience story currently, this is also *not* a message that you have been irrevocably damaged by your experience. Choose a different person who has earned the right to hear your story and keep going until you find a tribe of people that matches your vibe and has the capacity to hear, know, and see you as the beautiful human you are!

When is a good time to share your resilience story?

There are many good times to share your resilience story. However, sharing your resilience story initially can be stressful, scary, or anxiety provoking, so set aside plenty of time to share your resilience story. Choose a time when other aspects of your life feel calm, not stressful. This is to ensure you have the time and energy to focus on sharing in a manner that allows you to feel you have the energy to make this leap of trust and faith.

GUIDELINES FOR SHARING YOUR RESILIENCE STORY PUBLICLY

The following are common questions I have received about how to share your resilience story and demonstrate vulnerability. I have found the answers to these questions create helpful guideposts for you to consider when sharing your resilience story with others publicly.

What if I get emotional when sharing my resilience story and vulnerable aspects of my life?

I ask myself: *Am I talking about my experience for catharsis or for the purposes of catalyzing others' growth?* Asking myself this question is important to determine if a resilience story is suitable for a general audience or only for my close friends and family.

One of the first times I shared my resilience story was to an audience that included David Rock, founder of the NeuroLeadership Institute (NLI). His presence made me even more nervous because I admired his work and watched his response to my presentation closely as I spoke. When I began speaking, he was typing on his computer. Then, he began to look up from his screen periodically. Finally, he folded his computer and put it away, giving me his full attention.

Afterward, there was a luncheon, and Rock asked me to eat with him. While we ate, he said: "I've never heard anyone tell a story the way you did. You went deeply into authentic emotions, demonstrating the power of vulnerability, but you didn't get stuck there," he said. "You brought the audience back out of the experience with you. It's one of the most incredible things I've seen onstage—to watch you go into the depth of the experience and to be able to bring yourself and us back out."

His words were an incredible compliment and summed up the importance of recognizing that you can share your emotions and use your insights from your resilience stories for the right audiences. I was able to take people on the journey that Rock described because I had already done an extensive amount of healing, and I knew I wouldn't be overcome by my emotions. If you're feeling vulnerable or emotional about your resilience story, this is likely not a story you are ready to share at work or publicly. Feeling all your feelings is important. Sharing a story that is cathartic isn't meant for a public audience and is better suited for close friends and family until you've done more work on healing the experience.

Don't violate the expectation of the relationship.

This means that when sharing resilience stories, your level of vulnerability will work best when it matches the nature of the relationship you have with a person or a group. It's not fair or justified for a therapist to ask their client for guidance on personal matters. It violates the expectation of the relationship if I ask my keynote audience to take care of me because I am crying onstage when, as the speaker, I am meant to be taking care of the experience of each person listening to me.

Alice Sebold, author of *The Lovely Bones* and *Lucky*, was asked in an NPR interview if her writing was ever cathartic. She responded that cathartic writing is very different than writing a compelling story for a mass audience. When we share our resilience stories, this experience can be cathartic and healing. Yet, sharing resilience stories publicly when our healing is still in process violates the expectation of the relationship we have with a wider audience.

Share from a place of wholeness, not lack.

Last, but not least, it is dangerous to share our resilience stories with the hope or expectation that we will receive feedback that validates or heals us.

When we are in a vulnerable place of healing and reconciling our resilience stories, the comments and responses of others become supercharged with meaning, and opening ourselves up during this tender time can do a lot more harm than good if we are not sharing our resilience stories publicly from a place of wholeness. If you hope to receive something from your audience when sharing your story that is healing, you may be violating the expectation of the relationship and potentially exposed to being hurt rather than healed.

HOW IS THE PRACTICE OF VULNERABILITY LIKE CANDY?

I observed that each of us has a natural set point for how we tend to express our vulnerability. Our default comfort level with vulnerability is

part of our personality. The extent to which we tend to express our vulnerability can be understood and categorized as candy.

Are you a gummy bear, Blow Pop, or Jolly Rancher?

Vulnerability is like candy. I have observed that our natural capacity, our natural state of comfort, with The Practice of Vulnerability can be characterized by three types of candy: gummy bear, Blow Pop, and Jolly Rancher. Can the environment we live or work within impact how or to what extent we express our vulnerability? Of course. Can the people we interact with dictate whether we choose to show more or less vulnerability? Absolutely. However, how we express our vulnerability tends to be a personality trait that is consistent.

I have found that exploring our vulnerability as a candy makes the self-reflection on vulnerability feel more fun and less judgmental because everyone enjoys candy. With all of the fear and anxiety that surround vulnerability, using candy to represent our vulnerability preference can add some levity to the conversation. Not to mention, talking about vulnerability as a familiar candy helps everyone have a shared understanding of each person's natural vulnerability set point.

What's your vulnerability style?

HOW ELSE MIGHT YOU DEMONSTRATE VULNERABILITY?

Sharing your resilience story is a great way to enhance your vulnerability, but it isn't for everyone. In addition to The Vulnerability Checklist, here are a few practical suggestions for taking the next steps to enhance your vulnerability right away:

- Be willing to say things like "I don't know," "I feel afraid about what the future holds," and the three most difficult words in the English language (and many other languages), "I need help."

- Recognize that the only insane thing is to be the sane one all the time. Lean on your relationships for support, and don't fall into the trap of believing you have to hold it together for everyone else. It's okay to not be okay.
- Start time with friends or meetings with a check-in that taps into your vulnerability. Some of my colleagues and I like to use "Rose-Bud-Thorn," where we go around the in-person or virtual room and share:
    - Rose: A success or point of pride
    - Bud: Something emerging
    - Thorn: A failure, challenge, or something difficult
    - Each person takes ninety seconds to two minutes going around the (virtual or hybrid) room. You'll be amazed how much you learn about the lives of your colleagues and friends that amplifies the vulnerability of everyone involved.
- Some Entrepreneurs' Organization (EO) chapters begin their meetings by going around the room and inviting everyone to complete the sentence: "If you really knew me, you'd know ___________."
- Many times, being vulnerable isn't about what you share, but breaking down the defenses that exist between yourself and other people, especially those that are different from yours. You can practice your vulnerability by watching a film or series and attempt to empathize with a character who is different from you by asking yourself questions like, "What is their underlying need? What drives them?"

These practices give you an opportunity to practice your vulnerability, along with your authenticity and empathy, by thoughtfully asking and answering questions, while also listening carefully to the responses of others.

A VULNERABLE CALL TO ACTION

When you tell your resilience stories of fear, loss, brokenness, pain, trauma, hurt, and disappointment, coupled with triumph, transformation, change, and growth, you enhance your vulnerability, and by extension you tap into your resilience to a greater degree because:

- There is greater alignment between your internal self and the outside self you share with the world, which conserves energy, because the more congruent your internal and external selves are, the less energy you need to exert to maintain different versions of yourself.
- When facing challenge, allowing your internal self to more closely match the external self you share with the world, allows you to receive the resources, support, and knowledge to effectively face those moments.
- You create stronger connections with others through your authenticity and empathy. By becoming real, you are no longer hiding, pretending, or walking around with your inside self misaligned with your outside self.

When you tell your resilience stories, free yourself from The Vulnerability Bias and by association your Vulnerability Cage, and when you practice The Vulnerability Checklist, you stop living in fear and start living as you truly are. In doing so, you embrace all parts of yourself and your experience, even the disowned or unacknowledged parts, and demonstrate even greater authenticity, empathy, and connection.

5
The Practice of Productive Perseverance

The Practice of Productive Perseverance is what we do when the grit hits the fan. At its core, it boils down to this question: "Do I stay, or do I go? Do I persevere, or do I pivot?" This is the resilient practice that supports you in your intelligent pursuit of a goal, knowing when to stay the course, when a setback is a setup for your next big success, and when, in the face of diminishing returns, you adjust and pivot in a new direction.

You may have asked yourself questions about whether you stay or go at various points of your life, whether it was a job, completing an advanced degree, continuing as an entrepreneur, or staying in a romantic relationship.

MAKING A LEAP AND HITTING A WALL

I, too, have asked myself the pivotal question of whether I stay or go at many inflection points across my lifetime. In June 2019, I accepted what I thought was my dream job with one of the most iconic brands across the globe, Nike. As part of my commitment to "speak dangerously," I took the stage at a human capital conference and shared The Five Practices of Highly Resilient People, along with my resilience story. Contrary to what The Vulnerability Bias would have us believe, that The Three L's will occur—that people won't like us, won't love us, and might leave—sharing my work did just the opposite; it opened doors for me that I hadn't known were possible.

Unbeknownst to me, there was an HR executive from Nike who heard my talk and saw the opportunity for resilience to be part of their strategy to develop their leaders and support their athlete partners. After many conversations and not one, but two, invitations to the Nike World Headquarters, just outside of Portland, Oregon, I couldn't believe my ears when I was presented with the opportunity that I thought was destined to only remain a dream. First, I was offered the role of head of Nike's executive development, leading a team to oversee the development of the C-suite and four hundred vice presidents, along with supporting our athlete partners in further developing their resilience. Within a few months, my role was expanded to include heading talent strategy, how we evaluated our leaders' performance and potential. In a matter of a few years, I had evolved from the woman who thought she would never work in this industry again after losing my first management consulting job to leading executive development for one of the most recognizable and sought-after global brands.

In the years leading up to this opportunity, I had led global leadership development at Cigna across eighty-six countries, initially moving my family to Hartford, Connecticut, for this role. Now, living in Philadelphia, where I shared custody of my two sons with my former husband, I would commute across the continental United States weekly to be present at Nike's Global Headquarters Monday through Wednesday—then take the red-eye back to Philadelphia Wednesday evening, and work remotely Thursday and Friday so I could spend the weekend with my sons before leaving Sunday afternoon to do it all again.

For the first few months, I came up with strategies to make the commute more palatable. I invested in several neck pillows until I found the one that most comfortably propped my head up on those overnight flights without giving me a headache the next day. While I was navigating the commute, I was also navigating a position that was brand new for Nike. There hadn't been a head of executive development and talent strategy before, so there was no template, no best practices. Alongside not having a road map, I also had the opportunity to blaze a new trail.

Beginning with our leaders in the C-suite, we began offering meaningful assessments for our highest leaders to appreciate their strengths, talents, and opportunities for growth. For many, even in advanced leadership roles, this was the first time they'd received meaningful leadership development that included leadership assessments, development plans, and executive coaching.

Despite the fulfilling work, the opportunity to build out my new role and team, and the storied campus that is Nike's Global Headquarters (where I might say "Hi" to the towering LeBron James while waiting for my latte), a persistent question kept floating into my mind: "Could I do this resilience work full-time?" The Nike job was an opportunity of a lifetime, but as I walked from meeting to meeting on the beautiful corporate campus, I found myself contemplating a more independent path as a consultant, coach, and speaker built on The Five Practices. That concept had resonated so strongly with Nike's leaders that they offered me this position. I was excited and flattered about that. I also was intrigued about the prospect of striking out on my own to share my work on resilience more broadly, to even more clients and corporations. Maybe you've felt this way at one time or another too? I thought Nike would be a career "summit," but when I arrived at the top of the peak, the experience provided a new point of view. When my work with resilience kept tapping me on the shoulder while I was in the role I imagined would be the ultimate opportunity, I thought that perhaps it was time to listen.

My job became even more interesting when then Nike CEO Mark Parker announced he would leave his post and become executive chairman of the company. While preparing for Mark's transition, examining the background, traits, and skills of his prospective successors, I began thinking if it might be time for me to make a transition too. And so, I got to consider if I was ready to make the leap: "Do I stay, or do I go?"

I reached out to friends and colleagues in human resources, leadership development, and talent management to gauge their interest in partnering with me on The Five Practices framework. I found a highly receptive audience. I was invited to lead executive coaching engagements, give keynote addresses, and facilitate workshops.

By the time I'd departed from Nike in January 2020, I had agreements in place to replace my income for the next six months. I created my own company, the Resilience Leadership Institute, and though I felt that old sense of fear that crops up anytime I step outside my comfort zone, I steeled my resolve and prepared to bring my work on resilience, mental health, and well-being to the world.

Sometimes the world has other ideas. My timing was not so fortuitous. One month into my new career, the World Health Organization (WHO) and the president of the United States declared a public health emergency due to the COVID-19 outbreak.

All the promising business that was supposed to replace my income as I transitioned to ensure I could still pay my bills as a single mother and head of my own household evaporated by mid-March. Instead of being a busy entrepreneur, I was home with my two sons, navigating virtual learning while I tried to reformulate my business plan.

My departure from Nike felt like one of the dumbest things I'd ever done. I agonized over what to do next. *What would happen if I couldn't pay my mortgage? If my home was repossessed? If I lost everything? If I had to move into a homeless shelter? How would I support and see my children?*

I was certainly not alone in my worry, fear, and uncertainty. Like so many others, I tightened up on all expenses, buying discounted groceries, applying for COVID-19 relief on my mortgage, and sewing my sons' pant knees and socks when they sprouted holes, instead of purchasing new ones.

Then, Arianna Huffington deemed *resilience* the key word for 2020. As an expert on the topic, I was biased, agreeing that this concept was critical for all of us. I needed it as much as anyone. For the first several months, I thought about folding up my start-up's tent and applying for another corporate position.

I kept practicing what I preached, and, fortunately, as the rest of the world adjusted to the new realities of the pandemic, clients came knocking. Organizations began reaching out to me to speak on cultivating resilience. I was ready and willing to share my own stories of uncertainty, confusion, and fear as part of my teaching, alongside the two decades of learning that had gone into The Five Practices.

I began to think that maybe my timing wasn't so bad after all: *If I can make it with this company during a pandemic, I can create a solvent business in less chaotic times to come!*

The pandemic had tripped me up initially, but I had a feeling that if I weathered the storm—patched enough pants and ate enough peanut butter sandwiches—my business concept might have even greater appeal as individuals along with leaders, teams, and businesses searched for ways to develop resilience in face of challenging times.

I focused on creating a vision for my business and set about bringing it to reality. I'd spent two decades researching resilience. I was the undisputed international expert on the topic for those seeking ways to survive and thrive in business and life. I had the expertise, relationships, and work ethic to be successful, when (I reasoned, thinking positively), not if, the clients signed up. I trusted my intuition, worked diligently toward making my vision a reality, and focused on using my training and expertise to allow myself and my company to be of service to add value during those trying times.

THE RESILIENT PRACTICE OF PRODUCTIVE PERSEVERANCE

When facing any trial, we often receive conflicting advice: stay the course versus shift gears. The Practice of Productive Perseverance is the intelligent pursuit of a goal. It requires the ability to know when to maintain the mission, and when, in the face of diminishing returns, to make a pivot, small or large, in a new direction.

Being able to pursue goals intelligently is the hallmark of this practice. Productive Perseverance is about pursuing a goal even when you don't know if you'll "make it," and doing your best to navigate the complexities of your journey. We've all seen people rise above ridiculous obstacles and achieve a lofty goal in the face of naysayers and few, if any, believers. We've also seen those who chase an unachievable goal too long with diminishing returns. The Practice of Productive Perseverance is about the art and science of knowing the difference.

At the close of 2021, Arianna Huffington deemed "Resilience+" her word for the year, likely the decade. Just as your computer and smart phone are continually updating their operating systems, resilience is the continual upgrade required for our human operating system (HOS) to function. Resilience is not a destination, an end state, but rather an always evolving set of skills that equip us on our journey in this life.

The Practice of Productive Perseverance exemplifies the ever-evolving circumstances of navigating the constant presence of the three C's. Resilience, along with The Practice of Productive Perseverance, isn't about achieving normalcy once and for all; it's about navigating our shifting environment one step at a time. Productive Perseverance demonstrates that we get to evaluate our environment routinely and determine if pursuing a goal is worthwhile, despite challenge, or if pivoting in a new direction, in the face of diminishing returns, makes more sense.

Despite the advice to never quit, The Practice of Productive Perseverance tells you that giving up, or at least making a pivot, small or large in a new direction, is now a hallmark of resilience and the ability to effectively pursue your goals, not a sign of weakness. Gone are the days when simply putting your head down and charging toward a goal no matter what obstacles emerge is a sign of resilience. These days, our lives are defined by flux, disruption, and ambiguity, making it even more important that we take stock of our conditions before engaging dogged determination to arrive at the outcome we hope to achieve, no matter what.

GRIT IS NOT THE SAME AS BEING RESILIENT

I am often asked whether grit is the same as resilience. The answer is, No, they are not the same thing. However, grit one is a component of The Practice of Productive Perseverance.

Grit, a concept Angela Duckworth has researched extensively, is the metal that allows us to keep going when the going gets tough.

If you want to be a US Navy Seal, graduate from Harvard, or win the Scripps National Spelling Bee, grit can be a healthy attribute. In these instances, there are a clear set of requirements that don't change much inside a relatively predictable environment. Therefore, having the mentality to stay the course will often create the desired results.

Yet, when environments are being disrupted by technology, health concerns, political realignment, or economic shifts, grit may not be so great when it comes to demonstrating resilience and achieving your goals. People and companies have failed, not for lack of grit, but for being too gritty, too determined to reach their goals, while ignoring signals that the circumstances of their marketplace were changing. Blockbuster video stores and Borders bookstores (which began in my hometown of Ann Arbor, Michigan) were supergritty, and yet they are now extinct. Grit is not synonymous with resilience. In fact, in turbulent and distruptive times, grit may be the opposite of resilience. Grit works well in stable and consistent environments, yet plowing toward our goals, come hell or high water, in environments characterized by disruption and uncertainty, can have a deleterious impact. Your coping strategies and goals can easily become outdated when your environment changes to a significant degree, and you fail to adapt.

A RESILIENT MINDSET

There are three common qualities that encompass what I have come to refer to as a Resilient Mindset:

1. A clear desire: Those who flourish are unequivocal about their goal or imagined achievement, and unflinching in exactly the vision for what they wanted to create.
2. A defined purpose: Those who flourish are unambiguous about their purpose and desire for a specific outcome.
3. A dogged determination: Those who flourish possess an unwavering focus and passion to achieve their goal.

Those that engage in a resilient mindset focus extensively on what they are creating, but release control over how their dream comes true. They often report that their vision became a reality but emerged in a different manner than they anticipated. This balance of relentless commitment, coupled with an open-mindedness around how the desired results would manifest, allows them to focus only on what is within their realm of control while releasing the details outside of their control.

Those who flourish set high standards, are demanding of themselves and others to achieve excellence, yet remain prescriptive in how the vision would emerge, allowing space for dynamic forces outside of their control to interact with their best laid plans. What looks like a lucky break from the outside is, in fact, a resilient mindset that fosters the persistent belief in what was possible.

Any invention, advancement, or evolution seems impossible until it's discovered. If I told you thirty years ago that humans would devise a way to send messages to one another through the air, you would have had my head examined. Yet today, far from being impossible, it's called the internet.

SHOULD I STAY OR SHOULD I GO?

If your business or living environment has changed, you may have to adjust to have the career and life you want. If the environment is still favorable, then the key is to stay, to persevere, long after others have given up and gone home. The moment just before you're ready to give up may well be the moment just before the miracle happens. That was certainly true for me and my business, and it has been true for many of the successful people I've interviewed.

Now, that's not to say that I haven't done my fair share of leaving, cutting my losses and bailing out in search of something better. Within the last decade and a half, I've left two significant relationships, changed employers several times, and have resided in seven different US cities. In short, there has been more pivoting than staying the course in my adult life. Yet, growth is often nurtured by our willingness to face difficulties and learn from them.

The measure of who we are, our character, is often how we behave and respond when things don't go our way. Continued learning requires that we stay long enough to learn the valuable lessons of our experience. It requires that we stay at least long enough to confront the discomfort. Not running from what feels painful, humiliating, or scary, at least long enough to face the thing head on, ensures that we don't continue to repeat the same lessons. Rather than our discomfort driving us to go, staying gives us the presence and the power to learn and grow.

THOSE THAT STAY

At the University of Michigan, painted on the wall for the football team is a quote from the late Bo Schembechler, "Those who stay will be champions." Schembechler promised his players that if they remained on the team, they would receive a championship ring for winning one of the bowl games during their college tenure. I've often wondered if Schembechler's words were true only of his team under his leadership or if there is something to the idea that if we persist long enough, we will be champions of our craft or career.

Earlier in my career, I was not progressing as quickly as I desired. I received an offer to move cross-country to head the department of learning and leadership development for an enticing company with a large team and plenty of engaging work. It was an opportunity to build out the learning and leadership development strategy for the entire company. I "should" want the job, I reasoned. That "should" in my head signaled that my expectation of what I thought I ought to want, and feel, didn't match what was true for me.

I hesitated. I wanted the opportunity, yet I was excited about what I was building and creating with my current company. What felt most ideal was if I could stay and continue to advance right where I was.

Looking for guidance, I shared the opportunity with my manager at the time, our vice president of talent management. We talked about the prospect openly, the pros and the cons, and what might happen if I chose to stay versus go. She didn't offer me more money or a promotion to stay. She did offer me her time and counsel. After the conversation, I felt heard. Understood. In speaking to her, I had the opportunity to ask for what I wanted. She gave me space to articulate my needs and desired career path. While my next career step wasn't immediately apparent, I got to speak my truth, and I felt empowered to chart my path with my current organization.

I felt as valued in those conversations as I did in considering the shiny new career prospect. I learned that sometimes, though you may think you want to leave a relationship or a company, what you really want to leave behind is something within yourself or a feeling, like my frustration at progressing more slowly.

I learned I didn't want to leave my company. I wanted to feel valued and know that my company saw opportunities for advancement and expansion in my future. I turned down the other offer, choosing instead to stay the course with my current organization. Within a year, my role and team were expanded, and shortly after that, I received my next promotion.

STAYING POWER

Staying isn't always easy. If it was, everyone would do it. Fortunately, there are strategies to stay, sustainably, at least long enough to learn the lessons life is placing in your path. When faced with the decision to stay or go, to stay and grow, consider:

- *Choose self-compassion over self-criticism.* Acknowledge what you did right. Beating yourself up reduces mental and emotional strength. By giving yourself space for grace and gentleness with yourself, you enhance your capacity to learn, grow, and try again. For his album *Divide*, Ed Sheeran wrote more than two hundred songs, but went on to release just sixteen of his creations. When he wrote a song that didn't make the cut, he didn't chastise himself. Each song was part of the creative process that led to the songs that he ultimately featured on the album.

- *Don't do more, get back to the core.* More isn't necessarily more. Often, we think whipping up more work, productivity, or output is the answer. Sometimes, it is. But sometimes, it isn't. Having the courage to sit and be with your circumstances can often teach you more than doing more.
- *Focus on small wins.* Ask yourself what is working as opposed to fixating on what isn't. Do more of what is working. Celebrate wins. Envision a successful outcome. When distance swimmer Diana Nyad successfully swam the grueling 110 miles from Havana, Cuba, to Key West, Florida, she shared that, when the swim got difficult, her best friend encouraged her by instructing her to take just five more strokes at a time. In the end, the small wins added up to a big achievement.
- *Remember your freedom of choice.* Choose to go. Choose to stay. Whatever you do, the most important aspect is that you give yourself the freedom to choose. There is freedom in exercising the simple power of choice. Remember, you are not a born winner. You are not a born loser. You are a born chooser.
- *Your history doesn't define you.* Reconciliation is not about remaining within circumstances that diminish you, let alone do not support your highest purpose and growth. Stay long enough to learn. Be open enough to accept how you contributed. Understanding your history can be healing. Forgiveness is often transformative. Be mindful of how and to whom you offer a second chance so that second chance doesn't lead to the same lesson. We can forgive AND leave.

- *Try one more time.* This might sound at odds with my last point, and it is. If you decide that staying is the right next decision, you can realize success, even after failure. There is a high likelihood that success will occur even after a failed attempt. When the United States launched Explorer, its first successful satellite into space, it did so just one month after a failed launch of the satellite Vanguard, which exploded on the launch platform. We learn more from failure because we scrutinize these experiences more closely. Life is composed of infinite tries, and the willingness to continue to try, even after failure. Don't let failure deter you.

KEEP AUDITIONING

On the streets and alleys of my hometown, Philadelphia, Terrill Haigler is known as Ya Fav Trashman. The city's most celebrated and decorated sanitation worker has his own Instagram account with thousands of followers. In 2021, he was named Most Valuable Philadelphian by a local news organization and invited to the White House for a barbecue in his honor.

Haigler joined me on my *Flourish or Fold: Stories of Resilience* podcast, and recounted how he rose to prominence during the early days of the pandemic when trash pickup delays became a major issue. He launched his Instagram account, @YaFavTrashman, with the promise of giving his followers "the inside look, with a lil comedy, of what it's like to be a trashman."

The civil servant's ample charm gained him media attention and a large following. He used the platform to explain delays in trash pickups and to advocate for his fellow sanitation workers, asking followers to support hazard pay, better masks, and "prick-proof" gloves for those in the city's trash trenches.

As his fame grew, I was among those who took interest in Haigler's backstory, which is as colorful and inspiring as his personality. He is a classically trained dancer with a theater background, and he only became a sanitation worker after failing in his attempts to make it as a performer.

He auditioned for a play at the Freedom Theater four or five times, but never won a role. Some might have taken that as a rejection of his talents, and decided that he wasn't good enough. Instead, Haigler decided that he would never stop auditioning to become the best he could be, at whatever he did.

"Now, as a father, I never give up, you know, auditioning as a dad for my kids. I never give up auditioning as a productive citizen in, in society. I never give up. I may not get what I want.... As long as I show up to the audition, there's a possibility I could get the job. So, that's how I like to structure my life."

It is easy to believe that rejection is earth shattering and unrecoverable; however, rejection is not the worst possible outcome. Success is an answer. Failure is an answer. Not trying is a lifetime of not knowing. Haigler knew the worst outcome wasn't rejection, it was self-abandonment, not believing in himself enough to keep auditioning. Although Haigler never received the role, he learned to believe in himself relentlessly, to always keep trying, and to be his own best cheerleader.

BUST A MOVE AND FLOSS LIKE A BOSS

A few years ago, I was Halloween trick-or-treating with my two sons when we turned onto Delancey Street, which is a lovely area lined with large homes. It is also where the movie *The Sixth Sense* was filmed. The residents embrace Halloween with over-the-top decorations, including some with special effects and other frightful features worthy of Hollywood horror films.

"Mom! What is that?"

My oldest son Samson nudged me and pointed toward a clown breaking it down. It was a street performer, dressed as Pennywise, the super-creepy clown from Stephen King's *It*. This impersonator also did Michael Jackson moves, and as he danced, a flash mob of *Thriller*-inspired ghoulish dancers emerged from the crowd to perform with him.

Soon, trick-or-treaters were joining in.

Now, my Samson is an expert at flossing—not the dental thing, the dance thing. In the world of street moves, flossing involves moving your arms from side to side behind and in front of you. It almost looks like creating an optical illusion.

I looked at Samson's face, and read his expression, his eyes fixed on the dancing clown in pure awe. "Why don't you go out there and floss?" I asked him, knowing he was thinking the same thing.

But my son shook his head sadly, no. He was afraid.

I knelt down to look into his eyes and said, "Look, you will have other chances to floss. But you won't have this chance again. So, you get to decide what you want to do right now, because this moment won't come again."

Samson didn't say a word, so I continued: "Later on tonight, when we get home, what will you wish you had done?"

Samson thought a while longer and finally said, "Mom, hold my candy."

I watched his red-hooded Power Ranger head bob through the crowd and into the open dance circle next to Pennywise. At just the right moment, Samson unleashed his floss moves, and the crowd roared with approval.

As a parent, it's a proud moment to see my child trust himself and his talents, and to face his fears so that he can experience the joy of expressing himself. Samson decided to go for it and created a memorable moment in the process. Looking back, he tells me that he is grateful I pushed him, so he didn't miss out on that moment. Although he was initially scared, reminding him that this opportunity would only come once encouraged him to not miss the opportunity to floss with Pennywise.

MARKERS

Many people I have interviewed talked about scanning their environment for "markers" that gave them information to support their decision to persevere or pivot. People talked about looking at the outcome data to determine if they should have surgery. Prospective parents looked at success rates for in vitro fertilization (IVF) or evaluated adoption programs to determine the best way for them to begin a family. In business, people talked about looking for leading and lagging indicators, to assess the likelihood that a product launch would be successful or to look closely at factors that may disrupt their business model.

How to Prepare for the Pivot

Supermodel turned television personality, model, businesswoman, producer, actress, and writer Tyra Banks used markers in the modeling business to assess her longevity and plan for her pivot into even greater achievements.

From nearly her first trip down a runway, Tyra began planning for the end of her career, including how she would exit modeling and pivot into new realms. Many people plan for the pivot when they're nearing the end of a career path, facing a failure, or finding themselves at a crossroads, but resilient people are always looking for the next opportunity to rise above and beyond past achievements as well as developing an exit strategy, knowing that the only constant is change.

Instead of waiting until her daughter's career was on the decline, Tyra's mother began talking to Tyra about her pivot when she was at the top of her modeling career. Her mother knew that runway modeling would not be a long-term career, given the narrow dress size and age range at which models peak. Her mother encouraged Tyra to blaze new trails by creating her own brand that would open up greater opportunities.

Tyra went on to become a multimedia mogul, serial entrepreneur, and philanthropist whose Bankable Productions created the hit television shows *America's Next Top Model* and the Emmy Award–winning *Tyra Banks Show*. With her mother's help, Tyra prepared for and staged a remarkable pivot and a multifaceted, multimillion-dollar career that continues to this day.

THE 16TH SECOND

In 2019, high school student Kyle Martin gave a valedictorian speech that became a viral sensation on social media because of his searing candor and insight. With wisdom beyond his years, he reflected on the importance of relationships, not achievements, as the central focus of our lives. In the speech, he talked about competing to become his class valedictorian and how he sacrificed his relationships and took on immense stress to win the honor, earning an astonishing 4.64 GPA.

Martin noted that when he received the coveted award before the graduation ceremony, he felt wonderful. Elated. But only for about fifteen seconds. What happened in the sixteenth second? He thought to himself, "That's it?"

While wondering why he felt so empty, he examined his expectations. Had he imagined there would be a parade, balloons dropping from the ceiling, and all his problems would go away? Or that his insecurities would disappear?

He offered his classmates and the audience lessons he'd drawn from the sixteenth second onward. He concluded that pursuing and achieving goals is important, but hard work shouldn't be undertaken at the expense of relationships, if it requires sacrificing elements of our lives that are truly important.

"Working hard is good.... But it should not be done for the sole purpose of a goal's sake or at the expense of relationship with others," he said. "Looking back on this year, I realized the stress of this goal was paid for by the lack of attending to relationships in my life. Lesson learned, and self-reflection accomplished."

By the way, as of the fall of 2022, Kyle Martin is an honors student at UCLA, majoring in microbiology, with plans to become a physician one day, and despite continuing to crush academic goals, he has learned early on the value of both persisting in his goals and pivoting to focus on the experiences and relationships that matter most.

GIVING TOO MUCH AWAY

When engaging in The Practice of Productive Perseverance, many people I interviewed discussed not only the benefits of their goals, but also the cost of pursuing their dreams. We often sacrifice a great deal: free time, along with time with friends and family, hobbies, and even healthy habits like diet, sleep, and exercise, to make short-term investments in what we hope will be long-term gains.

However, the shadow side of pursuing goals at all costs is giving too much away. Of the top five regrets expressed by people at end of life, the second-most-common regret is "I wish I hadn't worked so hard." No one gets to the end of life and wishes they would have worked more.

One element of Productive Perseverance is not only knowing when your investments are yielding diminishing returns, but also being aware of when you are giving away too much of your time, energy, attention, and focus.

How do you evaluate opportunities that seem amazing at the outset, have the potential to have a big upside, but also may cross a line into requiring that you give too much of yourself away? One of my coaching clients partners with developing nations to create infrastructure and opportunities for the country's people. Although he dreams of helping others, he often finds himself immersed in bureaucracy, mired in red tape, and, at times, navigating the complex political relationships that exist within the developing nations he serves. In our work together, we identified what drives him, his purpose, and his values so he can monitor his involvement and ensure that he doesn't compromise himself or sacrifice his health or time with his beloved family members to an extent that he'll regret later on.

FINDING YOUR PURPOSE IN THE PAUSE

Sometimes, the decision is not whether to stay or go, but when to put a project on pause. A pause doesn't mean giving up, it means not yet or not now. It doesn't mean not ever. You may need to pause because the market isn't ready for your product, the technology you need hasn't been developed yet, or you don't have the resources to bring the team together. For most people with whom I have worked, life purpose is more elusive than being discovered all at once; typically our purpose is revealed little by little over the course of our lives, rather than all at one time. The following are some ideas for how to reflect on your purpose and determine how to move forward during a pause:

- *Does your goal or dream still motivate you to jump out of bed in the morning?* If you're not feeling inspired, perhaps it's time to assess why your motivation is waning.
- *Remind yourself this project, initiative, idea, or undertaking is important to you.* A pause can be an opportunity to remember why you're involved in this engagement and reignite your passion.
- *Ask yourself who you're doing this for.* Is this work for you? Others? Is this initiative right for you or are you doing it for someone else, because you think you ought to, or because you're trying to please or appease someone else?
- *If you can't create the project on the scale you imagined, perhaps you could run a pilot program?* How can you make smaller investments that allow you to try out new things and learn?
- *Seek out members of your community to collaborate, partner, or serve as a mentor.* Engaging those who may be able to help you see different perspectives, opportunities, or pathways can help you gain perspective on your pause and determine when the time is right to resume.

FINDING PERSPECTIVE

In a Western culture where productivity and accomplishments are pursued with abandon, one of the most difficult decisions we make can be to pause, rather than persist. We can't run before we walk; sometimes, we must slow down to go faster.

When Camilo Andrade, a senior brand director at Nike, heard me speak on resilience to his international team, he hadn't anticipated using the skills I taught that day to such a significant degree. Andrade awoke one morning to find his arm numb, and despite not having pain, in a dream he was told to go to the hospital. Upon arriving in the ER, he was rushed into surgery for blood clots in his arm, shoulder, and neck.

He was extremely concerned about taking time off for his health condition, especially because, being from Colombia originally, he'd achieved career successes of which he never could have dreamed in his home country and therefore he felt the weight of responsibility to not let his family or his country down. Yet he knew he would need to reprioritize his investments and focus on his health to undergo several painful surgeries and periods of recovery to ameliorate his blood clots. "I was afraid of taking that pit stop. I had to fight that demon, to step to the side of my career, knowing it could affect my performance and perception, so that I could be intentional about taking care of myself, my wife, and my baby."

We often expect our progression to be a direct route from Point A to Point B. The Practice of Productive Perseverance demonstrates that rarely are our paths a straight line, and we should expect fits, starts, and pauses as part of the process, rather than as the exception to the rule.

In a talk he gave to his colleagues at Nike, entitled "The Power of Perspective," Andrade described his journey to the audience by saying, "It's not linear, it's not fun, it's not always pretty, but it's real."

For Andrade, resilience is about being relentlessly conscious of his perspective. He appreciates how his reverse bucket list experiences, growing up in the narco war and an unstable country, both politically and economically, gifted him an outlook on the world that would be of pivotal importance when he faced his greatest challenge yet, life-threatening blood clots.

On that surgery table and in his recovery, he found the seeds of resilience that had been planted months before during my keynote had germinated in his mind and began to take root at just the moment when he was desperately searching for strength and inspiration.

"In those dark days, resilience will find us," Andrade told me. It was the night after one of his surgeries, alone in his hospital room, in pain and facing an uncertain future, that he recalled The Five Practices, and those seeds that had been incubating since my talk began to push into his consciousness and sprout, just at the very moment when he most needed hope to blossom.

The Five Practices not only carried him through the times when he needed to access resilience, his pause has refined his purpose and perspective. He's now writing a book on his experience to help others in their darkest times, to create his own resilience movement, and to pay forward the support he received from The Five Practices, when he needed them most, to help others.

WHEN TO SURRENDER

"Sometimes you have to let go and see what happens." That's how Heidi Powell, former cohost of ABC's hit reality television series *Extreme Weight Loss*, found the courage to make space for what she truly wanted in her life and let go of what she didn't. As a guest on my podcast *Flourish or Fold: Stories of Resilience*, she discussed how surrendering is often confused with laziness or not caring.

That couldn't be further from the truth. Surrender is about both growth and trying not to control things. Relinquishing control is, of course, easier said than done. Fear is very often the driver of control, peddling the faulty belief that if we exercise more control, we will be free from the discomfort of failure, mistakes, and uncertainty. Paradoxically, the ability to let go, to surrender the outcome, expands our perspective and often the opportunities that are available to us, when we're not trying to force our agenda.

The first time Powell surrendered, she described being frightened and feeling as though she was stepping off a cliff into a void of nothing, uncertain of what was on the other side. She waited for her next steps to emerge without exercising control. She couldn't control what happened next, but she could control what she did next.

Powell found that when she had the courage to let go of things in her life that were not serving her, relinquishing these projects and relationships first created a void in her life. Then, that space created room for new experiences to enter her life that were more aligned with her desires and dreams.

Sometimes, our most daring moments are not about taking on more but being brave enough to do less. To be willing to let go of aspects of our lives so the new experiences and opportunities we crave can emerge. Some were learning experiences, like cofounding a beauty brand, while others have been shining successes, like her sixty-day healthy living challenge, and a new fulfilling relationship with a man she describes as her best friend.

For Powell, surrender means letting go of what we'd planned in favor of something even better. When we release the outcome and simply take the next step, we allow a future that is chosen for us, instead of a future we attempt to control.

ANSWERS

Ambiguity is difficult for the human mind to tolerate, let alone integrate, which is why we often focus on the opposite of ambiguity, closure. Closure clears away the murkiness of ambiguity and gives our human mind that much sought-after certainty. The human brain loves clarity and certainty. It's clean, it's neat; we know exactly how to make sense of a relationship or experience when it is unambiguous. Despite the good feelings we receive from closure, the capacity to tolerate ambiguity allows us to become more resilient. Let me share a story with you to tell you what I mean.

One evening, in an Uber with my dear friend and our three sons, from the back seat, I could see that the glass monitor on the vehicle's dashboard was shattered. When my friend, sitting in the front seat, asked the driver what had happened to his monitor, sheepishly, he told us that, during an argument, his ex-girlfriend had struck the monitor with her phone, shattering the screen.

As he recounted the incident, serendipitously, a text from the ex-girlfriend, the woman responsible for the shattered monitor, flashed across his cell phone screen as he navigated us to our next destination. "You're still speaking to her?" I asked incredulously from the back seat, as though this was any of my business at all. "Yes," he self-consciously admitted. "But what can I do?" he asked.

Now, I don't know about you, but when I get into conversations with my Uber drivers, it's gotten deep, and fast. Knowing I had about five minutes to impact this man's life before he dropped us off, I said, "You get to think about why you allow someone who treats you this way to continue to be in your life."

He thought for a long moment and there was silence among all of us in the vehicle. "Yeah," he finally said, "I guess I'm just trying to get closure."

"Listen," I said, my voice soft with empathy, remembering how much I had longed for the delicious security of closure in past relationships. "You're never going to get closure because there is no good reason for this behavior. You're never going to understand why. She can't tell you why. You get to decide the answer to the 'whys.' Then, be done."

Our Uber driver's story is a prime example of how, when we get caught in ambiguity, we can stay in circumstances that do not serve us to seek the elusive closure. We want to make sense of what happened. We want to understand ourselves, others, and our relationships.

While clarity can help us move forward with a clean slate, staying too long in relationships that don't honor us, or worse, are detrimental, does not support our resilience. The continued quest for closure can keep us connected to people who diminish us instead of developing us. We think, if we just keep talking, texting, staying connected, if we can have one more coffee, we'll understand the answer to the "why" question of what happened between us, and we'll be able to make things right. Instead, the belief that closure is attainable keeps us engaged with negative energy. If we keep reaching back into a tumultuous relationship in the name of closure, we may be perpetuating an addiction to drama, not our development. Resilience means learning to tolerate ambiguity and that closure isn't something we get, it is something we decide. Detox by moving forward and answering your own "why" questions.

There are moments when we lose things, and we are certain our life is over. I thought my life had ended more times than I can count. Of the hundreds of people I have interviewed on how they have effectively faced significant challenge, about half of them report that when a challenge emerged in their lives, they, too, were certain their life would end.

When I lost my first consulting job paying $75K, I thought my life was over, for sure. Now, I own my own consulting firm and have a larger salary than I dreamed was possible. When I moved out of the condo I'd stretched to buy with my former husband by waiting tables to make extra money in graduate school, and into an apartment in a neighborhood not nearly as nice, I thought my life was over. Now, I live in a much more beautiful home and neighborhood and have a second investment property.

When I lost my best team member, I thought my life was over. Then, someone even better came along. When relationships that I thought were forever ended, I thought my life was over. Since then, the ending of those relationships has brought new beginnings, and allowed me to meet new people. Just when I thought my life was over, my circumstances found a way to turn out for the better.

It's tempting in the face of loss and disappointment to search for solid answers. I have learned that the answers I seek are not outside of me, but within me.

I've learned that surrender means allowing myself to not know the answers for a period of time, trusting the process, and believing in the possibility for something better to emerge. Answers feel safe and ambiguity feels messy. I'm embracing the messiness of ambiguity, learning that for a new season to begin, others must end.

PACE YOURSELF

One of the most difficult elements of The Practice of Productive Perseverance is being patient with the pace of change. Typically, we want growth, healing, and the removal of discomfort to happen faster than it does. Those that flourished, rather than rushing, paced themselves, taking time to understand and integrate their experience mentally, to heal physically and psychologically, along with time for rest.

Amberly Lago, author of the best-selling book *True Grit and Grace* and a guest on my podcast *Flourish or Fold: Stories of Resilience*, knows firsthand the importance of pacing ourselves when facing tragedy. After suffering a devastating motorcycle accident that nearly took her leg and left her with a severe nerve disease, complex regional pain syndrome (CRPS), dubbed the "suicide disease" because of the high number of people that take their lives with this diagnosis, she found herself thrust into a new life that she didn't recognize.

Lago describes herself as the type of person that had always pushed through pain, yet with CRPS, she needed to listen to her body more, not less. In 2016, one in five people in the US lived with chronic pain, and 85 percent of chronic pain patients were also diagnosed with severe depression. Like so many others, for Lago, the pain wasn't going away. One evening at the dinner table, her husband said, "You know, Amberly, you really need to pace yourself." She remembers feeling defensive, but when it came to the pain, she found that only one thing made a difference—pacing herself. So, she developed the PACER framework (which stands for perspective, acceptance, community, endurance, and rest) to support her perseverance.

For Lago, her focus on rest and recovery has been key to getting through one minute, hour, or day with CRPS. As she points out, rest is often the most undervalued aspect of resilience. For many people, rest can be equated with feelings of giving up. Yet, quite the opposite, rest is taking the time required to recover. To begin, Lago suggests strategic resting, taking planned time each day to refuel, recover, and reassess. Instead of constantly striving, taking time to rest allows time for reflection, which leads to being more productive, instead of believing that engaging in the constant hustle, the all-on 24/7 lifestyle, is the key.

PLAN B

Unlike those that found resilience in staying the course, resilience is also demonstrated in our ability to pivot in a new direction, especially in the face of diminishing returns. I was reminded of this when I read an article about the fashion designer Vera Wang, who at the age of seventy-two is still considered to be at the top of her game, especially as a wedding dress designer and fashion icon. The article I read wasn't so much about her amazing career longevity, however. Instead, this story focused on her appearance at a 2022 movie premiere. Photographs of her showed a radiant woman of ageless beauty, triggering a storm of online comments and questions seeking her secrets for remaining so youthful, fit, and fabulous.

I loved her response. She told one interviewer that her secrets included "work, sleep, a vodka cocktail, not much sun." Vera also noted that pizza, doughnuts, and Cheetos were favorite snacks, even though her online posts show that she still has an incredible figure.

Many of her fans, including young celebrities like Paulina Gretzky, who wore a sheer Vera Wang–designed dress for her 2022 wedding, are probably not aware that Vera is also known for her resilience and perseverance.

As a child of immigrants from Shanghai, Vera grew up in a household on Manhattan's Upper East Side. From a young age, her passion was figure skating, where she excelled; featured by *Sports Illustrated* as an up-and-coming athlete to watch in 1968, she dreamed of one day competing with the US Olympic team. But her dreams of Olympic success were dashed when she did not make the Olympic team. Rather than continuing to persevere, she felt that training and waiting for the next Olympics four years in the future offered her diminishing returns, so she decided to pivot in a new direction. But what to do next?

In addition to figure skating, Vera had developed a love for haute couture, and decided to focus her passion to that for a new career goal. After she graduated from college, she imagined she'd attend design school next, but her father said, "No. Get a job." She worked through her last two years of undergrad at a boutique, and when she graduated, she went to work at *Vogue* magazine as an assistant. She impressed her bosses and was named the magazine's youngest-ever fashion editor. Yet, after fifteen years as a fashion editor with *Vogue*, she was disappointed again when she was not chosen to become the magazine's editor in chief. Rather than persisting at writing about design, she left *Vogue*, and focused on trying her hand at becoming one of the designers she'd been writing about all those years. In 1987, she was appointed as a design director at the prestigious Ralph Lauren fashion house.

Nearing age forty, Vera was shopping for a wedding dress, but couldn't find anything that felt suitable for her as a mature bride. Everything was too lacy and frilly, while she was looking for something simpler and more elegant. Unable to find the wedding dress she envisioned, she decided to create her own. It's been several decades since she designed her first wedding dress, and now Vera Wang has expanded her business to include lingerie, jewelry, home products, and even desserts, branching out from haute couture to have her own lines in stores like Kohl's. According to market sources, the retail value of goods bearing Vera Wang's name is estimated to be upward of $1 billion per year. Now in her seventies, Vera Wang has hit her stride. Had she made the US skating team or been appointed as *Vogue*'s editor in chief all those years ago, she may never have become the designer she is today. Her rejections became redirections, and her setbacks became setups for her next great career successes. In an interview with *The Cut*, when asked about past disappointments, Vera discussed how she sees her failures as necessary parts of her journey toward success, not the opposite of what she has achieved today. She said, "Don't be afraid of failing. I think not trying is worse than failing. Have the courage to try. Otherwise, what are we here for?"

Productive perseverance is both an art and a science: knowing when to maintain the mission, despite challenge, and when to pivot in a new direction, in the face of diminishing returns, because each situation is slightly different. Yet, we can take the lessons from our past decisions and apply them to our present and future challenges, changes, and complexities to hone The Practice of Productive Perseverance.

KNOW THE DIFFERENCE BETWEEN BEING PATIENT AND WASTING YOUR TIME

One aspect of Productive Perseverance is being able to, with practice, get better and better at projecting what investments require patience and what investments, whether a personal relationship or a professional endeavor, given the changing economy, marketplace, or demand, are a waste of time and energy.

Vera Wang's willingness to engage her resilience and pivot, rather than persevere in the face of diminishing returns, allowed her to find success in her Plan B, while continuing to pursue a career that was meaningful and true to herself. Does this then mean that you should always have a Plan B to fall back upon? Surprisingly, research shows that having a backup plan is not helpful in achieving your goals. In testing, those who made backup plans ended up performing worse on the task at hand. When researchers asked follow-up questions, they learned that this was due, at least in part, to a diminished drive for success.

Having a backup plan can lead to a more restrictive mind-set, less time to focus on other interests, and not having as many options. There can be big, unintended costs associated with thinking through a backup plan. Fortunately, pivoting to a Plan B doesn't require you to have the plan fully formed and ready to go.

Those who flourish delay making a backup plan until they've done everything to accomplish Plan A. A backup plan, when given too much time and energy, before you know it, can become your main plan. Still, flourishing also means being able to pivot when required, having an open mind, clarity of focus in a changing landscape, and the time and space to evaluate what is and is not working. Oftentimes, the difference between flourishing and folding is knowing when to pivot, which can be much harder than simply putting our head down and persevering.

6
The Practice of Connection

While The Practice of Connection may be the most intuitive, I know that from experience it may also be the most difficult aspect of resilience to practice. In 2020 and 2021, when I was delivering keynotes remotely, I spoke to tens of thousands of people, members of associations, leadership teams, nonprofit organizations, and for-profit companies across the globe. I developed a multiple-choice quiz question for each practice, and the quiz question for The Practice of Connection went like this:

You've been invited to attend an event, but you don't want to go. If you do not attend this event, people will be disappointed. Do you:

A. Attend the event
B. Attend the event, but sneak out early
C. Agree to attend the event, but contract ahead of time that you will only stay for two hours
D. Decline to attend the event, even though you know you'll disappoint people

I included this question in my keynote speeches to illustrate the paradox of connection, the moments when our internal and our external connections are at odds. Overall, when I administered this quiz question, at least 65 percent of people said they would attend the event. Sixty-five percent! Almost two-thirds of people, even though they did not want to attend an event, even though they had two other options, to sneak out early or to contract to attend the event for only two hours, chose not to leverage those options and attend.

This quiz question highlights the intersectionality of connection, and the encounters when the connection we have with ourselves has quite different desires than the desires of those to whom we are connected outside of ourselves.

THE RESILIENT PRACTICE OF CONNECTION

The Practice of Connection is the connection we have with ourselves, internally, as well as the connection we create with others, externally. Internally, connection is the willingness to know ourselves deeply, listening to ourselves and cultivating our voice, knowing our value, and trusting ourselves.

Externally, our natural tendency is to reach out to others and build or maintain a supportive community that includes the connections we have with our friends, families, places of work, and neighborhoods. Oftentimes, communities are created for various points in life, especially when we are facing a challenge and we find a community that is specifically equipped to provide support.

YOUR CONNECTION WITH YOURSELF

Internal connection is about knowing ourselves, listening to ourselves, learning to trust our gut and intuition, and knowing our value and inherent worthiness. The Practice of Connection is focused on creating and deepening the connection with ourselves, including developing our intuitive abilities to listen to our inner voice. How we connect within ourselves determines our ability to connect with the outside world.

Consider, for a moment, the wisdom of the human body. When the heart cleans and oxygenates our body's blood, what organ does it pump this fresh blood to first? Itself. The heart gives itself the nourishment of the clean and oxygenated blood first because without the heart, our body cannot survive. Similarly, The Practice of Connection is concentrated, first, on our internal connection with ourselves, since it is the lifeblood that drives and nurtures all interactions outside of ourselves.

We receive immense benefits from this connection to ourselves:

- Knowing ourselves makes it more likely that we'll be able to express our needs and desires, as well as articulate what we want and don't want.
- When our outside actions align with our inside feelings and values, we experience less inner conflict.
- Trusting our gut and relying on our internal voice helps us make decisions that support the person we are and the person we desire to become.
- Taking time to appreciate our strengths, talents, and gifts means we're more likely to value ourselves and know our worth.
- Cultivating and listening to our internal intuition means we're less likely to make choices or engage in relationships that we may regret later.
- Knowing ourselves, our "why" statement and core values, means we have a clear framework from which to make decisions and solve problems.
- When we connect with ourselves, we know what motivates us to resist bad habits and develop good ones, increasing our self-control and the positive outcomes we create.
- When we are grounded in our own values and preferences, we are less likely to say yes when we want to say no.
- Knowing ourselves means we know what brings us joy, makes us feel most alive, and makes our experience of life richer, larger, and more exciting.
- Connection with ourselves means we are less likely to have regrets later in life because we didn't listen to our internal voice, trust our gut, know our worth and value, or live authentically.

LIVING AUTHENTICALLY

My colleague Ben Nemtin describes an idyllic life while growing up on the beautiful island of Vancouver, British Columbia, surrounded by mountains and the ocean. He was mostly a happy guy, a good student and superior athlete who made the Under-19 National Rugby Team while attending university.

But then, while training for the team and still in school, he began to experience flashbacks and nightmares to his high school championship rugby match in which he'd missed an important kick.

"It haunted me," he said in an *Ideas Elevated* podcast interview on Comcast NBCUniversal LIFT Labs.

He became obsessed with the fear of missing another big kick in the World Cup if he continued with the national team. That fear of failing became so powerful that he spiraled into a depression.

"I kept thinking, 'What if I botch it?' and I couldn't sleep because of the anxiety and the pressure," he said.

His fear became paralyzing. He couldn't go to class, so he dropped out of school, losing his scholarship and his spot on the rugby team. He moved back in with his parents. His depression lasted for months. At first he didn't want to leave the house. His parents tried to encourage him to get out and to seek counseling, but he wouldn't listen to them.

Eventually, some friends convinced him to move to a new town and work there with them. They were highly motivated, creative, and inspiring people and open to talking with him about his fears and depression, which gave him the courage to see a counselor and a therapist.

His recovery was slow at first, and came in stages, but over time, he began feeling better and found it helped to surround himself with friends, and also to help others with their struggles, including a Minnesota girl who was recovering from years of cutting herself and wanted to speak about it publicly as part of her outreach therapy.

Since she was opening up, Ben started to talk about his own mental health challenges to heal himself and help others find healing. One of the key things he shared was that, over time, he learned to be more aware of his thoughts, to listen to them, and to recognize when they were turning negative.

"I can see the signs when I am going down this path and I need to change something and get more sleep and take time off and spend time with friends and family," he said.

Ben also came to see that there are two types of passion: obsessive passion and harmonious passion. His obsessive passion for perfection had driven his fear of failing in rugby. It is the sort of passion in which there is no separation between what you do and who you are. Obsessive passion can be good for getting things done and accomplishing goals, but it is not healthy over the long term, he said.

Harmonious passion, on the other hand, is healthier because it encourages you to have more balance between your work and your relationships, social life, and pleasures like your hobbies and your "bucket list" goals.

"Your bucket list is a framework for understanding, to remind you that your goals exist so they don't get buried," said Ben.

Ben built up his resilience by increasing his self-awareness, monitoring his thoughts, and taking corrective actions to manage his response to fear and other triggering emotions. Now, his story is of particular interest because Ben's path to resilience led him to an unexpected career as an author, public speaker, producer, and podcaster.

He and three friends decided they were fed up with their day-to-day lives and wanted something different. They'd each connected with the essence of themselves, and acknowledged that they were seeking adventure, not the staid routine of their daily existence.

As a guest on my podcast *Flourish or Fold: Stories of Resilience*, Ben described how the friends borrowed an RV, bought a video camera on eBay (these were the days before filming video on our phones), threw a good-bye party to raise gas money, and hit the road for what they thought would be two weeks.

Ten years later, they are still on their mission. They first asked themselves, "What do I want to do before I die?" And they set out in search of their bucket list experiences. They soon realized that sharing their adventures and helping others achieve their dreams was as fulfilling as pursuing their own. For every item they complete on their bucket list, they help other people achieve something on their bucket lists as well.

Ben and his friends' efforts turned into the MTV show *The Buried Life* and they've written a #1 *New York Times* bestseller, *What Do You Want to Do Before You Die?* They have found purpose by listening to themselves and forging internal connection with themselves. Then, they had the courage to authentically pursue the lives that spoke to them, while helping others pursue their dreams too.

On their website, the authors write, "It's easy to think what others want for us but rarely do we truly listen to our gut and our heart, and that is where a bucket list should begin. If nothing in the world were impossible, what would you do? Even if it is impossible, what do you want to do before you die?"

We often sacrifice ourselves for what other people want rather than living authentically to ourselves. Ben and his *Buried Life* compatriots embody The Practice of Connection in their ability to know themselves deeply and to live authentically.

THE POWER OF "I AM"

I used to think the most valuable real estate in my life was the home I rented or owned. Today, I know the most valuable real estate is not the physical residence I live in, but the real estate of my own mind. Our mind is our emotional, cognitive, and spiritual home.

The home we create for ourselves in our mind can be a nice place to live, where we speak to ourselves positively with kindness, empathy, and grace. Or the home we create for ourselves in our mind can be filled with negative self-talk that is unkind, degrading, and cruel. What we say to ourselves in our own mind, our self-talk, determines not only how supportive and hospitable our mental home is, but it is a significant determinant of whether or not we reach our full potential.

When we speak negatively to ourselves, we say things that we'd never allow others to say to us. If someone else said these things to us, we'd have ended that relationship or drawn a boundary in a heartbeat. Yet, for some reason, we tolerate this negative self-talk from ourselves. Look, the world is hard enough. Do we need to be hurtful and mean to ourselves inside our mental home too? No, we do not.

What you say to yourself in the real estate of your mind significantly shapes the person you are becoming. No matter how many trials they face, people who flourish continue to encourage themselves with positive self-talk. People who fold speak to themselves using negative self-talk to berate and belittle themselves.

I've found that what follows "I am ________" follows you. This means that when we fill in the blank after "I am _______" with productive, positive, and loving comments, this is the person we become. When we reinforce our goodness, our strengths, and that we are doing our best, we become the best of ourselves as we listen to this repetitive positive self-talk over time. When we fill in the blank after "I am _______" with negative self-talk, unproductive, hurtful, and condescending remarks, we become the worst of ourselves. The words we say to ourselves in our mind become the map to our future, laying the groundwork for the person we will become.

Take a piece of paper and draw a line down the middle of the page. On the left-hand side, write all the things you say to yourself, the positive and negative self-talk you engage in. Once you've written down everything that you can think of that comes after "I am _______," review what you wrote. Which of those words or phrases do you want to change? On the right-hand side of your piece of paper, write down the words or phrases you would like to say to yourself to replace negative self-talk. If you have trouble coming up with a replacement for negative self-talk, ask yourself questions like, "What if I am more capable than I know? What would happen if I believed in myself? What if it did work out?" to come up with positive words to say instead.

If we're going to speak to ourselves in our own mind, why not say something positive to ourselves, rather than something negative? Why not say "You're a genius," instead of berating our intelligence? Sometimes we get so comfortable with the symphony of negative talk that fills our head, we don't even realize the detrimental music we're playing on Repeat. If you're not sure how to speak to yourself differently, ask yourself, "What would I say to someone I love and admire?" Then, say those same things to yourself. The way we speak to ourselves matters. In fact, the words you say to yourself in the real estate of your own mind are some of the greatest predictors of the person you'll become and the extent to which you'll realize your full potential.

IN PURSUIT OF HAPPINESS

We are responsible for our own happiness. No one can "make" us happy. Happiness is an inside job, not the pursuit of external accolades and possessions. We often believe we must "do" work to "have" things, and then we will "be" happy. This is a faulty script that keeps us chasing happiness and joy as an experience that is only available to us once we work for it.

Rather than pursuing happiness, happiness and joy are available to us in this very moment. We don't have to find a partner, start a family, lose weight, or get a promotion to be happy. Happiness is derived from our state of mind, not our situation. Instead of the "do-have-be" script, flip it and follow "be-do-have." We concentrate on "being" the experience we want to "have," and our "doing" results from being in the desired state of contentment, peace, happiness, and so on. This means focusing on being happy in this moment, not on the other side of an experience.

Like resilience, happiness is available now. Just as resilience can be developed through The Five Practices, Professor Richard Davidson at the University of Wisconsin–Madison has demonstrated that we can increase our happiness by routinely practicing tangible skills to increase our happiness. Rather than expecting that happiness will spontaneously emerge in our lives, we have to practice be-do-have to create more happiness in our life now. No matter where we are in life, we can find joy in the journey, because the word JOY is in the word JOurneY.

LEARNING TO LOVE AND CULTIVATE YOUR VOICE

Chase Bell had a problem. He has always been a natural with instruments. Given an instrument, he'd learn to play it beautifully in a few days. There was one instrument, however, that was causing him some trouble: his own voice. Unlike other instruments, Chase didn't like the sound of his own voice, and he couldn't figure out how to manipulate the instrument within himself. He wanted his voice to resonate from a deep place of truth, strength, and clarity and to love his own voice, but how?

Our vocal muscles are tiny and when stretched too far, easily become rigid. Chase learned from working with some of the biggest musical artists of today that emotional incoherence constricts the throat and tightens the muscles. If he wanted to expand his ability to express a deep sense of love, rather than agitate his vocal cords, he was going to need to learn to accept and love his voice to relax vocal muscles he was unconsciously tightening.

As a singer-songwriter, Chase spends much of his time singing from his authenticity (along with writing, developing, and performing songs with other musical artists). Yet, his experience is not so different than those of us that are cultivating our own voice. We stay silent because we don't like the way we sound.

As a guest on the *Flourish or Fold* podcast, Chase shared that to change his vocal tone and quality, he needed to spend a lot of time gently guiding it. His goal: to feel his voice resonating within his body. Chase expressed gratitude for how his voice sounded at that point in time, knowing full well it would doubtlessly change for the better given proper time and attention.

Chase said everything changed when, rather than being at odds with his voice's sound and quality, he recognized the importance of accepting what was being emitted from his body, mind, and soul. It wasn't until he loved his voice completely that his voice changed to sound lovable to his own ears. In other words, Chase discovered that he had to love his voice completely, as it was, to make a change.

Today, you can hear Chase's voice clear as a bell (I couldn't resist the pun) and experience his songwriting genius with other luminary artists. Learning to love his voice allowed Chase to create an even more beautiful voice for both himself and his fans. I feel fortunate to have been able to support Chase as he has continued to grow and evolve as a musician. Chase's music has been so meaningful in my life, and one of my personal favorite songs is the yet-to-be-released song entitled, "When I'm with YOU."

YOU HURT ME, AND I LOVE YOU

How can we cultivate and learn to love our voice more? It starts with authentic communication. When we communicate inauthentically, we say, "You hurt me, but I love you," denying our feelings in favor of making someone else feel comfortable. This short-term offering of comfort creates a long-term denial of our experience. Other times, when someone we love hurts us, we'll deny our feelings to minimize the importance of the relationship, so the offense doesn't hurt so much by saying, "I love you, but you hurt me," negating the love, and instead privileging the feelings of pain.

The next time someone you love hurts you consider saying, "I love you, *and* you hurt me." Learn to say both. This is the art of the "and": the ability to honor both the love of the person and the pain for the offense. Learning to speak to both the love and pain, rather than negating one aspect, cultivates our voice by speaking the truth, rather than staying silent or only giving voice to one part of your complete emotional experience.

TRUST YOURSELF

Another important element in our internal connection to ourselves is the ability to trust ourselves. Trusting ourselves means trusting our internal voice, experience, and intuition, as well as trusting what we hear, see, and feel. I caught up with NFL player and All-Pro linebacker Seth Joyner, who played seven seasons for my hometown Philadelphia Eagles as well as several other teams, on my *Flourish or Fold* podcast where we talked about the importance of trusting ourselves even when others doubt us. I was surprised to learn in our interview that Seth had to deal with many who doubted his abilities to make it in the NFL early in his career.

After all, Seth, who is now a football analyst for NBC Sports in Philadelphia, won a Super Bowl Ring with the Denver Broncos and was once named NFL Player of the Year by *Sports Illustrated*, among many other honors.

But he told me many people, including loved ones, family members, and friends, didn't have faith in his ability to play in the NFL. His high school guidance counselor was one of those early doubters, Seth recalled.

Instead of encouraging Seth to go to college and play football after high school, the counselor told him, "You know, I don't think you can handle the academics on the division one level."

The counselor had his file and his grades, but he didn't know the passion in Seth's heart, nor did he grasp that Seth could up his game in the classroom too.

Seth recalls thanking his counselor politely but feeling rage inside as he walked out of their meeting determined to prove him wrong.

"He was basically telling me my dream of playing college football was unattainable. That's when I set my mind and my heart to do whatever I wanted to do," Seth told me.

He did succeed in getting a college football scholarship at the University of Texas in El Paso, where Seth found yet another source of motivation—his mother.

"Don't come home," she told him, meaning that she wanted him to stay focused on studying for classes and developing as a football player so that he could create a new and better life for himself.

She had been a single mother, struggling to raise him without many resources, and her determination inspired her son. "You know, I'd made my mind up before I went away... that I was going to be the one, one of the ones in my family to break that chain."

Other family members, friends, and people in his community expressed doubts that Seth could make it, but he was determined to prove them wrong.

"I wasn't going to allow them to steal the joy of my dreams," he said.

Now, Seth did well enough in college to impress NFL scouts and he was drafted by the Eagles in the eighth round in 1986, but then he was cut in training camp. That might have been a devastating blow to some, but Seth Joyner had learned to be resilient from all his years of proving the doubters wrong.

"It's almost a badge of honor for someone to express doubt in me," he said, because it only made him stronger and more determined.

The Eagles re-signed Seth later in the season. He still had to prove himself when his position coach didn't think he should be a starter, but within five years, he was selected for his first Pro Bowl. He started at linebacker for the Eagles for eight seasons and the team inducted him into their Hall of Fame in 2018.

Seth Joyner proved that he was too resilient to let his critics discourage him from achieving his dreams. He knew what he was capable of and trusted in his ability to keep learning and growing. Even when others doubted him, he believed in himself. This is a powerful lesson. When you accept others' beliefs as your own, you:

- Settle for what you're offered instead of selecting your opportunities
- Live a life that is smaller than what you're capable of instead of signing up for bigger, more expansive opportunities
- Allow others to tell you who you are, instead of knowing yourself, your talent, strengths, and power

HOLY GROUND

The connection to ourselves, especially knowing our worth and value, is critical to effectively practice resilience. When I am asked to speak to associations and organizations, I won't speak about wellness and self-care unless I am able to also speak about worthiness. The sooner we value ourselves, the sooner we understand that our body and mind are a sacred temple, that our very body, mind, and spirit is holy ground to be cared for with the utmost respect.

Radical self-care is spelled W-O-R-T-H-I-N-E-S-S. Worthiness and radical self-care go hand in hand because, to care for the temples of our body, mind, and spirit, we must believe that we are worth caring for. One of the best ways to improve your relationship with yourself is to intentionally prioritize radical self-care. What is so radical about it? Making ourselves a relentless priority, rather than allowing the needs of our work and relationships to crowd out the time to take care of ourselves, may sound simple, and it is. Yet, practicing self-care is also revolutionary.

When life gets chaotic, it becomes far too easy to neglect our personal health. Taking care of ourselves is the most important task on our to-do list. By taking small, meaningful steps to improve our mental and physical health, we will become more in touch with our internal cues and connect better with ourselves.

The three areas of self-care that are most important are sleep, exercise, and a balanced diet. Focusing on these three aspects of our life make a significantly positive difference on our overall health. Period! They may seem basic, but making small deposits in our health over time leads to big differences.

Radical self-care is not just about meeting our physical needs. It is about eliminating negative self-talk, keeping the promises we make to ourselves, not self-rejecting or self-sabotaging, uncovering and addressing triggers, expanding limited beliefs, creating health boundaries, reducing perfectionistic tendencies, and rewriting our story to become a more conscious narrative. The Practice of Connection is critical to guard against burnout, stress, and exhaustion because there is not a person who experiences these who hasn't compromised their connection to themselves. Cultivating and protecting our connection to ourselves both builds resilience and protects against burnout. When we do not care for ourselves for extended periods of time, especially, we are more susceptible to health concerns and stress-related illness along with being prone to burnout, exhaustion, stress, and overwhelm.

FEELING ALL THE FEELS

As a society, Western culture tends to be uncomfortable with people's discomfort. We often pressure anyone who has feelings outside a narrow range of acceptable emotions to slap a smile on their face. If someone is angry, depressed, or disappointed, we want them to suck it up or cheer up. How much better would it be if we allowed ourselves and the people in our lives to have a rich, varied, nuanced emotional life? If we allowed people to work through their challenges in a way that they connected to themselves and honored their feelings?

As an advocate for experiencing and expressing the full range of our human emotions, I came to deeply admire Elizabeth Edwards, the estranged wife of politician John Edwards. She supported him through two unsuccessful bids for the US presidency even as she battled with cancer. Elizabeth was an attorney, like her husband, and had a successful career. She dealt with incredible challenges, including the death of their sixteen-year-old son in a car accident, her long battle with cancer that eventually proved fatal, and her husband's infidelities that led to him having a child with another woman.

Through it all, Elizabeth maintained her dignity and became an advocate and inspiration to women facing challenges. She wrote in her book *Resilience*, "In the end, there is peace. If we are strong, if we are resilient, if we are stubborn and filled with hope, if we know how to love, there is peace before that, too. And, honestly, that is enough."

No matter what we're feeling, our emotions give us important messages about how to process our experience, and denying, numbing, or ignoring our emotions means we're repressing our experience along with reducing our ability to understand the impact of the events that are troubling us.

Going back to Albert Ellis's shame-based "shoulds," when we exert pressure on ourselves or others to bury our emotions, by suggesting that a person "should" feel a different way, we deny ourselves and others the healing information of the emotional experience. When we allow ourselves and others to accept all emotions, through honoring our emotional processes, we connect more deeply to ourselves and know ourselves to a greater degree, as well as the lessons we learned from our experience.

GRANTING YOURSELF GRACE AND FORGIVENESS

Forgiveness is important in relationships with ourselves and others. Forgiveness is something we do for ourselves, to free us from being tied to the past and to allow us to experience the expansive possibilities of our present and future.

Forgiveness is very much a learned skill that we get to practice over and over, sometimes with the same person or when exposed to a repeated offense. Often, we find that even if an offense only happened once, we may need to be intentional about working through forgiveness multiple times. Rather than expecting we'll be perfect at forgiving, we get to practice forgiveness, even when it is difficult. Especially when it is difficult.

Many times, the most difficult person for us to forgive for pain and allow ourselves to be at peace is ourselves. When we seek compassion for ourselves and others, this often makes forgiveness more accessible; even though what they did was wrong, we can see that they might have acted the way they did because of their past or circumstances. When we allow ourselves to be imperfect, flawed, and messy, and still be worthy of forgiveness, our capacity to forgive others when they are imperfect expands as well.

PERMISSION SLIPS

If we like to please and are focused more intently on the experience, thoughts, and feelings of the people around us, our external connections, rather than first connecting to ourselves internally, making some of these changes may feel scary or difficult. We may wonder where to begin. Connecting with the internal aspects of ourselves means honoring the person within our skin, before we take in the needs, desires, and wants of the people to whom we are connected externally.

To combat burnout, stress, and exhaustion, you may want a permission slip to care for yourself, slow down, or take on less. If these changes feel like you'll be letting others down or falling short in some way, permission slips can help give you the gumption you require to put yourself first. Sometimes, you may feel you need permission to be different. Rather than looking to others for permission, you can look to yourself and grant yourself the permission you need to make a change or a different choice. Whether you would like permission to take care of yourself, speak your mind, or authentically express yourself, the permission is there for the taking.

I have included some permission slips you may want to give yourself when you need them. Feel welcome to take these permission slips for yourself, and if you need to, write yourself other permission slips as you see fit!

MEET YOURSELF IN THE MIRROR

Meeting yourself in the mirror means finding a mirror and looking yourself in the eyes. This gaze isn't about self-criticism, finding imperfections, or the daily tasks of self-care like brushing your teeth and washing your face. Meeting yourself in the mirror is about really seeing, acknowledging, and knowing yourself. It's about, eventually, looking lovingly into your own eyes, the way you would a romantic partner and saying, "I love the shit outta you." It's about locking eyes with yourself and saying, "No matter what happens, I won't give up on you. I won't abandon you."

Connecting with ourselves internally means that we do the work of showing up for ourselves and not abandoning or self-rejecting. Our internal connection means that we honor promises we make to ourselves as though those promises were made to another person, and that we don't degrade or sabotage ourselves.

Sometimes, rather than being our own best friend, we're our own worst enemy. Go meet yourself in the mirror and apologize for any ways that you have let yourself down, compromised your standards, not trusted yourself, or stifled your intuition. It's not too late to make up with yourself and have a positive relationship with the man or woman in the mirror. When all else fails, it was always only ever you. Meet yourself in the mirror and rely on, trust, and honor yourself, now and for every year of your life yet to come.

YOUR CONNECTION WITH OTHERS

Once we have connected with ourselves, we get to crosswalk our internal connection with our external connections to find, rely on, and gain encouragement from existing or created communities, friends, family members, and colleagues. The Practice of Connection allows us to dive more deeply into relationships with other people. Living and working in community, fostering collaborative partnerships, sharing information, and working in teams are key leadership behaviors, and even more important during times of change, challenge, and complexity.

The critical importance of connection to others, outside ourselves, cultivates greater resilience as we draw strength from the support of others. Those who feel more connected to others have lower levels of anxiety and depression. They also have higher self-esteem, greater empathy for others, and are more trusting and cooperative. Our external connectedness generates a positive feedback loop of social, emotional, and physical well-being. Relationships aren't just protective. Lack of external connectedness predicts disease and death beyond traditional risk factors such as smoking, blood pressure, and physical activity.

The more we practice connection both to ourselves and others, the more we realize how we are not as separate from one another as we might have thought. It's easy to believe, when we face hardship, that we are completely unique, that no one has ever encountered our experience, yet we know that we are all connected universally.

The practice of connection reminds us that we are never truly alone. You have, within yourself, the resources to handle trying experiences, the wisdom, fortitude, and empathy that is necessary to make meaningful connections. Externally, you have or can find connection to other people who will support you in your journey, across your life span, or at particularly important moments in time when you need them.

THE OTHER SIDE OF LONELINESS

In a world of unlimited digital connectivity, we still experience loneliness and feelings of profound disconnection. In a landmark *Loneliness and the Workplace* study conducted by Cigna, 61 percent of those surveyed reported feeling lonely. Loneliness not only has adverse implications for mental health, but it was also as detrimental to physical health as obesity and smoking a pack of cigarettes daily. As humans, we are pack animals.

It goes against human nature to be isolated, experiencing life through a screen, limited in our mobility with the mandate to physically distance. Of the 330 million Americans who indicated being lonely or very lonely, these people also reported dramatically reduced productivity, greater absenteeism, higher risk of turnover, and lower quality of work, demonstrating a direct link between the power of personal experience and business profitability.

LONGING FOR BELONGING

Most of us have experienced loneliness and isolation. Many fewer of us have reached out when we need support because it feels frightening and vulnerable to ask for help. One of my favorite books and TED Talks is Amanda Palmer's *The Art of Asking*, in which she discusses the art of getting the help we desire and need. Here are some suggestions to reconnect with others and enhance your external connections:

- *Assume positive intent.* We often shut other people out because we assume others can't or don't want to help us. Start from a place of assuming people are generally good and want to help. Then, go from there.
- *Be present.* Recognize feelings of aloneness and loneliness and what they mean for you in that moment. Is a current experience being magnified by other factors in your life or a reminder of an experience?
- *Allow yourself to be.* Reaching out when facing a hardship takes courage. In the spirit of The Practice of Vulnerability, it's okay to be imperfect, afraid, or honest. Belonging occurs when we show up with others, as we truly are. Don't wait until you're "all better" to share your experience. Share it now.

- *Break the silence.* Speak about your experience. It's scary, but necessary. *That which goes unspoken, becomes unspeakable.* When we trade our voice for silence, silence keeps us quiet, but it doesn't keep us safe.
- *Recognize that help is not about worth.* We're all entitled to receiving the support we need and want to be successful, and you're worth it.
- *Receiving help is not something you have to earn.* By virtue of simply being, you are entitled to tap into the grace, wisdom, and support of your fellow humans.
- *Inability to help is not a rejection.* If you ask someone for help, and they are unable to support you, this is not a statement about you, this is not a rejection; it's just a statement about the other person's capacity.
- *Offer help to others, who seek your assistance, in the manner that you would have liked to have received support.* Do better than offering the help you got (or didn't get).

The opposite of loneliness is togetherness and shared understanding. Connection with people outside of ourselves allows us to heal past wounds, create communities in which we belong, and impact social change.

Just look at the #MeToo and #TimesUp campaigns where people who had previously been isolated and alienated by sharing their stories came together to find support and even justice. *Give all those around you permission to support you by being savvy enough to know when you need help and brave enough to ask for it.*

MAKING THE TRANSITION

If she hadn't literally run into a supportive friend, Natalie Egan would likely not be with us today. She identifies, first and foremost, as a human being, as well as a mom, entrepreneur, athlete, and a trans woman. One of my dear friends and a rock star entrepreneur, Natalie joined me as a guest on my podcast, *Flourish or Fold: Stories of Resilience*, to share her incredible resilience story.

For years, she'd repressed her identity as a woman. She was ashamed to express who she truly was, so she hid, drowning out her internal voice under layers of masculinity, pretending she was someone else—for everyone else. In other words, instead of living the life that was hers, she was living the life she thought everyone else wanted her to live.

Then, things started crashing down around her, her marriage and business, as they do, when for too long we don't listen to the connection with our internal self. She called a friend of hers named Morgan, who'd transitioned, and told her she was going to be in New York and asked if she could talk to her about an urgent problem. Natalie met her friend at lunch and told her she had a cross-dressing problem that was ruining her life. What Natalie's friend said next shocked her. Morgan told Natalie she thought she was transgender. A notion that she immediately rejected and wrestled with for the duration of lunch. As they were paying, Morgan invited Natalie to continue the conversation later that evening.

That night, Natalie thought they were going to get dressed up and hang out in the hotel room. But instead, Morgan, Natalie's friend, insisted they go outside. Natalie had never been out of the closet in the world, so the act of walking through the lobby was a daring feat of authenticity.

Walking toward Madison Square Park on a beautiful fall night, arm in arm with her friend, Natalie recalls seeing the wind blow through the trees, watching the breeze flow down the street and curl back toward her. The invigorating feeling as it blew up her legs, skirt, and through her hair. She describes this as being her moment. "It was electrical, like lightning. I realized, *Oh my God, this is what I've been missing my whole life. Like, this is who I really am, and I've been denying it my whole life.* Everything finally made sense. I am a woman. I am transgender."

Natalie had the most amazing night, and the next morning, she had the worst hangover. It was an identity hangover. She'd had a glimpse of who she was meant to be, and there was no denying she was transgender.

Rather than embracing herself, she went into problem-solver mode. Because that is what entrepreneurs do. She felt like she needed to fix it. Fix the problem. Fix herself. Spare everyone the pain of her truth. Natalie recalls, "Pretty quickly I realized there is no answer for this. Sadly, the only answer was that I needed to kill myself. It felt like, Um, it's the only the responsible thing to do."

Fortunately, this isn't the end of Natalie's story. It's the beginning. She described having always looked down on people who'd taken their own lives, but now that her back was up against a wall, she understood their suffering for the first time to a greater degree. "I think it might have been the first time I had ever experienced empathy in my life. That's where empathy started for me."

Before she went to the car to drive home and end her life, she went to the corner convenience store to get a Gatorade and coffee to soothe her hangover. She stood in the line to check out and recognized the voice of the person standing in front of her. "I sort of like peeked over his guy's shoulder, and I was like, Alex, is that you?" Sure enough, it was Alex, one of her best friends from high school, standing directly in front of her. Alex took one look at her and said, "Egan, are you okay?" A host of improbable factors had to line up for Natalie and Alex to be in the exact same place at the exact same moment including the fact that Alex's client had just canceled on him last minute. Seeing that she was very much not okay, he invited her to go for a walk and talk.

Alex had been in her wedding. Natalie describes him as a traditional alpha male, lacrosse player, a "bro" kind of guy. She decided she was going to tell him everything she had just discovered, everything she had been hiding her whole life, except for the fact that she planned to end her life that evening, and just see what happened. After she recounted the story and said, "This is who I am, what should I do?" she thought he'd say, "Hey, wow. Thanks for telling me, but please don't tell anyone else…and you really should go get help." But he didn't. Instead, he looked her straight in the eye and he said, "Bro, I don't know how you're gonna do that, but you gotta be you."

In that moment, despite the irony of the word "bro," Alex saved her life. That moment changed everything for her because she thought to herself, "Wow, if Alex can handle this, maybe Matt can handle this too. If Matt can handle it, you know, and then maybe Pete and Jed can too. If they can, maybe my brothers and dad could too. That's when I was like, you know what? Maybe I'll just try this. I'll just try it, see what happens." That was seven years ago.

Since age thirty-eight, when Natalie came out as a transgender woman, she has lost a lot of people in her life. Countless friends, family members, and business partners that will never speak to her again. "It was eye opening. I experienced bias and discrimination for the first time in my life. Academically and theoretically, I always knew what those things were, but I'd never actually experienced the cold hard reality or the sting of marginalization." These experiences of marginalization and microaggressions were things like: people not taking her seriously, not looking her in the eye, and refusing her service, and feeling unsafe because of her identity.

Natalie's journey of a thousand steps began with her first steps toward self-awareness and empathy. Pretty quickly, she realized we can't understand one another better if we don't understand ourselves first. "It was a lightbulb moment for me," she says. Creating connections with people who are like us, who share our experience, background, and worldview, is relatively easy. By getting closer to people that are different from us, we drive out fear and "otherness" because fear cannot stand proximity.

Natalie, a serial technology entrepreneur, decided to build the technology to solve the very problem she was experiencing of inequity and unconscious bias. In her prior technology start-up, she created a change management software platform designed to help companies change their employees' hearts, minds, and behaviors toward a particular topic, all the while making the process measurable, scalable, and repeatable. So, then she said, okay, I'll build that same company, only this time the topic is: empathy. Today, Natalie's company, Translator, Inc., supports organizations by identifying unconscious bias, helping them measure their diversity, equity, inclusion, and belonging (DEIB) initiatives, teaching empathy at scale.

Her groundbreaking company would not exist if she hadn't had that single life-altering, really lifesaving, conversation with Alex. When it comes to breaking the silence, Natalie was brave enough to ask for help, and she learned she didn't have to take her own life to fix herself, but instead could be fully accepted by the people that matter most, just as she is. We can't overestimate the power of reaching out for help in our darkest moments, nor can we appreciate how much we've helped people in our lives, as Alex did, simply by being willing and courageous enough to make time to listen to people and encourage them in moments of despair. For Natalie and so many others, this is truly the difference between life and death.

I am grateful Natalie Egan did not end her life, and I got to meet her after I heard her speak on a panel at a women in technology conference on a cold snowy day in Philadelphia. I rarely go up to people at conferences. I found her story, intelligence, and perspective so compelling, I made an exception, and sought her out. Since then, we've become close friends, and when I got married, I asked Natalie to be one of my bridesmaids. She later shared with me that being chosen as a bridesmaid was a dream come true for her, and for me, having her as my friend has been dream come true too.

THE POWER OF ONE

Just as Alex played a heroic role in saving Natalie Egan's life, without knowing her plans to end her life, even just one close friend, mentor, or teacher has the power to create extraordinary impact in our lives.

While a community of connections is extraordinary, we only need one positive external relationship to enhance our resilience. There is immense power in just one close supportive friendship. External relationships with friends and family members influence us immensely and have the potential to enhance, as well as detract, from our resilience.

SHOW ME YOUR FRIENDS AND FAMILY, AND I'LL SHOW YOU YOUR FUTURE

Let's look more closely at how the people you surround yourself with enhances or detracts from your resilience. Your community, your friends and family, predict your future. This isn't a magic. It's math. We are influenced by the people and environment around us. So much so that Jim Rohn once said, "We are the average of the five people we spend the most time with." Take an inventory of the people you spend the most time with in your life. This is a call to be choosy about your community, the people in whom you invest time and energy, and those that invest time in you.

If you're the smartest person in the room, you're in the wrong room. You won't get any smarter or savvier or develop new skills if there aren't people in your community who challenge you and can help you level up. Surround yourself with people who push you to do and be better.

A good friend is there for you when you're down, and great friend is there to celebrate when you're up! Why? Because often, it's easier to be there for people in down times. Lifting others up is easier than celebrating another person's successes. Friends that are threatened by your drive, achievements, or success aren't friends, and their negativity will bring down your average. You need people to hold you to a higher standard to achieve your goals, not someone who will be envious of your achievements.

Give the people that bring jealousy or hate the heave-ho and hold on to the people in your circle who bring out the very best in you, and you in them! The fastest way to rise to the next level is to put yourself in environments with people who are already there. These people can be friends and peers as well as mentors, coaches, and bosses. Learning from others who have already blazed a trail you want to take yourself is an important way you surround yourself with people who increase your average.

Not sure which people to keep in your life? Ask yourself which people support your dreams, observe your boundaries, meet your expectations, or have shown up to consistently cheer for your success. These are qualities of people that will increase your average. The people who bring you down, whose presence tends to leave you feeling guilty or drained, and who make you feel like you need to apologize for your success are likely bringing your average down.

BOUNDARIES

Thanks to a host of factors, our natural boundaries have largely eroded. Working from home with no morning commute means we can sit in front of our computer for endless hours. With the convergence of work and home, we don't have alone time for ourselves. This can make us feel cramped, irritable, and resentful. That's how moving or removing one boundary allows work or other aspects of our lives to, well, take over our lives. Without naturally occurring boundaries like needing to leave the office before childcare closes or beating the morning traffic, there can be a spillover of external demands that, over time, may feel unmanageable, especially for *segmenters*.

Segmenters are those who avoid overlap between personal and professional lives with abandon and like to keep things, well, very segmented. People who are segmenters often describe themselves as having two different personas, a version of themselves at home and a version of themselves at work.

Integrators are a segmenter's worst nightmare. They like to blur the boundaries of personal and professional, befriending work colleagues and discussing business outside of traditional work hours. They draw fewer distinctions between work and home and tend to feel as though they are the same person in both spheres.

Whether you identify as a segmenter or integrator, we can all benefit from learning to draw boundaries, especially as our natural boundaries are eroding with the greater fluidity of remote and hybrid work arrangements.

Here are ten suggestions to help you draw better boundaries with your external connections:

1. *Know your lines in the sand.* Lines in the sand are behaviors, experiences, language, etc., that you simply won't tolerate. These are relationship-ending, or at least relationship-suspending, moves: if someone crosses your line in the sand, it's over. Know what your lines in the sand are, and communicate them to others so they can be aware of and observe your boundaries.
2. *Know your triggers.* Like lines in the sand, these are behaviors, experiences, language, etc., that you don't want to tolerate. Unlike the lines in the sand, triggers can be set off by a person who has good intentions but doesn't realize a particular place is tender for you. Know your triggers and communicate them to the people in your life so they can observe this boundary.
3. *Use your feelings as a guide.* When you feel drained, exhausted, or frustrated when interacting with a particular person or in the context of an experience, your feelings are strong data to signal that your personal time and space are being infringed upon. Listen closely to your feelings and evaluate your emotions.
4. *Speak to values, not incidents.* When setting boundaries, rather than pointing out the offensive incidents, set a boundary from your values. People can argue with incidents, but they can't argue with your values, so begin by sharing a value such as integrity, honoring personal time, or your health, and set your boundary using your value to guide the conversation.
5. *Examine access and privacy.* Boundaries should be set up like a castle with a moat and a drawbridge where people must cross over chasms of distance to connect with you, but they shouldn't infringe on

your privacy either. When setting a boundary, assess the trade-offs of the amount of access you would like to grant with the level of privacy you would like to preserve.

6. *Adopt an attitude of gratitude.* Initially, it's natural for people in your life to feel dismissed, rejected, or hurt by your boundaries. Respond to other people by thanking them for sharing their perspective, as in "I appreciate your perspective" or "I understand this is hard on you," and thank them for attempting to adopt your boundaries.
7. *Know your core community.* Be clear on the people in your inner circle whose perspective matters and stop absorbing energy and perspectives from people who are not part of your inner, trusted circle. In *Daring Greatly*, Brené Brown says it is easy for her to remember those in her core community because she keeps a list in her pocketbook.
8. *Be clear on your boundary exceptions.* At times, people will need you outside of the boundaries you've set. Friends and family will be in crisis, break up with a significant other, or need you urgently. Spend time understanding what emergencies are exceptions to your boundaries. You won't be able to plan for everything that goes down, but your planning can serve as a guidepost when these emergent moments arise.
9. *The pleaser and the old patterns.* It's natural when initially setting boundaries to feel all the feels about setting limits, especially if you've spent any time being a people pleaser. It's not uncommon to feel embarrassed, like you're causing trouble or being difficult, guilty, or even selfish. To support yourself, create a mental picture of how your boundary is creating the life you want, and revisit your vision if you feel tempted to compromise your boundaries.
10. *Bring out the boundary reinforcements.* If you have trouble holding fast to a boundary, designate another person in your life to be your boundary cheerleader. Friends and family members have the gift of objectivity, and when you're feeling self-critical or uncertain

about maintaining your boundaries, they can give you an outsider's perspective to reinforce that your boundaries are valid, while also cheering you on as you progress with maintaining your boundaries.

Boundaries are not meant to separate us from others, they are meant to create relationships that are safe and sustainable. By honoring your boundaries, you contribute to creating relationships that are strong, clear, and meaningful, as well as mutually beneficial.

CONNECTION, COMMUNITY, AND COLLABORATION

Boundaries allow us to do for ourselves what others cannot do for us, to protect time and energy to replenish and rest, so we can be the best versions of ourselves. Yet, our external connections often create experiences we cannot create for ourselves in isolation, like collaboration. Rich Curran reflects on the importance of his collaborative community spurring him on during some of the most trying times he'd experienced. At the end of February 2020, Curran, CEO and president at EXPO Convention Contractors, a company that produces trade shows and events, watched in horror as his business ventures vanished into thin air, culminating on March 20, 2020, which he describes as the worst day of his life.

Like many business owners did on that fateful day, he called his entire company together, looked at the faces of ninety people, and told them what they had to do to ensure the company survived. They were going to 100 percent furlough until further notice. It broke Curran's heart to tell his employees he could not sustain the payroll, including his own.

With over fifty events that were continually postponed or canceled, there was a heavy administrative burden to shoulder. Although there were no events, and therefore no revenue flowing into the company, the next thing that happened was remarkable. Employee after employee came to him saying, "Whatever you need, I will help us get through this." For

Curran, knowing that he had so many people that cared for him and the company helped him get through their darkest days. "If I had people that were willing to work for free, I knew I had to make it work." He recalls:

> Rather than look at what we didn't have, I decided to look at what we did have to offer. We were a creative team of sales, designers, fabricators, and installers. We first began building some basic Plexiglas face shields and barriers. Then as reopening protocols were being put into place, we saw an opportunity to work with restaurants and businesses to design and build COVID safety barriers with decor that matched their existing spaces.

Word got out about Curran and his team's special skill set, and soon they had new projects underway. They'd figured out how to pivot to respond to new opportunities. One of their most notable projects was installing Plexiglas barriers in all four locker rooms along with the press boxes and broadcasting booths at the Miami Dolphins' stadium. They created a new product line for a new type of customer. The Dolphins' stadium required high-end finishes and a timely install for the NFL to approve their season start. "We also began doing some commercial interior design projects and launched our own brand of high-end, contemporary furniture called Infinitum USA. This allowed us to create a vertical strategy for commercial interior design. We design modern spaces and fulfill with our own furniture and decor," Curran reflects thoughtfully.

In the fall of 2021, Curran and his team began to see a steady flow of event business. Yet, they've not abandoned their new venture and have continued to grow that division, even expanding into Los Angeles. One thing is clear: "My team is the reason we made it through this, and I wish I could express how grateful I am to them for not only getting us through this pandemic but making us an even more successful company on the other side."

Without his community's support, partnership, and collaboration, the organization might not have survived, they never would have been able to adapt and expand the business and respond to the market's changing needs.

GET YOU A UNIVERSAL DONOR

Not every relationship you currently have in your life is in your best interest to maintain. Not everyone who follows you is with you. When I was looking up my blood type, I noticed those with type O blood are "universal donors." A person with an O negative blood type can donate to all other blood types, but here's the catch: those with O negative blood can only receive blood from those that also have an O negative blood type.

This got me thinking. I wondered about the people in my life to and from whom I give and receive lifeblood: lending a supportive ear, wise counsel, and empathy.

As with blood types, a universal donor is a relationship in which there is reciprocal sharing and support, and overall, one person does not drain the vitality of the relationship. Balanced relationships are the ones in which we take turns donating lifeblood to one another. Not everyone in our lives will be able to support us in our times of need.

In the moments when we need a transfusion of support and positivity, it's important to turn to those in our lives who have the ability and the desire to support us. If we have too many people to whom we're giving support, but no one we can look to for an injection of friendship, perspective, or help, we may be leaving ourselves open to being depleted, exhausted, or worse, not having a way to recharge when it's critically important.

Conversely, perhaps we've been leaning heavily on our community for guidance recently, and it's time to offer an infusion to others, instead of being the recipient. To ensure you have the right people in your life, look at your relationships through these lenses: Who are the people to whom you give? Who are the people from whom you receive? Are there people in your life who offer equal support to you as you do to them? THESE people are your universal donors.

WHO IS IN YOUR RESCUE PARTY?

One of the most powerful and difficult aspects of The Practice of Connection is the paradox of what to do when your internal connection with yourself is at odds with the external needs and desires of others. When my patients sustained brain injuries, they described their social networks as getting smaller and denser, meaning their social relationships dwindled down to just a few people, family members and maybe a close friend or two. The reality is, if we experienced a catastrophic event tomorrow, only a fraction of the people in our lives would show up to help: the few people that would be part of our rescue party.

Just as I discussed, at the outset of this chapter, how 65 percent of people said they would attend an event they didn't want to participate in, we often make decisions based on other people that may not be long-term, core members of our external network. It's wonderful to have a large network of people. But do you know who your true friends are? Who in your network cares about you enough to be part of your rescue party? These are the people that, if you got thrown into prison tomorrow, would stop what they were doing and come to your aid.

As you make decisions going forward to spend time with and accommodate the people you have in your life, to nurture your external connections, it is worth taking stock of who your core rescue party people are. The people you would be willing to support and the people that you believe would support you. Not everyone is going to ride into battle with the resources to free you from a prison in the unfortunate event that you are wrongfully accused of a crime and locked up. Yet, knowing who your core trusted relationships are will remind you to nurture the people and connections that will be there for you when you inevitably face challenge.

7

The Practice of Grati-osity

In my first role as a management consultant, I received a call one evening asking if I could fill in for a colleague who was ill by speaking at an event in her place the following day. I didn't know the material, but I wanted to help, so I hesitantly agreed. As I reviewed the slides that evening, there was no speaking overview, and the slides themselves had very few words, so I didn't know what material I was supposed to present. Since the event was at nine a.m. the next morning, I cobbled my understanding of the material together the best I could, and off I went to give the presentation.

Given the limited time and resources I had to prepare, I didn't think the presentation had gone poorly. However, a few days later, one of the principal owners of the firm called me into her office. When I sat down, she shared that she'd received feedback that my talking points were confusing to audience members and many people left without clear takeaways. I could imagine how they felt because the material was very unclear to me too. Then, she went on to say that while she wouldn't be removing my speaking privileges on behalf of the firm, she would need to approve every event at which I spoke.

This sounded incredibly unfair. I had spoken to help my sick colleague at the last minute with no guidance and little time for preparation, and now I was being punished for my willingness to help? She didn't stop there. As I sat, stone-faced, disbelieving in her office, she went on to say that while I was a "passable" speaker, I'd never be—she paused for effect—a motivational speaker. I can still hear the intonation of those words rolling off her tongue.

I was horrified for two reasons:

1. I dreamed of being a motivational keynote speaker one day.
2. A person I admired was telling me that my dreams were not possible.

When I left her office, I was shaken. A dream that was deeply ingrained in the version of the me I wanted to become had just been dashed. Or had it? What did she know about my potential? Was she the ultimate authority on inspirational keynote speaking? No, she was not.

In the moment, I felt a sense of despair, then later, anger. It might sound strange, but today, looking back, I tell this story, and I feel grateful. Why? Because I can see the good in what happened that day when she called me into her office. She gave me the opportunity to solidify my dream and determine that no one, not anyone, was going to take that dream away. That was the day I resolved that I would achieve my dream of speaking in front of big audiences and inspiring people. Although her words were not supportive, because of that interaction and my focus, today I have realized my dream, and have the opportunity to inspire people by speaking to big audiences all over the world.

THE RESILIENT PRACTICE OF GRATI-OSITY

The Practice of Grati-osity is a hybrid word that combines the words *gratitude* and *generosity*.

Expressing gratitude, typically some time after The Three C's have occurred, means seeing the good in the experience, even if you would not have chosen the circumstance. For example, I have a friend who is a successful freelance graphic designer. She is often buried in several big projects at once, but instead of getting overwhelmed, she focuses on gratitude by saying to herself: "There are a lot of freelancers who can't find work, so I'm grateful for these opportunities."

Expressing generosity to enhance your resilience is created by leaning on The Practice of Vulnerability and being willing to share your resilience stories instead of remaining silent. By sharing your resilience stories with others, you encourage others to take strength in their own success over adversity.

You can gain wisdom even in times of tragedy, hurt, and loss. Rather than withdrawing in those times, resilient people allow adversity to amplify their experience through gratitude and generosity. I'm not suggesting that you be grateful for feeling grief or sorrow. Instead, this is about honoring the capacity for healing and growth that springs even from suffering.

Life's blessings are often well disguised. You might have to wait some time before understanding the benefit of the most challenging experiences. I've seen this with clients whose position was eliminated after years in one job. They will often feel hurt and insecure and angry after being fired. Yet, over time, many of them go on to even greater success in new jobs and they end up being grateful for the opportunity that was created when they were let go.

There is a strong positive correlation between gratitude, resilience, and feelings of happiness. Gratitude not only makes us feel great, but it also inoculates us against negative emotions. Our brain is wired in such a way that we can't feel afraid or angry and feel grateful at the same time.

Feelings of gratitude block other negative emotions in our limbic system, enhancing our overall mind-set, mental health, and well-being when we practice gratitude. Gratitude fosters adaptive coping mechanisms, triggering positive emotions like satisfaction, happiness, and pleasure, enhancing our emotional resilience. It also is good for our well-being and mental health, and builds our ability to manage stress.

We focus on obstacles and difficulties because these circumstances tend to disrupt our lives and require that we exert energy to return to our regular flow of life. Since we usually don't have to exert energy when good things occur in our lives, we tend to focus more on those times when bad things happen.

Practicing gratitude is the best way to expand our perspective and remind ourselves what is going well. Robert Emmons, one of the world's leading experts on gratitude, says, "When disaster strikes, gratitude provides a perspective from which we can view life in its entirety and not be overwhelmed by temporary circumstances."

By intentionally practicing gratitude, we create an invisible mental shield that protects us from internalizing negative psychological thinking. Rather than ignoring negative or troubling circumstances, gratitude is powerful because it expands our viewpoint to incorporate what is going well in our lives.

When we ask ourselves about the positive things we've learned from adversity, we create a new way of looking at old problems, which can shift our perspective in powerful ways.

Try it. Your brain forces you to choose. One or the other. You may not have good choices, but you can make good choices by choosing gratitude in situations where you are facing setbacks and rejection. Choosing gratitude helps change your mind-set so you can focus on how to make that setback a setup for your next success. Instead of feeling rejection when you lose a job or end a relationship, consider it time for a redirection.

GRATITUDE AS SELF-IMPROVEMENT

Gratitude is a wonderful tool that can help you achieve your goals and bring your vision to life. Researchers found that gratitude motivates and energizes us by encouraging us to move forward to achieve our goals. It helps you adopt a positive mind-set, which makes you more likely to act and be motivated to achieve your goals.

THE POWER OF SHARING POSITIVE EXPERIENCES

Often, it is only after losing what we have taken for granted that we fully appreciate what we already have. Practicing gratitude and sharing it with others leads to more resilient thinking. Enhanced resilient thinking is associated with less depression and anxiety, and greater well-being and vitality.

The ability to find positive meaning in adverse situations and to regulate negative emotions contributes to personal resilience. What's fascinating is that psychological resilience, as an enduring personal resource, suggests that experiences of positive emotions build long-term psychological resilience rather than just reproducing resilient responses.

Positive emotions broaden a person's array of behaviors to adopt so that more actions and solutions come to mind when faced with an adverse situation. Through the practice of mindfully replacing negative emotions with meaningful positive emotions, over time an individual adapts to develop a greater range of resources, fostering increased resilience.

This means that:

- Positive mood and shared joy explain the relationship between positive events and a resilient mind-set.
- A resilient mind-set is associated with better psychosocial health, physical function, and resilience.
- Shared positive experiences promote psychosocial health and resilience in midlife.
- Practicing emotions doesn't simply allow people to re-create that emotional state when facing difficulty; positive emotions increase the collection of behaviors they may draw on in the future, giving them more solutions and tools at their disposal than if they had not practiced cultivating positive emotions.

CREATING A PRACTICE OF GRATITUDE

Performing a gratitude practice once or even just twice a week can lead to a long-term impact on well-being. But it must be the right gratitude practice. You've likely heard about developing a gratitude practice, yet you may not know that a gratitude practice can significantly enhance well-being and mental health.

Research has demonstrated that people who practice gratitude are able to rewire their brains by focusing on what is going right, rather than scanning their environment for what is wrong. The positive neurological impact of gratitude means that focusing on feeling gratitude has benefits that extend beyond our emotions to our mental and even physical health.

Gratitude is alchemy. A regular gratitude practice is a potent way to move our mental and physical health in more positive directions, and the effects are very long lasting. Similarly, a gratitude practice can:

- Create greater integration of and tolerance for traumatic past experiences
- Create fewer experiences of trauma by shifting and rewiring neural fear networks in our brain
- Enhance personal and professional relationships
- Shift neural circuitry in the brain that activates the nervous system to enhance connection to ourselves

So, how do we get more gratitude in our lives?

An effective gratitude practice involves giving thanks by keeping a gratitude journal and writing down one to three entries that generated gratitude for you each day before bedtime. Gratitude journals begin to shift the circuitry of our brain as we instruct our mind to scan our environment for what is going right in our day, instead of what is going wrong.

An even more effective gratitude practice involves *receiving* thanks, as in this practice we internalize gratitude to an even greater degree because it is personalized. This practice includes things like reading a thank-you note from a friend or family member before bed and feeling all the emotions that the note evokes.

Perhaps you can write down the emotions of gratitude in a journal to solidify this experience. You don't need someone to share gratitude with you each day; instead, you can reread cards and call to mind times when people praised you and shared gratitude for your contributions.

Another effective gratitude practice is to watch stories about others having positive experiences and imagining what it would feel like to be grateful for that same experience. These stories can be in the form of a book, podcast, or film.

No matter which gratitude practice you choose, you will find that when you consistently engage in them for just one to three minutes a day, your mood, thoughts, and feelings will improve.

GRATITUDE TAKES TIME

Recently, a friend shared that he was facing a significant challenge. He had received some troubling information from his wife about their marriage, and when we spoke soon afterward, he was still reeling from the disclosure. In his moment of acute pain, he told me, "I think I'm supposed to be finding gratitude and wisdom in this experience, but mostly, I just feel awful."

"Yes, you can find gratitude eventually. But not right now," I responded.

While it is possible to feel gratitude early on, for many people, it takes some time, often needing some distance from the issue or the experience before they can truly reflect on their circumstances from a place of gratitude.

Most people don't feel grateful when receiving chemotherapy, changing a flat tire, or cleaning out their desk when they've been laid off. Gratitude typically emerges after some time, after we have perspective, after the shock of what has happened has been absorbed, and then, looking back, with a more objective perspective, we can see the good in the experience, even if we wouldn't have chosen the circumstance.

What appear to be some of the worst moments of our lives, in retrospect, can be the times for which we feel the most gratitude. With a more objective perspective, we can see how that rejection was a redirection, how that breakup was a breakthrough, and how what we thought was a setback was a setup for something more magnificent.

When he was let go from his accounting job at Deloitte, Simu Liu recalls being devastated. He returned to his desk to collect his things just before being escorted out of the building, and he recalls on his Instagram page that no one "offered a whisper of encouragement or even looked in my direction." He remembers fighting back tears of humiliation and being certain his life was over. Today, a decade later, Liu can see that being laid off was the beginning of his life, not the end, and that now, rather than feeling bitter, he believes he owes Deloitte a debt of gratitude.

He didn't know it at the time, but his layoff set into motion a series of events that led to an even more beautiful dream coming true that would have been unattainable had he stayed at Deloitte, crunching numbers. Today, he is the star of Marvel's blockbuster film *Shang-Chi and the Legend of the Ten Rings*.

Every year on April 12, he pauses to reflect. Liu's manager's decision to sever his employment set him on a different path, toward pursuing his previously dormant dreams of acting and film. At the time, Liu recalls feeling like a failure, a disappointment to his parents, and today, he can see that the loss of his employment set him free, to live an even more expansive life he never could have envisioned from his former cubicle.

Over time, even if the experience isn't what we would have wanted, even if we wish we could undo it, looking back, we can often find the good in what happened.

One of my workshop participants from many years ago shared a wonderful characterization of how she was formed for the better by loss. She told us that her family had been well-to-do in her birth country, but when they immigrated to the US, they had very little money and had lost their social status. Whereas she was treated like a princess in her prior country, with beautiful clothing and lots of possessions, she had to leave those things behind, and when they arrived in America, she was expected to help her parents in the home by doing chores, and when she was old enough, earning an income to support the family. She told us that this experience "kicked the princess out of me." Although at the time, she certainly wasn't praising the hardship, like Liu she could see how emigrating, leaving behind a more affluent lifestyle and starting over from scratch, shaped her for the better.

THE RESILIENT POWER OF LANGUAGE

When you elevate your language, you enrich your life. The words you speak have a profound impact on your mood, mind-set, and experience. That is why you must be careful in the words you choose. Your brain believes what you express. Stephen Covey in *The Seven Habits of Highly Effective People* suggests that listening to your language creates greater self-awareness. Neurolinguists have found that it is not only your mood that influences your language. The language you speak has the ability to positively impact your mind-set, emotional state, and well-being.

Consider your to-do list for the balance of the day or even the week. If you can, tell someone in one minute or less what is on your to-do list, and invite them to do the same for you, sharing what is on their to-do list. If you don't have another person nearby, take a moment to say aloud to yourself, in a couple of sentences, what is on the list. Take note of the language you use when you speak about your to-do list and then refer to the discussion of reductive versus resilient language that follows.

REDUCTIVE VERSUS RESILIENT LANGUAGE

Reductive Language		Resilient Language
"I have to ..."	vs.	"I get to ..."
"I've been told to ..."	vs.	"I have the opportunity to ..."
"I've been tasked with ..."	vs.	"I chose to ..."
"I've got to ..."	vs.	"I'm looking forward to ..."
"I need to ..."	vs.	"I'm grateful to ..."

In my workshops and training, I find that when I initially ask people to share their to-do list with one other person, 97 percent of people use *reductive* as opposed to *resilient* language. The impact of using reductive language is that, hearing these words, people feel disempowered, demotivated, and depleted.

The good news is that this is a simple fix. Say your to-do list out loud again, but this time, use only resilient language. Do you notice the difference in your energy and mind-set? When I do this in small and large groups, the energy shifts almost immediately. Most begin laughing, smile more, and feel more motivated by the tasks they have ahead of them.

What's powerful about this exercise is that nothing changed on your to-do list or on the to-do list of the people I described. The change is in how you talk about your to-do list. So, if you want to lift your mood, create a more positive perspective, or feel more motivated, focus on using resilient, rather than reductive, language.

COMPARING YOURSELF TO OTHERS IS A TRAP

By avoiding the traps of self-comparison, expectation, and shame-based interpretation of challenge, you prevent experiences that steal your gratitude and allow yourself more space to choose gratitude.

Comparing yourself to others is a stealthy habit that compromises your ability to practice gratitude. It is that destructive voice that tells us that no matter how successful we are, no matter how many goals we achieve, we haven't done what someone else has done, so our success and achievements do not matter.

Social comparisons cause us to constantly recalibrate and redefine success, making our goals more difficult to hit. There is always someone else who has done things in a unique way or hit a different level or who makes it seem easier than what we have done.

Comparing yourself to others leaves you unsatisfied and feeling as though you are lacking. Avoid the trap of comparing yourself to others by finding your own measures for success. Keep a physical chart of your progress and celebrate the milestones you achieve along the way. Acknowledge the hard work that goes into your progress over time. True, competition can spur us to achieve more, but if the only metrics we have for success are external factors, we are setting ourselves up for misery.

Yoga taught me to stop comparing myself to others. Instead of eyeing my classmates and meticulously filling out my mental scorecard on whose pose was better or worse than mine, I ripped up the scorecard and focused on my own mat. Few life changes have felt so freeing. Up until then, there was a lot of meritless mental chatter as I compared myself to others: "Was he smarter?" "Is she thinner? Prettier? More accomplished? A better mom?" I mean, the list can go on and on. Candidly, it's exhausting. The quest for being better can be overwhelming and never-ending.

The Sanskrit word *mudita*, which means "vicarious joy," refers to delighting in other people's success. The success of others does not take away from your own success and well-being. But if you compare yourself to them, you can fall into the trap of being jealous, envious, and wanting what others have. That is a formula for poor mental and physical health, discontent, and unhappiness.

Practicing mudita, being delighted for other people, enhances a sense of well-being and contentment. The success of others shines a light on a path that you can follow to have your own success.

Scarcity

When we engage in the process of self-comparison, we also invite in scarcity. The belief that we must measure up to be good enough. To be worthy. Scarcity tells us there is only so much good to go around. Believing that there is no room for us all to be successful and valuable, scarcity tricks us into thinking that we must compete to be worthy when we engage in self-comparison.

Abundance

When we drop the self-comparison, we invite feelings of abundance. The belief that there is enough goodness for us all to partake. We can all be worthy. We can all be enough. It's not me *or* you. It's me *and* you. Are you better at cooking or baking or PowerPoint? Great! Can you teach me? Do you speak four languages? Awesome! Can you help me get better at French? Abundance leads to gratitude because, when I'm not judging you or me, I have time to appreciate and love you and me. As we are. Today. Right now.

EXPECTATION CREATES RESISTANCE

Expectation is the mental chatter that sounds like this: "It wasn't supposed to turn out this way." The existence of expectation creates resistance and blocks our ability to accept and find joy in what is. I'm not saying you shouldn't expect things from work, life, and relationships. When life hands you an experience that is different than expected, there is an opportunity to choose gratitude instead of disappointment.

I am dyslexic. For a long time, I expected not to be dyslexic. I expected that I would be a neurotypical learner like most of the population. I resisted being dyslexic. I attached negative (untrue) beliefs to being dyslexic, like "I am dumb."

Today, I am grateful for my dyslexia because although it made certain aspects of my education more difficult, it has endowed me with special talents: an excellent memory, the ability to see possibilities and patterns that are not available to many others, and skills with metaphors and storytelling.

Now, I know better than to fall into the expectation trap. Expectation creates disappointment. Disappointment is the result of unmet expectation. Instead of feeling disappointed by having a learning disability, I am grateful for the skills and strengths dyslexia has afforded me.

SHAME IS THE ENEMY OF GRATITUDE

Shame is a treacherous gratitude thief. Please don't misunderstand me. I'm not asking you to feel grateful for forking over your insurance deductible, getting a troubling health diagnosis, or losing someone you love.

While you don't (and shouldn't) feel grateful *for* the adversity, you can (eventually) feel grateful *for what came out* of the adversity. When handed the short straw of misfortune, you have a choice. The choice is to rail against the hardship, to feel angry, ashamed, and slighted, or to embrace the beautiful lessons and growth that inherently spring from suffering.

For a long time, as a survivor of trauma, I met the diagnostic criteria for post-traumatic stress disorder (PTSD). There was a part of me that felt ashamed of the challenges I'd faced. I am not grateful for the experience that caused my PTSD or the symptoms themselves. However, I am grateful for what came out of this experience: the capacity to connect with people more deeply through empathy.

My ability to create an environment of safety for others exists largely because I have walked the path of adversity myself. Experiencing trauma gave me the gifts to offer others hope in a time of crisis and solace in a time of pain. Today, rather than feeling ashamed of these experiences, I feel grateful for the gifts I have received. Gifts that I have received not despite my experiences, but because of them.

GENEROUSLY SHARING YOUR RESILIENCE STORIES

Generously sharing your resilience stories means that rather than giving advice or telling others what to do, you offer them in the spirit of mentoring, coaching, and advising others. Your stories of perseverance also encourage others to heal and grow. Your stories of resilience can become a survival guide for others.

Sharing reduces the power of faulty thinking that The Vulnerability Bias holds over you. It demonstrates that you can be liked, loved, and not left. It also signals to others that they are not alone in their challenges, changes, and complexities.

In sharing, you shine a light on the paths of others.

After I gave a keynote speech on The Five Practices at a global technology company, one of the attendees reached out to me and shared the following:

> Thank you so much for taking the time to speak to us today. Your presentation was incredibly inspiring. This also resonates with me because one of my dreams (albeit naive right now) is a world where we are celebrating our differences and we as humans lift each other up. I know we have a long way to go but that is something that I aspire to live my life by. The one question I did put in the chat which got missed was: The challenge I've had was I lost 3 members of my immediate family over the past 12 years. I've overcome that by leaning into trying to be the best person I can be because I know from those I've lost they would want me to do that. While that is a very intimate and personal story, it is something that defines me. This is where I can be reserved. Is this being "too vulnerable"?
>
> I believe in being my true authentic self, which means also not being afraid to share personal challenges. At first, I was very uncomfortable sharing that, but today it is something that defines me, and I guess I wonder if it is too much. Just curious on your thoughts.
>
> Thank you again and wish you the best, RJ

After thinking about this important question, I wrote back to him and said the following:

> We haven't been given a template to tell our resilience stories, so oftentimes, we're left wondering, "Was that too vulnerable?" Or sometimes we have a "vulnerability hangover" after we share something, suddenly feeling frightened or ashamed by what we shared.
>
> I am not saying this is your journey, this is just what happens for many people at times. Therefore, when I teach people to share their resilience stories, I like to teach them to first ask themselves, "vulnerability"

in service of what? What are you desiring to share, accomplish, or convey with your story?

What I hear you saying is this experience of losing three family members in twelve years has been a powerful catalyst that encourages you to be the best version of yourself. That you've transformed the pain to a purpose of making yourself the best person you can be, because you know in your heart, this is what your family members would have wanted.

My impression is you are telling a beautifully authentic and meaningful story about the challenges that have catalyzed your growth. It is only through challenging the fear associated with The Vulnerability Bias that we learn that fear is unfounded. Bringing our resilience stories out into the light reveals truth and burns off the fear once associated with being seen and known.

Dr. Taryn Marie

HOW OTHERS BENEFIT FROM YOUR RESILIENCE STORY

Even when you might not realize it, your words can have a positive power to influence others. The act of sharing your resilience story can truly inspire others. If nothing else, those who listen will realize they are not alone in their hardships. So often, we look up to successful people who have achieved great feats and don't see the tremendous amount of struggle and work it took to get to where they are.

When RJ shares his resilience story generously with others, he gives them the opportunity to learn vicariously from his experience. If you're grappling with finding the goodness in your experiences, take a step back, and write a story about experiences that make you feel grateful.

An icebreaker I use to warm up a group or team, to get them in the mood to reflect on gratitude, is to write the most positive story they can imagine, using only four words. When I ask teams to do this, people say things like "She believed she could." Or "My dreams came true." Or "Believe in the Lord." Or "*Una dia mas cera*," which means "one day closer."

Give it a try! Along with supporting others, when you tell your resilience story, you reinforce your own resilience, as well as pave the way for others to connect with and share their own stories of resilience.

HOW YOU BENEFIT FROM SHARING YOUR STORIES OF RESILIENCE

Generously sharing your resilience story also has personal benefits for you. Vulnerability is the cornerstone of authenticity and empathy. Often, vulnerability and authentic self-expression grow from the same root. Sharing what you have gone through brings the experience full circle and can provide you with a new and more positive perspective on how you demonstrated resilience.

The courage to share your resilience story can support you in creating a coherent narrative out of something that was chaotic at the time. Constructing the narrative causes cognitive changes in the brain that tell your body to relax and that all is good.

Taking time to organize your thoughts about an adverse event, trying to create your narrative, not just recount your story, gives you an opportunity to exert a greater sense of control over the event and can help move you toward making peace with the situation.

Research has shown that even brief autobiographical storytelling exercises, written or oral, can have substantial impacts on psychological and physical health even months after the storytelling. It's not just the telling or writing it down, but knowing that what you write will be read by others and the hope that someone else might be inspired or helped by your story. Sharing our resilience stories also supports the practice of external connection.

Paul Zak, who leads the Center for Neuroeconomics Studies at Claremont Graduate University, believes that reading or listening to stories triggers a release of oxytocin, the hormone associated with empathy, trust, and relationship-building. This brain activity strengthens social bonds and the psychologically powerful sense of being heard and understood by others.

MY LIFE, MY STORY PROJECT

The My Life, My Story Project is a national Veterans Health Administration (VA) interview program that aims to provide more humanistic patient care for veterans by sharing the veterans' resilience stories.

When the project was initially implemented, interviewers asked veterans what they wanted their health-care provider to know about them. Veterans have experiences of personal triumphs, hardships, and aspirations. Simply by being willing to tell their stories generously, veterans were able to strengthen the provider-patient relationship that existed between veterans and physicians, but the benefits did not end there.

Sharing their resilience stories even improved the medical care veterans received. The power of this, and the connection that is fostered between humans when we share our stories, as well as the impact on our relationships and our ability to influence and change ourselves and the people around us, cannot be underestimated.

Those that are most likely to flourish when facing challenge are those that practice Grati-osity by first finding the good in difficulty, even if they wouldn't have chosen the circumstances, and then, by sharing their resilience stories generously with others, solidifying their own resilience while amplifying it by allowing others to learn vicariously from their experience.

8
The Practice of Possibility

The late *60 Minutes* reporter Mike Wallace once interviewed a young woman who was in the process of launching her very own national talk show.

"How do you think it will go?" Wallace asked.

"It will do well," she said.

"And if it doesn't?" Wallace asked.

"And if it doesn't, I will still do well," she replied. "I will do well because I am not defined by a show. I think we are defined by the way we treat ourselves and the way we treat other people. It would be wonderful to be acclaimed as this talk show host who's made it. That would be wonderful. But if that doesn't happen, there are other important things in my life."

The young woman who believed she would do well regardless of the outcome of her talk show was none other than Oprah Winfrey. Yet, I thought it helpful to remind you that in her early days on television, Oprah, who was born into poverty and suffered horrendous abuse as a child, was unknown outside Chicago and not guaranteed national success by any means. Just look at how many other aspiring talk show hosts have failed over the years.

What made the difference for Oprah? Her unwavering belief in the infinite possibilities for success, not just in her career, but as a person of incredible resilience, who knew that a single show would not dictate her success or failure.

THE RESILIENT PRACTICE OF POSSIBILITY

Resilient people who engage with The Practice of Possibility are better able to recognize that the never-ending quest for perfection doesn't equate to excellence, often incapacitating us with unattainable standards, and to instead focus on progress. The Practice of Possibility is key during times of stress because, by nature, stress makes us more myopic.

However, by considering unique and novel ways to achieve a goal, you expand the array of options for creating results, and you leverage creativity to make your goals a reality. You also can more accurately appraise risks and opportunities.

The Practice of Possibility is, first, about focusing on progress instead of perfection, recognizing that the quest for perfection often paralyzes us with impossibly high standards. Second, The Practice of Possibility teaches us that to effectively navigate challenge, we get to examine the associated risks and opportunities inherent in every possibility. Those who flourish, rather than fold, become adept at creative problem-solving and finding solutions, even to seemingly intractable problems.

The Practice of Possibility, then, is about finding creative and innovative solutions, even in the face of fear and potential failure.

PERFECTION IS THE ENEMY OF PROGRESS

The world craves your presence, not your perfection. The deceptive aspect of perfection is that it is unattainable. It will always elude you and you will have nothing to show for it, no matter how long you chase it.

Focusing on progress is much more fulfilling, not to mention attainable. There is a strong relationship between perfectionism and the detrimental impacts of procrastination. When you try to be perfect, you feel pressured, and you may tend to put off doing what you need to do to make progress.

Sometimes, the self-induced pressure of procrastiantion produces your best work and sometimes it does not. The results are what they are. Then, you go back to thinking everything must be perfect, procrastinating, and dealing with the stress of doing everything at the last minute.

If you are like me, you probably are beating yourself up for procrastinating the whole time you are doing things at the last minute. You *know* you did it to yourself, but it's too late to do anything about it, so you are stressed out even more.

The solution here is to focus more on progress than on perfection. No one is going to precisely say the right thing every time or complete every task correctly on the first go. Just because every step along the way is not perfect, it doesn't mean the outcome won't be great.

So, rather than demanding perfection at every stage, focus on progress and achieving the desired result. Good enough is just that: good enough to get you where you want to go. As a graduate student, you can spend years and years toiling away on writing the perfect master's thesis or dissertation. But you're not going to get any special awards for staying in school to write a perfect research study. My classmates and I reminded one another not to fall into the perfection trap by reiterating that a good thesis or dissertation was a done thesis or dissertation. We focused on progress and the result.

MANIFESTATION DONE WELL

Manifestation is the process of intentionally making your desires and goals take form. If you would like to create more opportunities and explore the possibilities of what you can create, manifestation is a method for starting on a path to your dreams. Many people live in the uncomfortable space between the life they imagine and the reality of their life as it is today. Very few people know how to cross the chasm that exists between what is true today and the hopes and dreams of their imagined future.

Simply focusing energy from your thoughts can begin to bring your dreams to life. Desire is possibility waiting to be manifested into form. Mental creation precedes physical creation.

If you've spent hours visualizing your company's growth, your house on the ocean, or your wedding, you may be missing three key ingredients that are blocking the possibilities you want to create.

First, when visualizing the outcome, many focus on the result of what they most desire. They engage all five senses and imagine what it will look, taste, feel, sound, and smell like. They imagine their dress, see themselves on the red carpet at the awards ceremony, and think of the questions they'll ask when interviewing filmmakers and actors about their resilience stories—the lesser-known challenges encountered by well-known people to be nominated for the evening's award.

Or maybe that's just me?

Anyway, many tend to visualize the end goal. What they don't realize if they don't visualize the process of reaching their goals is this: they are not creating a mental path to make their desires become a reality.

When Michael Phelps was training for the 2008 Olympics in Beijing, his coach Bob Bowman would tell Phelps not just to envision the result, but to play the tape, which meant Phelps spent time each day envisioning each of his races, from start to finish, turn by turn, stroke by stroke. What Bowman understood from sports psychology is that envisioning the ultimate outcome is not enough.

To make our desires a reality, we also must envision the path, see ourselves doing the work, putting in the time, and making the deposits to bring our dreams to life.

While it's powerful to step into the possibilities and be willing to believe in the endless array of opportunities that await our investment, if you don't visualize yourself doing the work, as Phelps did, your mind will get caught in the chasm of today's reality and tomorrow's aspirations because you didn't give your brain a mental blueprint for how to go about creating those results.

Picturing the result is motivating—it's all glory when we achieve our dreams and win. To truly get those gains you're imagining, you've gotta visualize the guts of the goal too. If you want to lose weight, instead of just imagining yourself as thinner, envision yourself eating healthy, working through a sugar craving, passing up the doughnuts, working out even when you're exhausted after the kids are in bed, because you told yourself you would. See yourself taking the small steps toward your dreams, and you'll not only create the outcome, but you will also show your brain and body how to chart the path to get you there.

Second, recognize that gratitude is the rocket fuel of manifestation. Gratitude is your signal that your work is done. Your desires have been granted. When you visualize your path, and you see yourself attaining your goal, take time to express gratitude for the experience as though it already happened. This isn't a fake-it-until-you-make-it tactic. See your imagined outcome occurring, and smile, thanking yourself, God, the universe, and all the people who supported you for making this opportunity possible. The expression of gratitude seals the deal and is the message to our heart and mind that what we most want has already happened, and now, we get to put in the work and wait for our reality to catch up to what we've created for ourselves in the future.

Third, keep close track of the language you use when describing your dream. Just as we learned about reductive and resilient language, the words you use to share your dream matter.

Our words carry a vibrational signature that signal to our mind, body, and the matter around us the extent to which we believe in our dream. When we say things like "I'd love to create..." or "If we're successful..." or "I hope that one day...," we send the message that we don't completely believe in what we're creating.

Your language has betrayed you, because even though you say you are "all in" and focused, your words suggest hesitancy and disbelief. Instead of using language that sends the message that you're hedging, be intentional about using words that signal your headlong focus on your goal.

Say "I am creating..." or "When we're successful..." or "I know that one day..." Language has power. The truth of our belief is in our language. Leverage language to reinforce the viability of your dreams, not to diminish your desires coming to fruition.

DREAMS

It's not about the talent that you have. Oftentimes, talent is overrated. Talent is where you start, but it will take you only so far. Tenacity coupled with talent is the best predictor of your potential. When it came time for the band Journey to hire a new singer in 2008, Neal Schon went searching on YouTube. After days of sitting in front of his computer, he landed on the video of Arnel Pineda, a Filipino singer who'd grown up listening to and loving Journey's music.

Pineda had fallen on hard times. He was living on the streets of Manila and eating food off the concrete. Yet, even in his lowest moments, he never stopped believing (sounds like a good theme for a song, right?).

His life took a turn for the better when he signed with the band The Zoo. It was then that he began to perform on YouTube, where he belted out Journey songs with such soul that Schon invited him to try out for the real band.

Today, Pineda's life has been dramatically enhanced by the unanticipated opportunities he has been given as Journey's lead singer, a possibility he never even dared to dream about back when he was living on the streets.

When you work on your dreams, even when all seems dark, unknown possibilities emerge. A dream is not the one you dream at night while you're sleeping. Your dream is the one that won't let you sleep and keeps you awake at night. Go pursue that dream!

NAVIGATING AMBIGUITY

The Practice of Possibility requires that you gain a greater comfort with navigating the ambiguity associated with evaluating potential risks and opportunities. However, as we discussed your human desire for closure previously, your brain naturally prefers clarity and certainty to ambiguity.

Tolerance of Ambiguity (ToA) is decreasing for adults under age forty, compared to those over age forty. For younger generations, the ability to order items anytime with one click, avoiding uncertainty in navigation with Google Maps, Waze, and other tools, and growing up with parents who minimized exposure to ambiguity may be some of the reasons ToA is on the decline. However, this type of tolerance is an essential skill correlated with increased performance, enhanced job satisfaction, better leadership, and even higher earnings. In addition, research demonstrates that leaders who possess higher ToA create better performance-related outcomes for the team they manage.

Fortunately, this is a skill that can be cultivated as a by-product of The Practice of Possibility, and enhancing ToA contributes to enhancing resilience overall. To focus on enhancing how you practice Possibility along with ToA:

- *(Re)focus your actions to align with your effort and vision.* Even if your environment is uncertain, focusing on what you can control and returning to your vision, mission, or "why" statement can increase ToA.
- *(Re)claim your joy.* Tune into what brings you the greatest sense of fulfillment and aliveness to remind you why you do the work you do.
- *(Re)connect to your truth.* Tune into the internal connection you have with yourself for guidance and discernment in moments that feel murky, to gain more clarity and enhance ToA.

EVALUATING POSSIBILITY

One powerful practice to evaluate possibility is to begin by asking yourself questions about your current perspective: What is my perspective; how am I seeing things? How am I impacting others? Who are the others and what might their different perspectives be?

Now, you won't always be able to do this perspective shifting by yourself. Another way to step outside of your own perspective is to physically change your scenery and do something else. Listen to music, take a walk, take a drive in the countryside, spend time with someone you enjoy, or do anything that removes you from the midst of your current situation to gain new perspective and see things from another point of view.

You can also ask yourself questions, such as:

- How would the best version of me handle this situation? What would my perspective be?
- How would someone you admire handle this moment?
- What would happen if…?
- I wonder if…?
- Is that true?
- How might I…?
- How will I want to remember this chapter in my life when I retell the story?
- What can I learn from this moment?
- How can I choose joy in this situation?
- What am I grateful for in this moment?

The Five Practices are highly interrelated, and The Practice of Gratiosity can contribute to The Practice of Possibility. We need to engage our wonder and our imagination to train our eyes to see opportunities. With wonder and imagination, you tap into limitlessness. If anything were possible, what might happen? You can't limit yourself with past beliefs, with false ceilings. If you have always believed you are not artistic or that your boss would never allow you to do something that unusual, then you might not engage in creative activities.

The truth is that creative activities of one kind or another work for everyone. It doesn't mean you have to create works of art that everyone admires or that sell for thousands of dollars. It means that you engage a different part of your mind with an activity that you might not normally do, thereby awakening possibilities you might not have seen otherwise. Then, you can consider the possibilities you uncover, rather than discarding any of them.

RISK

You may also be wondering how you evaluate the risks associated with the new possibilities that emerge. Every opportunity carries risk. We can manage risk, but rarely can we completely mitigate risk. Knowing that risk is inherent in new opportunities, you can use the following strategies to evaluate risk:

- *Identify the risks.* Take time to think through what MIGHT happen.
- *Determine who might be impacted and how.* Start with your own perspective but also consider how others are impacted, being as specific as you can.
- *Use your paranoia to productively assess risk.* How likely is the hazard to happen? You don't have to be mathematical about this, but could just indicate low, medium, or high risk. And consider what could be changed to lessen the risk involved. You tape down cords that cross where people might walk or put a rug over the cords so that no one will trip, for instance. What could be done, if anything, to reduce the risk you identified in the opportunity?
- *Be brave enough to break your own business model.* Be willing to poke holes in and find the cracks in your business model. Examine what elements of your current approach might leave you open to attack or susceptible to certain conditions, leaving your business or idea exposed.
- *Write down your assessment for future reference.* If you choose the opportunity, you will want this assessment so that you can take

action to reduce the risks you have identified. Writing things down also helps us more thoroughly think through things as well as remember our ideas.

- *Periodically review your risk assessment.* As you grasp an opportunity and move toward your goal, things will change so risk needs to be reevaluated against the changing landscape, especially for longer-term opportunities. Remember that if you overfocus on opportunity and don't evaluate the risks, you are more likely to fail. And if you overfocus on risks, you are more likely to stagnate and not move at all.

It's important to be balanced in your assessment of both risk and opportunity. Those that engage in The Practice of Possibility most effectively, are those that are willing to take the time to evaluate both the potential and the pitfalls of a new possibility amid The Three C's. Of course, after you have trained your eyes to see possibility, have identified limiting thinking, and have evaluated the risks, then you get to act by embracing the best opportunity and moving forward!

FEAR KEEPS YOU SMALL

Recently, I had coffee with a promising young leader at our company. He wanted to write blogs but hadn't published anything since he'd written for his collegiate newspaper years earlier. He wanted my advice to help him get started.

"When do you plan to write?" I asked.

He began by saying, "Someday when I..." I interrupted.

"Someday isn't a day."

"What?" he responded, confused.

"Monday is a day. Tuesday is a day," I said. "But someday is not a day. You have everything you need to write a blog right now. Today. On this day."

Thinking we'll pursue our purpose "someday" virtually assures we won't, because we tell ourselves we are not enough today. The "somedays" keep us a safe distance from engaging with our true potential and passion.

While putting things off feels safe, it also keeps us small. There will always be a myriad of reasons not to step forward into the full complement of our capability: we imagine we need more experience, tenure, title, authority, schooling, credibility, and so on. *All* of these are small matters compared to the scale and scope of our strengths, the unique set of gifts we've each been given.

Don't let the little doubts stop you from chasing the big things.

FEAR ISOLATES YOU

Fear often tells you that, if people really knew your resilience story, they wouldn't like you, let alone accept, understand, or love you. So, fear feeds into The Vulnerability Bias and instructs, "It's better not to share your challenges, and stay separate."

Your challenges are display cases for your strengths. The vulnerability associated with telling your resilience stories of adversity allows you to integrate your experience holistically. Rather than being rejected for your adverse circumstances, the converse is true, your relationships have and will continue to become more connected.

My resilience stories have expanded others' ability to know, love, see, and understand me, as I am. Each one of us has at least one thing we don't do because we're afraid. Our society often sends the message that fear is bad, something to be avoided, a weakness, and therefore, you would do well to be fearless. I disagree. I don't know what it means to be fearless. But I know what it means to be afraid. I can speak so intelligently about fear because, thanks to my stalker experiences, fear is one of my most constant companions. I don't recommend we make fear our friend. More than any other emotion, it is fear that derails lives and careers and prevents us from being the best version of ourselves. Fear, if we let it, has the capacity to keep all of us tethered to the status quo and block our capacity for growth, change, and becoming more. I know a lot about what it feels like to be afraid. I have a lot of fears.

My rational and irrational fears, in no particular order, are that I am afraid of:

- not being _____ (fill in the blank) enough
- being too much
- success
- failure
- people listening to me
- no one will listen to me
- being seen
- being invisible
- being controlled
- being free
- being weak
- being powerful
- heights
- sharks
- wasted time
- wasted potential
- being alone
- not being left alone
- not having earned it
- trying too hard
- quitting too early
- missing my chance
- getting my chance
- disappointing others
- angering others
- not being liked
- not being loved
- being abandoned

Do any of these fears resonate with you? If I allow them, these fears will keep me small, scared, and quiet. These fears will convince me not to try, that I am not enough, and that failure is imminent. Yet, if I allow these fears to stop me, I have allowed fear to have the last word, to decide the landscape of my life. I have and will continue to actively choose to not allow fear to determine how I live my life, the opportunities I do and do not pursue, and to dictate the person I believe I can become.

WHAT SCARED US IS SACRED

Did you ever notice how similarly the words *scared* and *sacred* are spelled? These are the same words essentially, just with the *c* in a different place. This got me thinking: What if, considering the wisdom of the English language, rather than seeing fear as something to be avoided, to run from, fear is instead an experience we're supposed to run toward? What if the things that scared us are our most sacred opportunities for development and growth? When you learn to engage in your sacred journey, by facing the very things that have scared you and kept you stuck, you begin to recognize the feeling of fear as an opportunity to build resilience.

We all have a responsibility to make a difference now. Each. And. Every. One. Of. Us. No one is exempt. Fear can no longer be a reason for putting off being, doing, and giving what we are inherently meant to be, do, and give.

Why am I so invested in your facing your fear, embracing the possibilities, and making a difference? Because the difference that you do or do not make impacts me. Embracing your possibilities, your purpose, the difference you are meant to make, is for the collective good. If you let fear stop you, none of us reaps the benefits of the unique contribution you are meant to make within this world.

So, how do we know when to listen to the wisdom of fear and when to keep walking? Try these:

- Don't assume fear is a reason not to act or to act—fear is not a good reason for anything. Ever.
- The things which most scare us are often the most sacred aspects of our lives we need to engage with, rather than avoid.
- We can increase our tolerance for fear by asking ourselves where the fear is coming from: a past hurt, mistake, sensitivity? Sometimes, we must address our past fears to be more courageous in the present.
- Courage is not the absence of fear; it is the willingness to engage with fear.
- Instead of being deterred by the discomfort of fear, we can point ourselves squarely in the direction of that fear and engage with, unpack, and learn from it.
- Facing fear is a powerful teacher and leads to our formation as people and leaders.

It may sound counterintuitive, but those who face fear to pursue possibilities are often the ones that flourish, rather than fold, when facing The Three C's and demonstrating resilience. The Practice of Possibility is not about blindly pursuing opportunity or staying away from any form of risk, but instead taking the time to evaluate the relative risk and opportunity of each possibility that presents itself. Finally, it's easy to get bogged down in perfection, which can lead to procrastination. Instead, when facing The Three C's, don't expect you'll be perfect, but, like those who are more likely to flourish rather than fold, focus on making progress.

PART III

YOUR RESILIENT MOVEMENT— APPLYING RESILIENCE TO YOUR LIFE

Now, it's your turn to apply resilience to your life. To continue to make resilience the very essence of your humanity in the inevitable moments when you face challenge, change, and complexity (The Three C's). Part III of this book is all about the application of The Five Practices to various aspects of your life. Perhaps you're wondering how you can apply The Five Practices to your relationships, community, or parenting.

The following chapters are meant to serve as a practical source to guide you in applying these principles across all aspects of your life to choose resilience in every aspect of your life, create even greater momentum in your life by having the skills and tools to effectively address adversities, and to build on this momentum to create your own revolutionary resilience movement for you!

When you choose resilience, you create momentum. The momentum creates a movement. This is your resilience movement now.

9
Resilient Parenting

As I have crisscrossed the country, and the globe, speaking to organizations about resilience, attendees from my workshops, summits, and keynotes have approached me saying, "I wish my fifteen-year-old daughter could hear this." Or "How can I apply The Five Practices to parenting resilient kids?"

No matter what age your child is, you can enhance their resilience. Our children often look to us to determine how they should feel about experiences in their lives. Parents are often the most powerful and influential figures in children's lives.

We are their examples of what it means to be a man or a woman in this world, and our responses, attitudes, and approval have a profound impact on our children.

I don't have parenting all figured out. Not even close. I'm always learning. I've done a lot of things wrong. In the spirit of The Practice of Possibility, parenting is about progress, not perfection. Yet, I do have a few approaches to parenting that have worked for me, when I was married previously and as a single mother after divorce.

IS IT TIME TO PANIC?

My son Samson has always been a worrier. When he found a signed jersey he wanted to purchase at the mall, but hadn't yet saved enough money, he worried every day that someone else would purchase the jersey until he earned enough.

He also worries about safety, a lot. His safety and those around him. One morning, as we passed a pool, a father was launching his son in the air over the pool's water, and I asked Samson if he would like to do that with his father. He responded by saying, with an indignant tone, appalled at my suggestion, "Mom, that is so unsafe!"

My role is not to teach him not to worry. My role is to give him tools to navigate the worry. He will never not be anxious. He will never not worry. Never in the history of calming down did telling someone to calm down actually calm them down.

When we took a hot air balloon trip in Albuquerque, Samson was pumping me with questions on the ride to the launch site about what happens if the balloon is punctured, runs out of air to inflate, hits a power line, or the basket falls off in midair.

When we arrived at the launch site, the balloon pilot allowed my son to hold one side of the giant balloon while they inflated it; involving him in the preparation helped him gain confidence in the balloon's sturdiness to carry us through the air safely.

Just before boarding the balloon's basket, the pilot went over safety procedures. Our pilot told us that usually the balloon's basket lands upright, but when he lands in higher winds, the basket can turn sideways causing the passengers to spill out onto the ground, leading to what is known as a "Yeehaw" landing.

Just as the pilot spoke, another balloon landed in high winds, resulting in a Yeehaw landing. Samson flashed me an immediately horrified look, indicating he was already worried it would happen to us. Once we took off we had a serene flight over the New Mexico landscape. But then, it was time to land.

High winds were not our problem. There was no breeze at all. The pilot could not navigate to an open spot on the ground. We were just hanging there over highways and houses, and our fuel was running low.

Samson heard our pilot share our coordinates and discuss his plan for landing. My worrier son picked up on the pilot's anxiety, turned to me, and said, "Is it time to panic?"

"No, son," I said with a smile. "It's not time to panic just yet. But, when it is time to panic, you'll be the first one to know."

Our role is not to teach our children to never worry. Instead, we need to teach them how to worry well.

As our balloon descended over cars and trees and into a subdivision, I reassured Samson it *still* was not time to panic. Our pilot expertly guided us to a clearing, a thin strip of grass in a small park with a slide and swings, in a subdivision. Our basket remained upright. No Yeehaw landing for us.

Samson and his brother jumped out and ran to play on a jungle gym. No worries. Later, I reinforced for Samson what had gone right: we had landed safely, on the grass, and he and his brother were able to play while the team deflated the balloon.

Our role as parents is not to remove worry from our children's lives, but to teach them how to manage worry, anxiety, and fear. Here are strategies to use and teach your children, and perhaps yourself, if they (or you) have a propensity to panic:

- *Set aside time to worry, and then release.* Instead of telling children not to worry, invite them to set aside time for "worry sessions" to address their concerns. Set a timer for five minutes and ask your child to worry about every aspect of the concern. They can even write down all fears, anxieties, and concerns. Then, once the period is over, ask your child to release the worries and no longer think about them. If your child brings up worries again, share that they've already had their worry time. These worry sessions can occur daily, if needed.

- *Create a worry box.* Create a box or jar where your children can keep their worries, concerns, and anxieties. Have your child decorate it, and then write down each worry on a piece of paper and store it in the container. Tell your child that once it is in the box, there is no need to think about it anymore.
- *What's the worst that could happen?* When your child frets, ask them, "What's the worst that can happen?" This will help children feel more secure because they realize that the worst imagined outcome is not as bad as they thought. It helps give them perspective. If they are worried about not passing a test, tell them that if that happens, they can ask the teacher for more help, or get a tutor. Reminding our children that they are capable of handling even the worst-case scenario helps them see that most problems can be managed.
- *Ask, What is the best thing that can happen?* Children tend to imagine the worst possible outcomes, so encourage them to focus on more positive outcomes instead. I did this when Samson worried about the balloon ride, telling him to imagine soaring above the ground with the wind in his hair. This approach teaches children to have a more balanced thought process.
- *Point out and reinforce positive outcomes.* Talk to your children about the positive outcomes they've experienced to reinforce the good things that happen. I did this with Samson after we landed the hot air balloon safely to help him remember a time when his propensity to worry gave way to goodness. This will help him be less inclined to worry in the future.
- *Worry is not the whole story.* Remind children when they worry that worry is just one emotion, or one character in the story of their lives. Talk about other emotions like joy, happiness, enthusiasm, and excitement to put worry in perspective for them.

KEEP PASSING OUT THE PEANUTS

Even as adults, we look to others to gauge the seriousness of a situation, such as when our airplane hits turbulence. Parents get to walk the delicate tightrope of being authentic in our responses and shielding our children from fear and worry of the outside world. We are the airline flight attendant of our children's lives. In the book *Love Warrior*, Glennon Doyle, shortly after her divorce is finalized, reaches out to her friend, Elizabeth Gilbert, for advice on how to support her children in uncertain times. Gilbert says, "Glennon, your family is together on an airplane right now, and there is some serious turbulence. The kids are afraid. What do we do when we're afraid on an airplane? We look at the flight attendants. If they seem scared, we panic, too. If they seem calm, we stay calm. So, what I am telling you is that you are the flight attendant, and you've been through enough turbulence to know you'll all make it. Your kids are new to flying, so they are going to look to you to see whether they are okay. Your job right now is to stay calm, smile—and keep serving the freaking peanuts."

As parents, we are the flight attendants of our children's lives. Our children look to us and our responses to gauge how much concern they should feel in situations of ambiguity or uncertainty.

When we're on an airplane and we hit turbulence and the plane is bouncing around in the air, we look at the flight attendant's responses to see if we should be afraid. In the face of uncertainty, flight attendants are the barometer for how concerned we should be about a particular situation. While it's important for us, as parents, to be authentic in those moments of turbulence, it's equally as important for us hold a space for our children's psychological and physical safety; to send the message that they are safe, we've got what it takes to protect them, and amid their little plane being tossed around in the air, they can relax and trust that the pilot and the plane are sound. The way we send the message that our children are psychologically and physically safe is, like a good flight attendant, to keep passing out the peanuts. Due to allergy concerns, flight attendants pass out other snacks instead of peanuts. How can you metaphorically keep passing out the peanuts when life gets turbulent? When your child is worried or scared, take time to reassure, listen, respond thoughtfully to requests and questions, and support them by helping them learn to self-regulate their emotions.

EMOTIONAL REGULATION

While our personalities play a role, our ability to regulate our emotions is mostly a product of our environment as children and adults because this is where behavior is learned and reinforced or discouraged.

We all have meltdowns now and then, but when the behavioral response doesn't match the issue, or there are frequent emotional outbursts, there may be an opportunity for you and/or your child to learn to better regulate your emotions in a way that is healthy and socially acceptable.

Here are my tales of two meltdowns:

No. 1: The Case of the Child Meltdown

Years ago, when I was working for Cigna and the head of global leadership development, we had a charity run for March of Dimes, to which employees brought their families. I'd kept my sons out past their naptimes and let them have two doughnuts each. This proved to be a mistake.

When they wanted another doughnut, I said no. Samson took this well, but his younger brother Sawyer, who was around two years old, did not. To my horror, Sawyer squirmed out of my arms, walked a good distance away from me, and flung himself on the ground in full-fledged tantrum mode.

Remember, this was a work event. Naturally, my son went into his meltdown in front of Cigna's chief marketing officer and its chief technology officer. Embarrassed and appalled, I froze.

Meanwhile, Sawyer continued screaming, attracting even more attention from my coworkers.

I weighed my options, and my future with the company. If I rushed to pick him up, it would become clear to all of Cigna's corporate leadership that their head of global leadership development had lost control of her child.

What to do?

I took a deep breath and calmly walked over to Sawyer, lovingly scooped him up in my arms, gently kissed him on the head, and then said loudly enough for everyone to hear, for comedic effect, "Poor little guy, I'll try to find his mother."

No. 2: The Case of the Mom Meltdown

The second lesson occurred during the pandemic when I was living in Philadelphia. We'd been shut in for months, homeschooling, and witnessing riots, protests, and fires occurring less than a mile away.

As was the case for so many of us, my nerves were jangled and raw. I was feeding the boys breakfast before another day of online learning, where I would serve as their on-site teacher, determined to keep them online, on-task, and on-point for another day of lessons.

After a full day of virtual learning, we'd go outside to play, we'd have dinner, and then I'd put them to bed. Once my sons were asleep, my work day would begin. I'd work late into the night, revamping my business model, and struggling to keep my newly minted consulting practice afloat.

I was running myself ragged. Then one day, the boys acted up and I blew up. I yelled at them, which was unusual. When I finally, blessedly, calmed down, and realized I was in a galaxy way beyond overreacting, Sawyer looked at me, hurt and angry, with tears in his eyes, and said, "Are you done, Mom?"

Seeing his stricken face, I rushed to his side and apologized to both boys for losing my temper. I took the opportunity to reflect with them on what I should have done and to ask for their forgiveness.

Managing your response to emotions promotes resilience because it allows you to direct your energy in more productive and positive ways. Fortunately, emotional regulation is a skill that can be taught, learned, and practiced through a variety of tools.

Parents serve as the role model for our children in practicing these skills. When we manage our response to emotions, controlling them rather than letting them control us, our children observe and learn how to do the same. Children and adults with diagnoses like attention deficit hyperactivity disorder (ADHD) or anxiety, and others who have experienced trauma or a great deal of change, may need to be more vigilant with their emotional regulation.

The key for teaching emotional regulation to our children and practicing emotional regulation as adults is not to avoid difficult or upsetting situations, but instead to use these situations to practice these skills.

When my younger son, Sawyer, was entering kindergarten, there was a waitlist for his class, and it was not clear if he was going to be able to attend the same school as his older brother. We had told him for two years that he would be going there, so we knew he would be disappointed if that didn't happen.

As the summer was ending, I watched Sawyer's name inch closer to the top of the waitlist. It seemed likely he would be able to attend the school, but there was still uncertainty. Prior to school commencing, there is an orientation for new students and parents, and I asked the school's administrators if Sawyer could attend the orientation even though he was still on the waitlist. The school administrators responded with expressions of concern. "Why would you do that?" they asked. "What if he doesn't get in?" they questioned.

I explained that I'd told Sawyer there was a waitlist, and he was the second person on the waitlist. I prepared him by saying that while we hoped he would get in, there was a chance he wouldn't. I was introducing my son to the concepts of uncertainty and ambiguity. As parents, our job is not to figure it all out for our children. Our job is to give them the tools to recognize these situations and to figure out how to deal with them.

In the end, Sawyer was admitted to the school. Yet, in the intervening time between uncertainty and certainty, he had an opportunity to live with the ambiguity and to find ways to regulate his emotions. We can't eliminate uncertainty and ambiguity from our children's lives, or our own, for that matter. So, our children must learn to deal with not knowing if they will be chosen for the school play or the soccer team, or invited to a classmate's birthday party.

The tough part for parents is to be present and to guide our children in their emotional development without hovering or getting overinvolved. For me, overseeing homework is an opportunity to teach and model emotional regulation.

When the work is done well, I praise my boys, and then encourage them by saying, "I bet you can do the next paragraph on your own, and I am here if you have any questions." Then, I stay in the area, making dinner or doing my own work, so he has my presence, and he is relying on himself. I check on him every fifteen to twenty minutes and praise his progress. I also give him suggestions when he feels frustrated, such as, "Let's take a quick break and get a drink."

In this way, I am staying present to support him, not getting overly involved, and role modeling how to stay calm when the work feels difficult or frustrating, while encouraging and pointing out his progress.

When the assignment is complete, we celebrate! We might have a dance party to one of his favorite songs, play a short clip on YouTube that he's been wanting to watch, or play with a pet before we tackle the next assignment.

Here are suggestions for enhancing emotional regulation for our children and ourselves:

- *Respond instead of react.* This is a favorite tenet of mine from the Nonviolent Communication curriculum to enhance my emotional regulation as a parent and to role model emotional regulation for my children.

  When we allow someone else's emotion to lead to us reacting emotionally, this is a reaction. When we pause to separate ourselves from someone else's emotion, and respond from a place of calm and love, this is a response.

Here's the difference between reacting versus responding:

REACTING VERSUS RESPONDING

Reacting	Responding
is often immediate, emotional, and unthinking	is considerate, thoughtful, and guided by positive intent
is a "lower" version of ourselves, often driven by fear or control	is a "higher" version of ourselves, often driven from a place of personal values, calm, and love
gives away control to others by getting emotional	maintains control by remaining conscious
comes from short-term perspective	comes from a long-term outlook
hijacks the outcome	influences the outcome

To give myself the best opportunity to respond, instead of react, when I feel emotionally triggered, I:

1. Stop.
2. Breathe in slowly and recognize the emotions I am feeling in my body.
3. Label the emotions I am feeling such as afraid, sad, angry, disappointed, or frustrated. In our home, we've also developed the label "sad-mad" to characterize what it feels to be simultaneously sad and mad. I often feel the "sad-mad" when my sons are wrestling with one another, I ask them to stop because it's getting too rough, but they don't stop, and one of them gets hurt.
4. Respond by being nurturing, loving, kind, and calm, and assuming positive intent.

Responding instead of reacting means that rather than yelling, I can listen to my children's issue, and even if they react, I can role model how to emotionally regulate and respond.

- *Self-reflect.* In the moments we don't respond, all is not lost. We can still self-reflect. When parents respond to impulsive and inappropriate behavior calmly, we role model how our children can respond. Self-reflection involves reviewing behavior in a nonjudgmental, nonemotional manner by discussing what happened and how a similar interaction could go better in the future. Self-reflection takes emotion and lightning-fast interchanges out of the equation. Slowing things down allows children to reflect on their behavior and gain greater self-awareness, which leads to greater self-regulation in the future.
- *Catch 'em being good.* The difference between reactive and proactive parenting is that reactive parenting gives children attention for misbehavior, while proactive parenting gives children attention for being good. When we praise our children for being good—like when siblings are calmly playing together rather than arguing, or children say "please" and "thank you" without being reminded—we are reinforcing the behavior we want to see.
- *Give notice.* I noticed that when my boys were younger, when it was time to leave the park, they'd melt down, screaming and crying, and worse, I'd be *that* mom, chasing them around trying to get them to leave. "This is for the birds," I thought.

  So, I started giving them notice. I'd first get their buy-in. "How much longer would you like to stay at the park?" I'd ask. It didn't matter what amount of time they said. Whether it was two minutes or two hours, I said, "Okay." Then, I started counting down the time, letting them know when they had fifteen, ten, five, and one minute left to play.

  Then, I'd say, "You asked to stay fifteen minutes longer, we've stayed fifteen minutes more, and now it's time to go." This approach helped them feel like they were part of the decision-making process, and often we stayed the length of time they wanted to remain at the park, while also giving them time to mentally transition to the process of leaving as I counted down the remaining time.

- *Practice runs.* Any new behavior takes practice, especially emotional regulation. Taking your child on practice runs to build new capability is a great way to get comfortable with new behaviors. If your child tends to have a tantrum in the store when they don't get what they want, take them to the store when you don't have serious shopping to do. Stay for five to ten minutes and have them practice not touching items on the shelves. If they can go into the store and not have a tantrum about not buying something, they can get a point toward a goal or a dollar toward their allowance.
- *Set expectations.* When I began taking my sons out to eat, we would practice using silverware and napkins and other good behaviors before going out. Rather than telling them to be on their "best behavior," which gives them no real guidance, I try to be specific about my expectations. On the way to the restaurant, we walk through those expectations. First, we'll be greeted by the host who will seat us. It's important that we walk to the table calmly and keep our hands to ourselves. Once we sit down, we'll put our napkin in our lap and when the server comes, they will ask for our drink order. This way, my sons knew what would happen and the behavior I wanted to see from them. Telling them not to run around or kick each other under the table is instructive, but it only tells them what not to do, not what *to* do. I make a point to talk as much, if not more, about the behavior I want to see from them.
- *Expect that it won't go well.* A lot of parents get discouraged the first time they try to teach a new skill. I tell parents to plan for the new skill-building to not go well the first five times they try it. Think of children like puppies in need of training. We don't expect that the puppy will be potty trained the first or second time we try. It takes time and patience and consistent instructions.

- *Consistency.* Children test the limits, of course. They want to know, "Is this really a rule?" Being consistent provides psychological safety because our words and actions align, and over time, children learn what to expect from us, as well as what behavior is expected from them. Consistency communicates clarity and psychological safety, and allows children to relax and adapt to a new environment.
- *Judge your success based on your behavior, not your children's actions.* My husband and I frequently felt exhausted. Often, I've felt like a failure, even though our kids are generally good. Then, one night, it hit me: Instead of judging my parenting based upon the kids' actions, I should judge my own behavior. If everyone wasn't behaving or happy, I felt like a failure. I set myself up for disappointment. I began to give myself points for not losing my cool and for responding well, even if the child didn't like my decision. This epiphany allowed me to feel better about what was in my span of control and influence, and to not feel like a failure because of things beyond my control.
- *Success is not pleasing everyone.* When our family is laughing and smiling together, I bask in the shining moment, but I've gotten over my perfectionist need to always make everyone happy. I advise you to do the same. Consider it a victory if you manage your emotions through the unhappy times, react calmly, take deep breaths, rise above the chaos with a level head, and then explain why it is time to shut down the iPads and video games and go to bed, now!

LISTEN MORE, TALK LESS

The parent-child relationship is the most dynamic relationship of our lives. Most of us begin the journey with a helpless baby that requires care around the clock for every basic need, and then evolves from the littlest, most helpless human to, eighteen years later, a grown young person with entirely different needs. In no other human relationship does the dynamic evolve more completely than that of a parent and child.

I know many parent-child relationships where the parents stopped evolving and still treat their adult children as though they are teenagers, or younger. Parents need to evolve with their children and move from tell mode to show mode. When they become adults, we need to show our love by listening to them instead of telling them what to do.

In an exasperating moment with one of my children who questioned why I told him to do something, I gave the classic, bad mother response: "Because I said so!"

Not my best moment, but one that many parents have shared. There isn't much for a child to learn in that response, other than to avoid exasperating mom. Our goal should be to open two-way communication lines with our children at a young age, so those lines remain open into their adult years.

Sometimes we have conversations I'm not interested in having. Not about sexuality or intimacy or how babies are made. I don't mind those conversations so much because: (1) They don't make me uncomfortable; (2) I figure if my kids are going to learn about those things from someone, I'd prefer they learn about them from me; and (3) I wish those were the conversations I could have had with my adults when I was a little person.

The conversations I don't want to have are about Beyblades, Pokémon, World Wrestling Entertainment (WWE), Monster Trucks, what Mr. Beast did on his most recent YouTube giveaway, and who won, Spongebob or Deadpool, at Beatbox battles.

I wish I could say, "How was your day?" and our children would name all the interesting intricate details of their day for us to discuss while they eat their vegetables. But that's not how it goes for me. Instead, they mumble "Good," and go on to talk about a topic I have no interest in discussing. See above.

I've learned that if I want my children to listen to me, I must earn their attention by listening to them. For my children who may read this someday: It's not that I am not interested in these topics. It's that I am ONLY interested in these topics because they are interesting to you, my children, whom I love more than my own life.

SELF-LOVE STARTS AT HOME

Teaching our children to love themselves is one of the most important aspects of our job. Our capacity to love others is limited only by our ability to love ourselves first. When we don't love ourselves, we often look to others to make us feel valued and worthy of love.

What is self-love exactly, and is it vapid and self-involved to love ourselves?

Self-love means accepting ourselves fully. Some of this work is outlined in Chapter Four: The Practice of Vulnerability, about acknowledging and accepting all parts of ourselves. Self-love is not a state of feeling good, but rather, it is a state of believing we are good, an enduring appreciation for ourselves that is demonstrated by engaging in self-care to support our physical, psychological, emotional, and spiritual health.

Self-love means valuing ourselves to such a great degree that we take care of ourselves and engage in actions that nurture our happiness, growth, and well-being.

I'm not saying that people who have personal and professional achievements don't love themselves. What I am saying is that I believe much of our constant quest for success may be driven by a lack of self-love that exists within ourselves that we seek to replace with external achievements. I know this has been true for many of my executive coaching clients, and it's been true for me.

Why is it important to teach self-love to children and to ourselves?

As adults, the parts of ourselves that are unloved or have caused us pain will cause others pain if left unhealed. Usually the people we cause pain to are the ones closest to us. When children grow up without role models for self-love or without people in their lives to teach them about the importance of self-love, they may not learn to appreciate and accept themselves or know their inherent value. Without a core love for themselves, children may fall into people-pleasing habits and be more likely to put up with mistreatment and abuse from others because they've learned to value other people's opinions, desires, and needs above their own love for themselves. Teaching children self-love allows them to set their boundaries, fulfill their goals, and create healthy relationships with the people around them.

Children who have a positive view of themselves are more likely to have a growth mind-set; a way of seeing their world where they are willing to try out new possibilities, rather than being stuck in what exists in the present. Children with a growth mind-set are more likely to try new things, take on novel challenges, be less afraid of failure, and be less derailed by lessons, mistakes, and failure. Why? Because when children love themselves, they have a positive self-regard. They like who they are, see themselves in a positive light, and honor the skills and talent they've been given.

Developing and teaching self-love to our children is often a lifelong process. Like all essential life skills, it takes time and practice for children, along with parents, to learn.

Here are some ways to get you and your children focused on developing self-love:

- *Role model self-love.* You cannot teach children something that you don't know yourself. Your own behavior is one of the biggest influences on your children's development. When your children see you taking time to practice self-love, they are more likely to imitate this behavior.
- *Practice self-care.* The World Health Organization (WHO) defines self-care as "the ability of individuals, families, and communities to promote health, prevent disease, maintain health, and to cope with illness and disability with or without the support of a healthcare provider." Self-care is doing things for yourself that let you live a holistically healthy life.
- *Encourage positive self-talk.* Self-love is treating ourselves in a gentle loving way, the way we would treat another person whom we love. Often, we are kinder and more loving to others than we are to ourselves. We teach our children to talk to themselves with greater kindness by encouraging them to compliment, comfort, and motivate themselves. We do this also by helping them see their own positive and redeeming qualities.
- *Say positive things to your children.* As our children grow, our voice becomes the voice in their head, especially when we are not present. What we say to our children and how we say it matters. For example, I ask my children to clean their *place* after each meal, not clean their *mess*. Saying positive words to our children helps them develop positive self-talk. Long after we're gone, they will hear our voices in their minds, either cheering them on or telling them they'll never measure up. I want my children to hear me cheering for them. This is a legacy I would like to leave, to be the positive voice, loving them and encouraging them long after I am not here. When my children tell me a story, I say, "I love the way you tell stories. You're engaging." Or when they tell me a hilarious joke, I'll say, "I love your sense of humor." Our children learn self-love by seeing us love ourselves, and by seeing how we love them. When I am with my

children, sometimes I like to imagine that I am covered in mirrors, and with each interaction, I am reflecting to them their goodness, worthiness, and capacity to believe in and love themselves.

Here are some self-care ideas for kids:

- Drink plenty of fluids and stay hydrated by keeping a water bottle in their backpack.
- Choose healthy foods, foods that are good for their body, instead of food laden with sugars, fats, and sodium that simply taste good.
- Create a sleep-wake routine that allows for plenty of sleep and rest.
- Exercise, play sports, or spend time outdoors.
- Spend time with friends who are kind and supportive.
- Engage in favorite activities such as taking a bubble bath, playing catch, listening to their favorite music, reading, or playing their favorite game.
- Play with favorite toys, pets, or friends.
- Spend time getting organized at the end or beginning of the school day—packing backpacks and lunches, laying out clothing, etc., helps kids feel more at ease and less rushed in the morning.

What other ideas do you have for teaching children self-care? The process of teaching our children self-love, and by extension, self-care, gives us an opportunity to enhance the self-love we have for ourselves as parents, while teaching our children to have the self-love we didn't have the opportunity to develop when we were their ages.

BLENDED

I was once a "bonus" mom to two additional sons and a daughter. Blending a family is tough because taking the parts of two families and bringing them together to create a cohesive whole, when children have different rules, routines, expectations, and experiences, can feel like trying to solve a Rubik's Cube in the dark. No matter how many moves I made, all the differences just didn't line up. Most days, I felt very far from figuring out how to be, create, support, and blend a family of biological and bonus children, but I have figured out a few things.

Good news first: I am happy to report that I loved being a biological and bonus mom to five kids, and when we were all sitting around the table laughing, watching a movie together, or enjoying being with one another, there was truly nothing better. I loved the noise, the excitement, and the feeling that there is always something going on with so many children in the house at once. I worked hard to be loving and fair toward all the children, making it clear that I wouldn't prioritize my biological children over my bonus children, and ensuring that each child felt loved and valued.

There were also times that were difficult. Times where none of the children seem grateful, where it felt like I was just a taxi or social chair or personal assistant. Times when I was not making everyone happy. Times when I needed to discipline bad behavior rather than ignoring it or letting it slide by. In these moments, which often felt sticky or icky or both, first and foremost, I got to keep reminding myself to do and be my best, regardless of what is going on around me. Or, said differently, the most important aspect of being a bonus parent is reminding yourself that you are a bonus even when your bonus children do not think you are a bonus.

As a bonus mom for a blended family, I learned:

- *Patience.* Each child will come along at their own pace. Growth, healing, and gaining closer relationships isn't linear, and I got to be patient with each child's progress rather than trying to rush through the process.
- *It's not my job to rescue them.* It can be uncomfortable to listen to their feelings and experience. Sometimes my bonus children wanted

their old life back, for their parents to get back together and for me to disappear from the equation all together. Rather than trying to make everything better and rescuing them or denying their experience, I got to simply listen and accept that they felt what they felt. Validating what they feel, rather than trying to fix or rescue, is much easier.

- *A lot of new relationships are being formed.* A family of seven with five children seems large, but there is even more going on than I'd initially imagined. When I examined our family from the perspective of each person forming a new relationship with each other person in the family, plus realigning our personal relationship with ourselves in this new family, that means forty-nine unique relationships are being formed. That's a lot of new relationships. Realizing how much is going on for each person helped me be more patient as well.
- *Set aside individual time.* Yes, individual time for just you is important, AND what I mean is spending time with each child individually is important. With five kids, it's easy to lump all the kids together and do things as a family, which is important. In addition, it was meaningful for both of us to have our own individual time with the kids 1:1; whether that is going to sports, taking a hike, or playing a game, having our own special relationship with each individual child allows them to feel seen, known, and valued. Our effort to spend time and know each child as an individual person apart from the family unit reflects to them their value and how much they are loved, not to mention, gives us the opportunity to know our children as people, and for our children to know us as people, beyond being their parent.
- *Don't forget about date nights!* In addition to spending time with each child, my former husband and I protected our dates and made sure we spent time together, focused on our relationship, and (this is important) did NOT discuss the children.

- *Take time for you!* Second and third marriages are more vulnerable to divorce, and one of those reasons is the enhanced complexities of bringing together children from prior relationships into blended families, along with the strain this blending can place on the couple. I realized that if I was going to be able to care for six other people, I was going to get to prioritize my mental health and well-being. This meant that, rather than attending to every need, argument, and request, it was pivotal to make my own rest, reflection, and restoration a priority so that I could be the best version of me for myself and everyone else counting on me.

WHAT HAPPENED ISN'T YOUR FAULT, BUT HEALING IS YOUR RESPONSIBILITY

Healing past hurts, regrets, rejections, and traumas is important because we don't want those burdens affecting our parenting, or our children. We don't want to pass our pain and trauma on to our children, a process known as intergenerational transmission. In my *Flourish or Fold* podcast, I spoke with Heidi Powell, former cohost of the television show *Extreme Weight Loss*, about her healing process after ending a decade-long eating disorder and body dysmorphia. She said when she finds a pocket of hurt today, she sees it as an opportunity to do more work on her healing and growth so she can continue to be a person who doesn't carry shame with her.

IF ALL ELSE FAILS . . .

. . . be the big person you would have wanted when you were a little person. Even if you didn't have an example of a parent you'd like to emulate. Or you're faced with a parenting situation that you've never encountered and don't have a frame of reference for how to handle, that's okay. Because as a parent, you know what it is like to be a child.

So, you can go back to your little person self, check in, and ask yourself, "What did I or would I have wanted and needed in this situation?" We can use our child-selves as a guide for what to do as a parent. Whenever I don't know what to do next, I ask myself, "What would I have wanted a big person to do for me when I was a little person?"

50 POSITIVE THINGS TO SAY TO YOUR CHILDREN

- I enjoy spending time with you.
- You are interesting.
- You are fun to be around.
- I admire you.
- I could never stop loving you.
- You are more than enough.
- I love seeing you be brave, courageous, etc.
- Thank you for being so considerate.
- You put a lot of effort into what you've created.
- That's a good question.
- I believe in you.
- You are right.
- We can try out your idea.
- You make me a better person.
- I love seeing you evolve and grow.
- I love seeing the world through your eyes.
- I like hearing your perspective.
- That was a really good choice.
- I am interested in what you have to say.
- I love you.
- You're making me think about that differently.
- I support you being you.
- I will always like you.
- Your best is enough.
- Your actions were very brave.
- You have a great sense of humor.
- I admire your work ethic.
- I love the way you tell stories.
- I love how your mind works/how you're thinking.
- You are worth it.
- I will always be here to love you.
- You have a beautiful heart.
- I love your creativity.
- It's a joy to be your parent/mother/father.
- I trust you.
- I am in your corner, always.
- I know you did your best.
- What do you think we should do?
- You are a good person.
- It's a pleasure to be your parent/mother/father.
- It's fun to hear what you are curious about.
- You have good ideas.
- Seeing you happy makes me happy.
- I am listening.
- That's a good point.
- You're beautiful.
- It's okay for not everyone to like you.
- You can try again tomorrow.
- I forgive you.
- You/Your experience matters.

When I ask myself this question, I get good answers. I am reminded that I wanted my big people to celebrate all my A's before they pointed out the B's or C's and asked, "What happened here?" I recall that when I was sick or in pain, I just wanted someone to sit with me and tell me it would be okay. I wanted to feel trusted, valued, and heard.

Recalling what we wanted or needed as a little person helps us be the big person to our children that we may not have received when we were little, yet now, we can give the gift of what we would have wanted to our children.

10

Resilient Leaders, Teams, and Organizations

At the peak of the COVID-19 crisis in 2020, the entire airline industry was sent reeling. "The collapse in our revenue and finances was just breathtaking," said Southwest Airlines' chairman Gary C. Kelly, who estimated the airline was losing up to $25 million a day during that period.

Because of the airline's resilient team, Southwest survived, he said. "One of the real strengths of this company over our 50-year history is that we've been prepared for the unexpected and we're battle-tested as well," he said in a *CEO* magazine interview. "Our people are tough."

Resilience is key differentiator for leaders, teams, and organizations. When business and organization leaders enhance their resilience, their rising tide lifts all of those on their teams. Recent global challenges have demonstrated the critical importance of resilience. According to a McKinsey analysis, "Firms should strive as much as possible to embed resilience in the way they work, in a way that makes them better in normal times, not just in the face of unpredictable threat or change."

When Tim Cook, Apple's CEO, reflected on the company's progress during the October 2020 earnings call with Wall Street analysts, he credited team resilience for Apple's financial performance exceeding expectations, sharing that "resilience has been an essential part of how we have navigated this year."

I am often asked to give a keynote on The Five Practices to inspire and motivate team members with companies, foundations, and associations to harness their resilience. Recently, at a global financial services company, I was asked to address top executives at the CEO's meeting, and after my keynote, the CEO told me that my message on resilience was exactly what his team needed to hear to make sense of their shifting landscape and the complexity of their business.

The science of leadership, team, and organizational resilience has been poorly understood, with little agreement about what constitutes resilience in an organizational setting. My work through the Resilience Leadership Institute (RLI) has demonstrated that leaders, teams, and organizations that adopt The Five Practices markedly enhance their resilience, along with greater productivity, engagement, and innovation.

WHY, NOT IF, LEADERS, TEAMS, AND ORGANIZATIONS NEED RESILIENCE

Today, most of the work focused on teams and organizations is conceptual, versus offering tangible practices that enhance resilience instead of inhibiting it systemically. The management style of top leaders has the greatest potential to increase organizational resilience. They set the tone and tenor of the company culture, yet all employees can play a role.

Soft skills have become even more important in the modern business environment, including in leading change. Change leadership doesn't foster or disrupt resilience; rather, it is the management process of the change leadership that either facilitates resilience for the employees, teams, and organizations (e.g., the enterprise is perceived to go over and above to make sure people are on board with change) or inhibits resilience (e.g., the organization lacks the communication about the rollout of change leading to confusion).

In addition, an organization's pace of change may have a positive impact on resilience (e.g., the volume of change does not appear too demanding or taxing) or a negative impact on employee resilience (e.g., the volume of change is too overwhelming and large scale).

RESILIENCE IS A TEAM SPORT

When leaders, teams, and organizations manage a workforce in stressful times, it is essential to have a framework for creating and enhancing resilient behaviors. Oftentimes, we think about resilience as being an individual pursuit. Yet, increasing resilience, mental health, and well-being is a team sport. When one person invests in their resilience, the development and growth creates ripple effects that extend across the team, and have the ability to positively impact the entire system. The resilience of one member of the team has the capacity to enhance or detract from that of the entire team. The Five Practices of Highly Resilient People are a set of behaviors that can help any of us or the teams we're part of to operate in more resilient ways when we face challenges instead of freezing, fighting, or fleeing.

Elements of leadership, teams, and organizational resilience are built into the methodologies and The Five Practices we have discussed so far. Yet, the application of resilience to a business environment has special considerations. The demands of the workplace require that leaders and

THREE-STEP PROCESS FOR HARNESSING AND AMPLIFYING LEADERSHIP, TEAM, AND ORGANIZATIONAL RESILIENCE

1. Assess and identify strengths and opportunities.
2. Harness and enhance resilience through teachable best practices.
3. Create sustainable solutions and action-planning for resilience, mental health, and well-being.

teams are charged with navigating The Three C's in the marketplace, along with disruptions and unforeseen events, while also demonstrating collaboration and inclusion and looking after the well-being of employees.

To support leaders' and teams' energy and engagement, there is a significant opportunity to lead in such a way that both harnesses existing resilience and amplifies it across the organization. When my team and I work with organizations, we employ the following three-step process (also outlined in the chart on page 176) to assess and identify the resilience of individuals, teams, and organizations. We then recommend the best practices for harnessing and enhancing resilience, followed by the creation of sustainable solutions and action-planning for mental health and well-being.

Organizational health is made up of the combined resilience, mental health, and well-being practices of the collective employees. By providing individuals across the enterprise, along with teams and organizations, the tangible tools to enhance resilience, we can enhance engagement, productivity, and innovation at the individual level, which collectively enhances the health of organization overall, and makes the company stronger in the face of continued challenge in the future.

ASSESS AND IDENTIFY STRENGTHS AND OPPORTUNITIES

Based on two decades of research and work with business clients across the *Fortune* 500 companies in the United States, as well as global organizations, we have developed the Resilient Practices Inventory (RPI), a seventy-five-item diagnostic assessment that examines resilience, based on The Five Practices. There are fifteen items for each practice, to identify both strengths and areas of opportunity at the individual, team, and organizational levels, while also providing an overall resilience score.

Assessing and identifying resilience is highly effective, not just because you are enhancing resilience in yourself, your teams, and your enterprise, but because the qualities of team resilience are highly related to creating and nurturing high-performing teams. Teams that have higher resilience scores on the RPI are also the teams in which we observe higher performance. More resilient teams also appear to engage in The Three T's to a greater degree. They demonstrate greater:

1. *Trust:* An enhanced sense of psychological safety and the belief that their team members will support them
2. *Transparency:* Share with greater vulnerability, authenticity, and empathy
3. *Traction on collective deliverables:* In short, they get more done together.

Our approach in applying The Five Practices to individuals, teams, and organizations is to complement the work already created on mind-set and focus on behaviors and observable practices that are meaningful and reliable indicators of resilience.

When we look at resilience in an organizational setting, we assess The Five Practices overall, as well as fifteen items on the RPI assessment that provide information about each practice in three areas, with five questions each:

1. How one element of the practice of resilience is demonstrated by the individual person through formal or informal leadership
2. How the other pole of the practice is demonstrated by the individual person through formal or informal leadership
3. How a climate of resilience is created drawing on each of The Five Practices to provide formal or informal team leadership

For example, the RPI examines The Practice of Productive Perseverance, which navigates the polarity of maintaining the mission in the face of challenge versus pivoting in a new direction when presented with diminishing returns, and how the individual creates a climate of vision through their leadership with statements such as:

- *Productive Perseverance Maintaining the Mission:* "I demonstrate an ability to stay the course, even in the face of challenge."

- *Productive Perseverance Pivoting in a New Direction:* "I continually engage in 'outsight' by scanning my environment to anticipate potential disruptions."
- *Productive Perseverance Vision Leadership:* "I communicate vision in an inspirational manner that is both understandable and paints a positive picture of the future."

Therefore, the RPI identifies individual, team, and organizational strengths and opportunities for resilience, and the assessment data provides self-, team, and organizational awareness of their resilience, along with creating an opportunity to engage in leadership growth and development planning to further hone strengths and close existing gaps.

When I use the RPI with individuals and teams, I often am surprised by the power of the results to create greater self-awareness for individuals and teams and generate greater trust, candor, and humility. One of my favorite experiences was working with the technology leadership team of a *Fortune* 500 financial services organization. These leaders were essentially keeping the technological lights on, which allowed employees to stay connected to one another, while leading their teams remotely and protecting the organization from ever-evolving cybersecurity threats.

For our workshop series on The Five Practices, each team member completed the RPI, and we held confidential coaching debriefs of the assessment results with each person. Then, in our workshop series, we reviewed the team's overall resilience, along with their team scores on each of The Five Practices.

In the RPI individual coaching debrief sessions, team members enhanced their awareness of their resilience, understanding which resilient practices came most naturally to them as strengths and what areas of opportunity they had to increase their resilience. One team member said, "I know vulnerability is an opportunity for my growth, but until taking this assessment and seeing the results, I didn't know exactly how to be vulnerable at work, what that would entail."

In addition to identifying the key observable behaviors that demonstrate resilience, after completing the RPI, team members had a shared lexicon, and a common knowledge and language to describe their own and their team's resilience. Team members also found important insight into their leadership.

In an organizational setting, the RPI focuses on The Five Practices behaviors and actions used in a business setting:

1. *The Practice of Vulnerability:* The practice of engaging in individual vulnerability by allowing our inside selves, our thoughts, feelings, and experiences, to match the outside self we share with the world; appreciating The Vulnerability Bias, how vulnerability is the jet fuel of connection and humility, yet often feels incredibly scary; and being willing to create a climate of vulnerability where team members are invited to be vulnerable and valued for their authenticity and empathy that springs from a willingness to be vulnerable
2. *The Practice of Productive Perseverance:* The practice of maintaining the business mission and strategy in the face of challenge, and being willing to engage in pivots, large or small, when experiencing diminishing returns, along with not losing sight of the broader vision for the team and organization
3. *The Practice of Connection:* The practice of the connection to self, along with the connection to others through listening and participative management and creating an environment of connected leadership in which feedback is given, people are encouraged to voice their opinions, and team members feel their contributions are valued through the connections with the broader team
4. *The Practice of Grati-osity:* The practice of finding the good in challenge, having gratitude, and fostering the willingness to share resilience stories generously with others, along with promoting a climate where people are supported and encouraged in their demonstration of gratitude and sharing generously

5. *The Practice of Possibility:* The practice of evaluating opportunity and risk in a business setting along with the focus on formal or informal leadership to create a climate that promotes the appreciation of progress over perfection, with an emphasis on problem-solving and learning

HARNESS AND ENHANCE RESILIENCE THROUGH TEACHABLE BEST PRACTICES

Once we have identified individual or team strengths and opportunities, I'm often asked how employees can find time to focus on their resilience. The good news is, enhancing our resilience, mental health, and well-being is not about carving out time to do more.

Resilience, if you're a baseball player, is like batting practice. You don't need to do something more or extra; you simply adopt the practices of resilience into your development and the work you're already doing. Resilience is meant to be both accessible and practical.

After working in corporate America, I understand that each initiative is intended to build sustainable resilience practices that lead to true and lasting behavior change for their employees. For this reason, we work with our clients to cocreate experiences that can impact the organization in a manner that creates lasting meaningful change.

RESILIENCE CURRICULUM

While resilience and The Five Practices are at the center of our work, we see resilience as being the "hub," the central connector of how we work with individuals, teams, and organizations. We also recognize the need for topics and training modalities to meet our clients' needs.

The Five Practices is the core empirical model, the "hub" that informs the "spokes" of our practice that include building trust, engaging and retaining talent, supporting women in leadership, increasing innovation and creativity, along with promoting mental health, well-being, and

DEIB initiatives for individuals, leaders, and teams. The Five Practices model also supports initiatives focused on change leadership, burnout, stress, and exhaustion, as well as hybrid work, remote teams, and reintegrating to the physical office.

TALENT STRATEGY AND SUCCESSION PLANNING

Resilience is a critical leadership skill, and the ability to adopt and demonstrate it is a hallmark skill set of high-potential leaders. Therefore, many organizations have adopted resilience as a competency because they have an interest in gauging the resilience of their high-potential leaders, those on track for promotions and expanded roles.

My team and I work closely with companies to create talent strategy and succession planning centering on evaluating and enhancing leaders' resilience, as demonstrated by The Five Practices. At a high level, we use a five-step process where we:

1. *Define:* Understand and operationalize what resilience means for the organization and leadership, present day and for the future, mapping resilience to existing competencies
2. *Measure:* Identify strengths, opportunities, and themes of resilience for individuals and the organization, focusing on the resilience qualities that predict potential and performance
3. *Benchmark:* Compare internal talent to external industry and geographical benchmarks using talent analytics
4. *Enhance:* Develop and grow talent leveraging engagements that enhance resilience strengths and close existing opportunities to enhance talent in the pipeline for succession
5. *Evaluate:* Quantify the impact of The Five Practices and incorporate resilience in talent strategy and succession planning by tracking improvement over time and applying our outcomes-based methodology

DIVERSITY, EQUITY, INCLUSION, AND BELONGING (DEIB)

The Five Practices support the foundational skills needed to become proficient in having conversations that uncover privilege and unconscious bias, and further promote diversity, equity, inclusion, and belonging (DEIB) across organizations. We have found that teaching employees The Five Practices provides them with the toolkit to alchemize DEIB work so that people gain the necessary ability to have conversations that often feel vulnerable or outside their comfort zone.

Our high-impact practices support people in developing the necessary attributes to amplify DEIB initiatives by giving them a framework for how and when to demonstrate resilience when having conversations about sensitive, and often highly charged, issues.

We've worked with many organizations to teach workshops that give employees a playbook for having sensitive conversations with one another that are productive. We provide guidelines for how and when to express concerns around bias, inequity, and exclusion, as well as how to effectively listen in a manner that people can be present instead of defensive.

Enterprise DEIB initiatives are of critical importance, and teaching employees The Five Practices gives them a toolkit to engage more effectively in these conversations while together.

RESILIENT HIRING

Resilience is becoming an increasingly important and sought-after attribute in the hiring process. Can we evaluate someone's resilience in the talent acquisition process? The answer is, absolutely, yes we can!

We work with organizations to build interview questions that specifically uncover the extent to which the candidate demonstrates resilience in their work and leadership. We often begin by asking candidates to describe a significant challenge they've faced, and what they did in the face of that challenge to effectively address it.

Based on the candidate's answer, we can code responses for resilience to the extent they discuss demonstrating The Five Practices. We look for attributes such as demonstrating vulnerability: Did they seek out help or resources to face the challenge?

As they tell us about their challenges, we listen for key diagnostic behaviors such as empathy for self and others, an ability to persevere in the face of challenge or pivot in the face of diminishing returns, gratitude, generosity, and a focus on problem-solving and progress over perfection. We find that identifying resilience candidates for key roles is crucial to enhancing the resilience of teams and the organization.

Let's look at each of The Five Practices and understand how we can put them into action in the workplace to create sustainable solutions and action-planning for resilience, mental health, and well-being.

VULNERABILITY

Vulnerability is a hallmark of high-performing teams because it is the cornerstone of both authentic and empathetic leadership, two leadership practices that have become even more important in connecting with employees in hybrid and remote distributed workforce environments.

Conventional thinking says that leaders and teams should project confidence and mastery. While leaders celebrate success and growth, they also need to ensure they spend time recognizing and celebrating how their team effectively addressed challenges.

In addition to authenticity and empathy, vulnerability is also the cornerstone of a team's ability to build the psychological safety needed to take risks, innovate, and challenge one another. Teams that prioritize this practice by demonstrating vulnerability with one another try to share their successes as well as their failures and flops.

One key aspect of vulnerability is the ability for team members to ask for and receive help from one another. When team members are unable to ask for support, perceived failures, mistakes, and shortfalls are covered up, rather than being opportunities for learning and growth.

Psychological Safety

First and foremost, individuals and teams in an organization will not do the hard, and often scary, work of demonstrating vulnerability if there is not a sense of psychological safety among the team. An environment where vulnerability is welcomed and accepted helps foster it as a cornerstone for a company's culture, along with authenticity and empathy.

Psychological safety assures that The Vulnerability Bias won't rear its ugly head, and The Three L's won't occur. When I work with teams to create and promote psychological safety, we first contract around team norms and expectations. I tell teams we are doing important work that requires adhering to a shared set of expectations so that each person feels secure.

Creating a set of team expectations or shared norms for behavior is key. We spend fifteen to thirty minutes creating an overview of team agreements for behavior during this work, and most teams adopt these agreements for their meetings and interactions going forward.

A Safer and Braver Workplace

During this contracting period, I am intentional in sharing with the team that these agreements support us in creating a "safer" environment. Many facilitators talk about creating a "safe space," but I believe this is dangerous. There is no place that is truly safe. Even after we create our team norms and shared agreements, a team member could decide not to adhere to those agreements and harm the team dynamic.

When a norm or expectation is violated by a team member, the environment feels unsafe to the team members. What makes matters worse, if I have told the team this is a "safe place," and the team member's behavior has violated this promise, then their trust in me has been compromised.

Instead, I talk with teams about creating a "safer" space that allows us to engage in The Practice of Vulnerability with shared expectations and clear guidelines for what happens if those norms are broken by someone. I share with my teams that this approach also is meant to foster a braver workplace.

A sense of increased safety encourages team members to speak more bravely and honestly. The focus then becomes not on everyone being completely safe, but on creating an environment with some extra parameters for team members to feel safer and engage with one another in a way that is braver.

Empathy

Google's Project Aristotle was a two-year, in-house study of more than 180 teams to determine what makes them successful. Among the five factors identified in the study was psychological safety. I've found this is true especially when team members share a sense of empathy in which they truly care for one another and there is a shared belief that team members have one another's back.

One way that teams foster empathy for one another is by engaging in The Practice of Vulnerability by sharing their failures and challenges, in addition to their successes. With the idea that the practice of resilience in the workplace is like batting practice for a baseball player, skills directly necessary to enhancing our professional growth and leadership, empathy can be incorporated in our daily professional (and personal) lives without engaging in extra work.

Here are five suggestions to engage in empathy at work:

1. *Seek perspective:* Take time to walk in other peoples' shoes and view a situation from the perspective of another person, imagining their feelings and experience.
2. *Check in:* Take time to ask team members how they are doing, *really*, and listen carefully to the answer.

3. *Demonstrate care and concern:* When colleagues are facing difficulties professionally or personally, take them for coffee, lunch, or dinner to demonstrate your care and concern. Ask how you can be of support.
4. *Practice active listening:* Listen carefully without interrupting and reflect on what was said by paraphrasing to see if you heard your colleague accurately.
5. *Validate other people's perspectives:* Share an empathetic reflection, such as, "That must have been disappointing for you," when someone shares a difficult experience.

By practicing empathy toward them, team members will feel less judgment and a greater degree of acceptance and support, allowing each person to be more at ease while vulnerable.

Team Vulnerability and Resilience

I work with the CEO and cofounder of a cryptocurrency company in which the employees work asynchronously across the globe. Many had never met in person. During an off-site meeting, they asked me to lead the team through a series of experiences meant to enhance the team's trust, reliance on one another, and vulnerability.

We engaged in the reverse bucket list exercise as part of the meeting. Each team member spent a few minutes reflecting on a reverse bucket list challenge that had shaped them. As we went around the room, some told stories they had never shared with even close family members or friends. Their team members listened and connected deeply with their emotions.

The team left the off-site meeting feeling a strong sense of connection, appreciation, and trust for one another. It's a good thing we invested in the team's vulnerability, authenticity, and trust, because just five weeks later, the cryptocurrency market was rocked by one of the largest destabilizing events in recent years. Terra, the billion-dollar behemoth UST fund that had been widely thought to be too big to fail, began rapidly losing value. This resulted in millions in losses for the company I'd worked with.

When the markets finally stabilized, the same company had lost 35 percent of its financial assets. Although there was much to rebuild, the CEO thanked me personally, saying that in the moments of uncertainty, when Terra's value was sinking, the team had banded together as a cohesive unit. They rallied with deep trust for one another, making decisions in record time. The CEO said they worked so well in that time of fear and uncertainty because the team connected while sharing their reverse bucket list stories during my work with them.

PRODUCTIVE PERSEVERANCE

For resilient teams, having the capacity to adjust and fluidly navigate between the mission at hand and then shift in a new direction in a volatile marketplace can make the difference between high performance and missing the mark.

A leader, team, or organization can adopt The Practice of Productive Perseverence by:

- Setting long-term goals, while determining how to closely monitor the marketplace for fluctuations, disrupters, and emerging trends.
- Creating clarity on why a goal exists and questioning how the work aligns with the organization's broader purpose, mission, and vision.
- Recognizing the path to a goal is not a straight line from origin to destination. Climbing Mt. Everest is not a direct trek to the top. Climbers trek up and down the mountain, often backtracking to camps lower in altitude to acclimatize and gain strength to reach the summit. If the highest peak on the planet isn't climbed in a straight line, why would you expect something even more nuanced and difficult, like your development, growth, and achievement of complex goals, to be a seamless path to your destination?
- Designating a person to listen carefully to the conversation, and then add whatever needs to be said, while allowing contrary voices

to be heard. The goal is to ensure all perspectives are heard and valued. In our article entitled "Resilience Is a Team Sport," Keith Ferrazzi and I referred to this person as the Yoda. Every team should have a designated Yoda or Mr. Miyagi to have the express permission to point out what the team is missing.

One of the pivotal (no pun intended!) areas we focus on with individuals, teams, and organizations is the process of long-term planning, which is a challenge in our complex and rapidly changing times.

Many leaders feel tied to five-year plans even though they recognize that the speed of change makes best-laid plans relevant for six months to one year. First, we get to disabuse ourselves of the notion that a five-year plan is superior to having an agile and clear six- to twelve-month plan. Second, we can still engage in five-year planning, and make these plans our North Star if we check in on our strategy regularly, every three to six months, to evaluate what has changed, evolved, and emerged.

Rather than making the planning process the responsibility of the team leader, we engage the whole team, which makes them more resilient. Checking in regularly on long-term planning engages them in The Practice of Productive Perseverance. They can focus on addressing challenges as they emerge and monitor for diminishing returns for a product, service, or strategy to maintain relevance and revenue.

CONNECTION

Teams are the most resilient when their members have strong connections to one another, which cultivates self-awareness, good communication, and trust. Strong connections among team members also provides a support network in which high-performing team members receive encouragement from one another.

To improve The Practice of Connection, a leader may consider developing a team charter that creates alignment and focuses the team on driving work across the organization effectively. The Practice of Connection can be applied to structures from enterprise listening to processes for collecting input, to how to create more resilient report-outs that engage team members in the dialogue, rather than creating a passive monologue by the leaders.

Workplace Loneliness and Isolation

During my time as head of global leadership development at Cigna, we uncovered the debilitating and far-reaching effects of loneliness on both mental and physical health. It also had significant implications for employees and the quality of their work and productivity. Employee loneliness is both a significant mental-health concern and exceedingly costly to employers.

We found that 62 percent (nearly two-thirds) of Americans are considered lonely, and employees who are lonely may cost their employers a whopping $406 billion to the US economy. Therefore, it is important to invest in deepening connections between employees to increase mental health, employee engagement, and retention. Those connections ease loneliness and save corporations significant money over time.

Burnout, Stress, and Exhaustion

Given the significant demands of work, many employees neglect their own needs so they can focus on work. This makes them susceptible to burnout and exhaustion. Almost every person I interview acknowledges that neglecting their needs for sleep, diet, exercise, and good relationships leads to burnout.

Many lose their capacity for finding joy in hobbies, meditation, yoga, walking in nature, pets, and their favorite television series. They have no coping strategies, which makes them vulnerable.

Business leaders are responsible for their own mental and emotional well-being as well as that of their team members. They should serve as role models for self-care, so employees know these practices are acceptable. If senior leaders work nonstop and send emails from vacations or at night and on weekends, they set a poor example for their employees.

To foster deeper connections with their team members, leaders might try the following tools.

Employee Engagement Through Stay Interviews

One way to foster deeper connections with your people is to conduct "stay interviews." To engage leaders and reduce voluntary turnover, ask genuine questions to create authentic dialogue *before* an employee demonstrates an interest in leaving the organization. Stay interviews are an opportunity to take the personalized pulse of employees and to collect richer data. They also help employees feel their perspective is valued. This approach, when used correctly, is scalable, actionable, impactful, and very low cost.

GRATI-OSITY

Gratitude is demonstrated when teams reflect on challenges that changed them for the better. Teams engage in generosity by sharing their resilience stories openly. Rather than simply doling out advice, they can learn vicariously from one another's experience.

To engage in The Practice of Grati-osity, leaders can celebrate successes, regularly sharing appreciation and gratitude for team members. Positive intent is a key. By believing that your team is doing the best they can, you communicate support, patience, and empathy. Instead of assuming the worst of a team member, first ask if you might have missed an email or document or ask how you can collaborate with or support the person.

Sharing Your Resilience Story at Work

I often receive questions like this one:

Question: Do you have any suggestions for us on sharing our resilience story AND also how to respond when someone is being vulnerable and sharing their story?

Answer: Sharing our resilience story in the workplace can be frightening, yet our resilience stories have tremendous value in the workplace.

Sharing Your Resilience Story with Teammates

- Chose a resilience story that has work-related implications. Perhaps you lost a family member to a rare disease, which impacted your choice of profession. Discuss challenges you experienced on a work project.
- Remember to reflect on why you are sharing your resilience story to help others learn from your experiences.
- Prepare your team to hear your resilience story. If sharing your resilience story is not part of team development, growth, or bonding, ask the team for their support to share your resilience story so they are aware, and you don't take them by surprise.

Listening to Others' Resilience Stories

- Thank the person for their courage in sharing their resilience story.
- To combat The Three L's, tell the storyteller that you think more of them for sharing.
- Ask what, if anything, the person would like from you in response to hearing their story, to support them.

Sharing resilience stories is powerful for promoting greater resilience, vulnerability, authenticity, empathy, connection, and possibility in the workplace.

POSSIBILITY

Particularly resilient teams see possibilities even in the face of challenges. They're able to experience the danger and fear of failure, but they are not deterred by it. They focus on progress, not perfection.

To harness The Power of Possibility, teams should challenge themselves to stretch into new areas to address the opportunities and possibilities presented by the market, while also ensuring they effectively evaluate risk.

Great teams I've worked with make this happen through a process called "bulletproofing." After colleagues share their plans or reports in a group meeting, have the team break into small groups and "bulletproof" one another's work by offering one risk that the individual might guard against, one innovative idea the individual might consider, and one act of generosity that the group could offer by way of help.

Get Comfortable Getting Uncomfortable

Teams fail or succeed together, and members enhance or detract from one another's resilience. We need to avoid directly competing with others on our teams, thus avoiding detrimental social comparison. Instead, we should offer support and encouragement to one another.

Focus on this aspect of resilience by believing you and your team members are collectively responsible for the team's success. It is not about who crosses the finish line first, but instead, how you can support one another.

By engaging in The Five Practices, teams can enhance their collective resilience, and their collective performance.

GET COMFORTABLE GETTING UNCOMFORTABLE

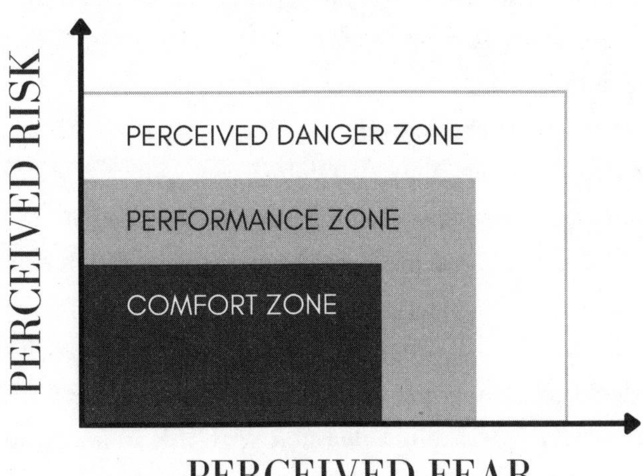

In business, you need to move out of your comfort zone and into your performance zone. Practical strategies for engaging discomfort and getting comfortable getting uncomfortable are:

- *If you feel uncomfortable, take stock of your physical and psychological safety.* Is there a good reason you're feeling unsafe? A feeling of danger? If so, rather than trying to get more comfortable with something that feels unsafe, you may want to consider removing yourself from the situation.
- *Listen first, speak last.* If you feel discomfort as part of a dialogue, spend time listening to and digesting others' perspectives. Understand where they are coming from before you offer your thoughts and perspectives.
- *Seek first to understand, not be understood.* Simply listening to another person's perspective or opinion that differs from your own may feel uncomfortable. Yet, the practice of trying to understand others' perspectives gives you an opportunity to expand your perspective and gain new insight.
- *Recognize discomfort is a necessary experience required for growth.* Discomfort is often a hallmark of growth. Just as we must break down our muscles for them to grow, experiencing the discomfort of lactic acid, discomfort is also required for us to grow in our understanding of the world.
- *Acknowledge your discomfort to yourself and others.* Drawing on The Practice of Vulnerability, you don't have to suffer in your discomfort alone. Lean on a trusted colleague or a friend on your team to share your discomfort and get his or her perspective on your experience.

For The Practice of Possibility to be effective, you must give up trying to be perfect because perfection is the enemy of possibility. Strive toward excellence. Perfection is an unachievable goal. It is an unrealistic expectation that leads to low self-worth and procrastination.

Bill Bowerman, one of Nike's cofounders, said, "Perfection is a luxury we can't afford." What I believe he meant is that the price tag for perfection is procrastination. A fear of not measuring up to impossibly high standards slows us more than it supports us in our advancement. Instead, focus on progress, constant improvement, and problem-solving to move the boulders out of your path as you and your team work toward your goals.

BUILDING RESILIENCE THROUGH ORGANIZATIONAL PROCESSES

I believe the need for resilient individuals, teams, and organizations will only continue to grow as a necessary ingredient for our ever-evolving world of work. With remote and hybrid work environments, individuals, teams, and organizations will gain a high rate of return on developing resilience as part of their strategy to equip employees with the necessary skills to navigate the business environment. It also can enhance DEIB and increase leadership skills for connecting people across the organization, managing through influence, fostering greater collaboration, and enhancing the ability for longer-range planning. All businesses and organizations need to increase their responsiveness and agility so they can adapt to constantly changing conditions.

To evaluate your organization's resilience levels, ask yourself the following questions:

- *How does our organization intentionally foster and develop individual and team resilience currently?*

  The most resilient organizations intentionally foster, promote, monitor, and develop resilience across the enterprise for individuals and teams, recognizing that resilience is an indispensable element of people development and leadership that has a high return on employees' ability to adapt and maintain agility in the face of challenge, while also promoting well-being and mental health.

- *How does our organization assess and evaluate our current state of resilience and how we grow our employees' and teams' resilience as part of our people-development strategy?*

  Resilient organizations focus on continually assessing and evaluating resilience through regular engagement surveys, conversations, soliciting feedback, and check-ins. The results of these ongoing touchpoints serve to inform current and future initiatives that focus on resilience to enhance deeper trust, engagement, or innovation across the organization.
- *How does our organization anticipate and support individuals and teams in developing their resilience and in guarding against stressors and experiences that erode resilience, mental health, and well-being?*

  The most resilient organizations develop methods and mechanisms to support individual and teams' mental health and resilience before they are in crisis and ensure that people are aware of and feel empowered to access these support services and development opportunities when they need them.

What I know for certain is that in business, every product or service is either bought, sold, or delivered. Resilience is required to do all three. So, by definition, leaders, teams, and organizations must be resilient. Today, more than ever, you get to be on guard for the unexpected and immense ways in which your global marketplace is constantly changing, evolving, and being disrupted. This means that in addition to building business resilience, you also get to think about guarding against seen and unforeseen events by investing in resilience that will support your organization in the future.

11

Resilient Women

In a 2014 Super Bowl commercial break, viewers were surprised to see sanitary pads advertised on television for the first time. The ad was part of Proctor & Gamble's Always feminine products "Like a Girl" campaign. Their goal was to address preteen girls' plummeting self-confidence at a formative time.

The advertisers noticed that the phrase "Like a Girl" is often used as an insult directed at young women, instead of a compliment. The advertisement showed how, when both girls and boys were asked what it meant to them to run, throw, or fight like a girl, they imitated wimpy, weak actions. Yet, when early elementary school girls and boys were asked the same questions, they demonstrated running, throwing, and fighting with strength and vigor. When asked what it means to run like a girl, one young girl responded, "It means run as fast as you can." The campaign demonstrated that though young girls begin their early years with confidence and a positive self-concept, seeing their gender as something positive, by the time they reach adolescence, something troubling has happened, and now they see their gender as being weak and ineffective. This was a real-world portrayal of what happens to women all too often. From a young age, females are taught that their strengths, talents, and unique approach to the world are not valued, and the erosion of confidence and worthiness for many women occurs before they even graduate from elementary school, before they even reach adulthood.

LIKE A WOMAN

Unfortunately, the harmful messages sent to girls do not recede after puberty. As we mature into women, we receive hundreds of thousands of messages about our lack of worthiness that become internalized over time.

These messages persist and make it even more difficult for women to navigate the workplace. They are discouraged from being assertive, competitive, emotional, ambitious, or aggressive—all traits valued in their male counterparts.

Dave Mayer from the University of Michigan's Ross School of Business wrote an article, "How Not to Advocate for a Woman at Work," in which he describes how men can unintentionally undermine female colleagues by making comments that refer to women as "warm" and "nice."

Mayer cites research indicating that when women are described in communal terms, such as "friendly" or "helpful," they are less likely to be seen as a competent. According to Mayer, if you describe a woman as being community-oriented, connected, warm, nice, kind, or friendly, no matter how well intentioned, you're doing her a disservice, and reducing the likelihood she'll be considered as a viable candidate for promotional opportunities.

Conversely, there is an exceedingly high price tag for women who are described as aggressive, emotional, or ambitious. These women, while on the opposite side of the spectrum, also receive fewer opportunities for promotion and advancement, and talented team members are less likely to want to join their teams.

In her best-selling book *Lean In*, Sheryl Sandberg, who stepped down as CEO of Facebook in the fall of 2022, cites an experiment conducted at Columbia Business School in which researchers selected the résumé of a real-life female entrepreneur by the name of Heidi Rosen. For the study, half of the business school students were given a résumé with Heidi's name placed at the top, and the other half of the students were given a résumé that read "Howard Rosen." Otherwise, the CVs were identical.

Then, students were asked a series of questions about Heidi or Howard's competence and likeability. The responses were nothing short of remarkable. The students rated Heidi and Howard as equally competent. However, Howard was judged to be more likeable and thought to be a colleague with whom the students would like to work, while Heidi was viewed as aggressive, selfish, and deemed to be someone who would not be a team player, someone with whom the students would not like to work.

Why does this happen? How can highly educated male and female students in a top business school make such vastly different assessments about a person's likeability, based solely upon gender?

This is the prescriptive bias, a framework for how we expect people to behave, based on gender, at work. Societal and cultural expectations of men and women are very different, and this becomes amplified in the workplace. As Mayer points out, positive societal traits for women, such as friendliness, helpfulness, and likeability, do not translate to traits that are valued for leadership.

While it's detrimental for women to be too nice, kind, and helpful, on the opposite side of the continuum, the prescriptive bias also expects that women are not too successful, ambitious, or focused. The prescriptive bias is a form of unconscious bias, held by both men and women, making it even more insidious because it is not an active, calculated judgment or intentional discrimination.

It's not about changing the compliments women receive; we need to change the entire conversation in our places of business—increasing the value placed on authentic feminine qualities.

THE IMPACT OF LABELING WOMEN "AMBITIOUS"

When women are too nice or friendly, they are not seen as leaders, yet when they are accomplished, the prescriptive bias holds them back, casting a shadow on their likeability.

Sallie Krawcheck is known as one of the most powerful women on Wall Street. She is the former head of Bank of America's Global Wealth and Investment Management division and currently the CEO and cofounder of Ellevest, a digital financial adviser for women.

When she asked her mother if she planned to vote for Hillary Clinton in the 2016 presidential election, her mother shocked her by saying no.

Sallie persisted, asking, "Haven't you been waiting your entire life to see a woman in the White House?"

"Yes," her mother responded, "but not Hillary; she's too ambitious for me."

Decades of social science research has found that women face distinct social penalties for doing the very things that lead to success. For women, being ambitious often is seen by men as being "am-bitch-ous."

While women are applauded for delivering results at work, there is a backlash for violating the prescriptive bias and acting in an authoritarian manner. They are then reprimanded for being "aggressive," "out for themselves," "difficult," or "abrasive."

These confusing conclusions are all too familiar to the multitude of women on the receiving end of these penalties, causing many to doubt themselves, lack confidence, and feel insecure about pursuing careers.

THE CRITICAL IMPORTANCE OF BEING ENOUGH

Many women have had enough. Yet, we also grapple with being enough. The Five Practices focus on how we enhance resilience when we encounter challenge at the individual, team, and company level across an organization.

It is important that we don't blame women for the societal inequities. We should not ask them to be solely responsible for remediating these biases or suggest that women are not impacted by the broader culture of society. However, women can take responsibility for their own behavior and actions. That means not ignoring the societal context, and not being limited by it.

These are key points for women focused on enhancing resilience and creating change:

- The critical importance of being enough
- Learning to be self-full
- Capitalizing on confidence
- Embracing failure
- Supporting one another in allowing our strengths and talents to shine

Let's explore how each of these topics contributes to enhancing resilience, allowing female leaders to flourish, develop, and grow. Being enough means we feel confident in our own capabilities. We believe in ourselves. We value the rare and beautiful gifts each of us has to offer.

Women often don't appreciate their own accomplishments, somehow believing that what they created could have been better, more flawless, or more perfect. While we might believe that these high standards are the secret to our success, in truth, never being enough keeps us exhausted, insecure, and ever on a quest believing that we need to prove our value.

Why is being enough seemingly so elusive? Many women spend too much time in the relentless pursuit of being enough, which makes us feel we are not measuring up to expectations. As we hustle to achieve our goals and objectives year after year, how do we calibrate our exertion? How do we know when to ramp up or scale back? How do we know if our efforts are truly enough?

THE THREE PITFALLS OF NOT BEING ENOUGH

When we feel we are not enough, we're willing to accept the scraps rather than believing we deserve the whole meal. We settle for what we're offered instead of selecting our opportunities. We live small when we are meant for bigger, bolder, and more expansive experiences.

When women don't allow themselves to feel that they are enough:

1. We stay too long in situations that don't serve us or deserve us.

When we stay too long in compromising circumstances, we lose out on other, better, more life-fulfilling opportunities. There is an opportunity cost inherent in being enough. Instead of settling for the opportunities we're given, we can be choosy about selecting the opportunities we want.

Drawing on The Practice of Productive Perseverance, we can engage the art and the science of knowing how and when to intelligently pursue our goals. Allowing ourselves to be enough also means knowing our value. When we stop feeling valued and appreciated, this is a strong signal to leave the situation.

Do you know your value or are you selling yourself short? Think of it this way: A bar of iron cost $5; made into horseshoes, its worth is $12; made into needles, its worth is $3,500; or made into balance springs for watches, its worth is $300,000. Like the bar of iron, your own value is determined by knowing your worth and what you decide to make of yourself.

2. We don't advocate for ourselves.

We aren't stewards of our own contributions: the music we write, the screenplays we create, the results we achieve. We minimize our contributions. Or worse, we aren't even aware of the unique talents we possess. **When we don't believe in the value of our work products, and advocate for them, our gorgeous creations may never see the light of day.** Many women don't consider jobs unless they meet 100 percent of the qualifications, whereas men will consider a role when they only have 60 percent of the qualifications.

What would happen if we subscribed to the 60/40 ratio for a role? If next time there is an open assignment and you know how to do 60 percent of a job, will you believe you can learn the other 40 percent and be successful? Instead of allowing "enough" to paralyze us, we can, instead, choose to have faith in ourselves and advocate for ourselves.

Looking back now, Barbara Corcoran, real estate mogul and host of *Shark Tank*, can appreciate how being her own advocate changed the direction of her life completely. When she thinks back to the time her boyfriend and business partner announced he was leaving her for her secretary, she sees that he attempted to deal Corcoran a crushing blow as he exited her life. He told her that she would never succeed without him.

She had two choices: to believe him or not. She chose not. He went out of business, and three months and twenty years later, Corcoran sold her real estate business for $66 million. Talk about it paying to believe in yourself! This story makes me so proud of Corcoran standing on her own two feet as an entrepreneur, determined, while she grappled with heartbreak and betrayal. I feel like we should start calling her Barbara Corcor-*can*!

3. We say yes when we mean no.

Sometimes our connection with ourselves is at odds with our connection to others. We acquiesce to agreements or circumstances that compromise our potential, joy, and capacity.

In 2003, I had front row tickets for John Mayer's concert in Washington, DC. For months, I had saved my precious money, while barely scraping by in graduate school, to purchase these coveted tickets. I had looked forward to the experience all summer, and when the time came, I requested the evening off at my waitressing job.

But when the restaurant schedule came out, I was down for the evening of the concert. I pointed out to my manager that I had requested the time off and asked if he could adjust the schedule. My manager said he needed me to work and if I did not work, he could fire me.

Despite my best efforts, I was unable to find someone to cover my shift, and when the evening of the concert came, rather than enjoying Mayer's beautiful music, I worked.

Looking back on that evening, I long to whisper in the ear of my younger self and tell her she doesn't need that waitressing job. I want to tell her she can work in another restaurant that values her and the aspects of her that make her feel alive.

I wish that rather than setting her tables, shining the silver, and polishing the glasses, my younger self decided to bolt for the door, untying her apron, and allowing it to flutter to the ground behind her, as she went to the concert and never looked back.

BEING ENOUGH IS NOT ONCE AND FOR ALL. IT IS A PROCESS.

We are all on the potter's wheel, being refined and shaped by each experience. As we spin, with each revolution, hopefully there is also a revelation. It's easy to wonder when we'll be finally formed. Done. Complete. But we are never complete. And when we consider the alternative, of being glazed and fired in a kiln, to no longer have a flexibility for change and evolution, to be put on a shelf for display to collect dust, staying on the wheel sounds much better.

I still ask myself, every day, some version of "Are you good enough?" On the best days, I allow this to be a challenge, a friendly wager between the person I am today, and the person I am becoming. On the worst days, I can say negative things to myself and feel unfit. I'm still learning. I am still on the potter's wheel. There is no place I'd rather be.

In her 2022 commencement speech at the University of Michigan, Maria Shriver admitted that she almost didn't agree to address the students at graduation. She was hesitant because of her insecurities and fears of not being qualified to offer advice.

Fears of inadequacy come in many forms.

Shriver said she worried she wouldn't be influential enough, that students would be disappointed, or that she wouldn't have compelling advice to share on such a momentous occasion. Rather than listening to her fears, she allowed what initially scared her to become her sacred opportunity to challenge her own fears. She took the stage that day and called for each student to "Go forth, believe in yourself, and act as if this world awaits your authenticity, your wildness, your guts, and your bravery. Because it does."

Some things aren't meant for us. You might fail. You might flail, but these experiences are data, an opportunity to learn, not to beat yourself down. If your deepest desires and dreams go unfulfilled despite your best efforts, it means there is something better in store. Keep showing up to be formed.

ENERGY MANAGEMENT

Being enough is related to a critical element of leadership: energy management. When we exert mental and physical energy worrying about being good enough, we have less energy for creativity, innovation, and problem-solving. Many women find themselves feeling drained and beat up by their career pursuits, even by their successes, instead of feeling energized and alive.

Being enough means we focus our energy on believing in the intrinsic value of our own strengths and talents, versus *doing* enough, where our energy is focused on preservation, proving our worth.

When we don't allow ourselves to be enough, this mind-set and view of our capabilities zaps our energy, and we lose out on opportunities, relationships, experiences, and contributions because we believe we are lacking.

When I became pregnant with my first son, I still wasn't sure I wanted to be a mom. I felt guilty and ambivalent my whole pregnancy. I also felt ungrateful knowing so many of my friends were trying to get pregnant. As a woman, shouldn't I want to be a mother? Shouldn't I feel a desire to nurture another person in my bones? I didn't. It's something so few women talk about. Yet, so real.

I was afraid of losing many things: connection to myself, my career, freedom, and so on. It didn't help that everyone said, "Life as you know it will change." Or "Say good-bye to free time as you know it." I felt that being a mom just wouldn't be enough.

My son must have known I needed a little more time, because he waited until his forty-second week to be born, and even then, he had to be induced. When he finally arrived, I fell in love. Our eyes locked, and I felt he had chosen me, and I had chosen him to journey together as mother and son in this lifetime. I experienced a fullness and joy that I hadn't anticipated or ever known.

Two and a half years later, my second son was born. I wasn't ambivalent or afraid this time, because my first son had shown me that the gifts of motherhood outweigh the sacrifices I'd feared.

It turns out that I didn't lose the things I was afraid of losing. I've made a point of deepening my connection with myself: trusting my intuition, listening to the voice within, and knowing my worth and value to be the best role model and mother that I can be.

My career has still grown and expanded. Yet, my sons' presence has given me a different lens, and now different things are more important: family, love, and relationships. My career is focused more than ever on making the world a better place and financially supporting my family, rather than on my advancement.

I did lose a lot of my freedom. But I don't mind. I love being home with my sons. Learning about them, hearing their stories, understanding how they see the world, and teaching them.

Mother's Day is a celebration for me of how I have evolved as a human and been blessed to contribute to life and learning through these precious humans. Maintaining a career, let alone becoming a single mother for a period, and founding a business certainly hasn't been easy. Yet, I wouldn't trade these lessons or this love for anything!

IT'S NOT SELFISH

Focusing on your own growth and development might sound selfish. It's difficult for us to pull away from our busy lives, from the demands of our family, friends, and coworkers so we can focus on ourselves. Research demonstrates that focusing on self-care and self-development is particularly difficult for women. We are more than twice as likely as men to sacrifice personal desires for career aspirations and, instead, serve as caregivers to our children or aging family members. During the pandemic, we saw millions of women turn in their laptops, quit their jobs cold turkey, and leave the workforce so they could care for their children at home.

SELFISH, SELFLESS, AND SELF-FULL

The worst things my parents could say to me when I was growing up were either that they were disappointed or that I was selfish. Since then, I've vacillated between not wanting to be selfish, and at times, believing that I needed to be self*less* to be liked, loved, and appreciated.

Yet, if selfish and selfless are the two poles on the continuum, there must be something in the middle, and my term for this is *self-full.* Being self-full means putting our needs, wants, desires, and dreams at the forefront of our lives.

This gives us permission to set appropriate boundaries in our relationships, and reject behavior that demeans, diminishes, and abuses us.

Being self-full means:

- Allowing ourselves to want things and have things we desire
- Putting ourselves first when it makes sense
- Refusing to always come in last
- Giving ourselves the rest, self-care, and respect that we are worthy of

Women are more likely to buy into a belief that they need to be selfless. Women are more than twice as likely to sacrifice their careers to be a caregiver to young children or adults in need. During the pandemic, we saw millions of women leave the workforce to care for children in the absence of school and daycare, and this large-scale departure was not true of men.

More than two million women left the workforce in those first few years as their personal and professional worlds collided. Many felt they had to choose between the two. While women tend to sacrifice their career, men tend to sacrifice their emotional connection with themselves and access to their feelings, a result of being told as boys that they should be tough and not emotional.

BECOMING SELF-FULL

If you feel focusing on your own development and growth is selfish, I encourage you to be self-full instead by nourishing yourself so that you can nourish others. Being self-full means embracing your strengths, having confidence in yourself, and allowing yourself to express emotions. Being self-full means fueling yourself first, so you can sustainably be and bring the best of yourself forward to the world.

If you believe that developing your resilience is selfish, think about it as being self-full, instead. This is an investment in yourself. Know that your growth and development will uplift those around you.

If it still feels selfish, remember that a rising tide lifts all boats. By way of you investing in yourself, your personal investments will pay off by enhancing the lives of the people that you do and will touch in the future.

WHY (PERCEIVED) FAILURE HITS WOMEN (AND GIRLS) SO HARD

As a card-carrying perfectionist who has been in recovery for some time, I know how deeply frightening the fear of failure can be. You do not have to avoid failure to succeed. Susannah Wellford, founder of Running Start, has trained more than fifteen thousand young women for leadership roles. She told *US News & World Report*: "You don't get to the top without significant failures."

If we're going to change the future, and value vulnerability, we've also got to flip the script for women and men around failure being a detractor, rather than a necessary and expected part of our development. When my team looked like they had bad news to share, and told me about a mistake they'd made, I would ask them, "Has this happened before?"

"No."

"Good," I would say. "The first time it happens, it's a lesson, not a mistake."

If, and only if, we fail to learn from our lessons and repeat the same behavior, then, and only then, is it a mistake.

You build confidence by learning from your failures, losses, and boo-boos. If you keep beating yourself up for failures, you have missed the point completely. Learning from failures makes you stronger.

Given that women tend to buy into the belief of perfectionism more than men, we tend to take perceived failures harder. But learning from our mistakes enhances our resilience.

SHINE ON

While there are broader systemic issues that we need to address to enhance opportunities for advancing women and women in leadership, there are also many ways each of us can encourage broader changes across our society. First and foremost, women, we have an incredible opportunity to embrace one another to a much greater degree.

Do you see that beautiful, intelligent, kind, accomplished woman standing across the room? No, you're not going to hate on her because she makes you feel insecure. She's not your competition; she's your next great collaborator. Her achievements don't diminish you; they enhance you.

Let that cascade over you. That's right. It's called the Shine Theory, coined by Ann Friedman and Aminatou Sow, coauthors of *Big Friendship*, and cohosts of the podcast *Call Your Girlfriend*. Rather than operating from a place of scarcity, believing that there is only so much light to go around, we can cultivate a belief in abundance, that there is enough light for all of us, and together, we shine even more brightly.

Female rivalry is relic of the bygone days when there was room for only one woman at the top. The truth is that, today, by celebrating the accomplishments of our fellow women, we benefit from what Ann and Amina call "the associative property of awesomeness," or the ability to shine brighter when we surround ourselves with stars.

As women, we do ourselves a great service when we focus on cooperation, rather than competition. Ending competition and being focused on collaboration begins with each one of us changing the way we think and behave.

An old friend once shared that when she saw my LinkedIn profile, she had to be mindful of not being threatened by me. She acknowledged her faulty, competitive thinking and then rejected it by saying, "She's the triple threat, smart, successful, and beautiful. If my girlfriends and I saw her out, we'd hope she was a bitch."

By circling up with our girlfriends and belittling women who make us feel less than, we are blaming others for our insecurities, rather than taking responsibility for them and healing.

When will we stop blaming women for being intimidating, and instead take responsibility to work on ourselves to be more confident? When will we stop accusing other women of taking up too much space, instead of taking responsibility for taking up so little? And when will we stop complaining that the lights of other women are too bright, instead of running up our own wattage?

Together, let's stop the rivalries with other women, and instead, revel in our shared accomplishments. That beautiful, intelligent, kind, accomplished woman standing across the proverbial room is not the reason you feel bad about yourself. She is not a threat; you are allowing yourself to buy into a mentality that her accomplishments threaten you.

I WOKE UP LIKE THIS

I woke up like this. Like a woman. As women, we have strengths, talents, and skills that we can harness and elevate to enhance our resilience. It's fascinating to me that the word *emasculate* means to deprive a man of his masculinity, yet, in the English language, there is no word for the removal of a woman's femininity. My femininity, our femininity, is so powerful that it cannot be confiscated or taken away.

While addressing the systemic elements of our society and workplaces that create confusion and perpetuate inequity, we can also focus on embracing our authentic feminine talents as leaders in the workplace. We can enhance our resilience as women by buying into our own enoughness and cultivating our ability to be self-full, confident, supportive of one another's "shining," and able to recover from failure.

12

Resilient Living—Rituals for a Resilient Life

How do you make the most of The Five Practices of Highly Resilient People? You begin with one new habit, practice, or ritual, and take one step at a time. How do you use The Five Practices to ensure you flourish rather than fold? This book is a message of change. New possibilities exist to bring you more harmony and balance. Know that any positive changes you make in your life will not only benefit you, they also will create ripple effects. Your constructive changes will enhance you and uplift those around you.

HOW DO WE CREATE MEANINGFUL CHANGE?

Start with just one small but meaningful change. On a separate piece of paper, ask yourself these questions and write down the answers:

- What are you willing to do differently to live your dreams?
- What are you willing to let go of to reach your dreams?
- How do you want to continue to heal from past trauma, loss, disappointment, and rejection?
- What limiting beliefs can you replace with more positive beliefs to create a more resilient life?

Once you've answered these questions, then ask yourself:

- What is the smallest meaningful change you can make today?

Then, write down that answer and put it in a place where you'll see it each day, like your refrigerator or your bathroom mirror.

DO ONE THING DIFFERENT

Resilience, fortunately, is not difficult to practice once we understand the framework of The Five Practices. Yet, many people think it is too hard, too difficult to understand, too lofty. You don't have to completely overhaul your life, go away and meditate for a month, or be in therapy for years to see real change when you practice the proven behaviors associated with The Five Practices.

To enhance our resilience,
we only need to do one small yet meaningful thing differently.
One new perception…
One new interaction…
One fresh thought…
One act of surrender…
One change of heart…
One change in the language we use…
One leap of faith…
One new behavior…
One new practice…

Every practice has the power to change your life forever, for the better, and by extension, the lives of your loved ones. Resilience isn't just nice to have; it is a critical set of behaviors focused on becoming and being the very best versions of ourselves. Our ability to practice it in the face of life's challenges determines, in large part, the quality and trajectory of our human lives.

Resilience runs the gamut from allowing us to show up each day as our best self, equipped to deal with life's challenges, to informing the extent of our ability to pursue our life's purpose. Even the degree to which we believe in and, ultimately, exercise our own talents and gifts over the course of our lifetime.

Now that you are aware of The Five Practices of Highly Resilient People, it's time for you to decide how you would like to incorporate this new knowledge into your life. To begin to create real and lasting change in your life, I would like to invite you to do one thing differently. Not more than one thing. Just one simple thing.

What will that be? This one small yet meaningful change is about enhancing you and your life, it's not about deprivation or restriction. Doing one thing different is about choosing a new behavior that feels good and makes you feel excited and engaged when you think about this new action you're going to take.

When we do one thing different, we have a more than 80 percent chance of success. But when we try to do two things differently, our chance of success diminishes by an astonishing 57 percent down to 33 percent.

Do not take on more than one commitment to yourself, one small but meaningful change at a time. We can't multitask important change. Don't do two things at once. What are some examples of small yet meaningful changes that my clients have taken on to kick-start change? Here are some ideas:

- Get eight hours of sleep.
- Drink one full 8-ounce glass of water each morning before breakfast or coffee or tea.
- Journal for ten minutes daily.
- Set aside time for a walk each day.
- Write down three things you are grateful for at the end of each day.
- Limit television and screen time to thirty minutes.

- Give one compliment to yourself and one compliment to someone else daily.
- Hang up your clothing at the end of the day.
- Make your bed.
- Recycle all materials that can be reused from your home.
- Bike to work one day per week.
- Write two pages of your book or novel five to seven days of the week.
- Engage in cardio for thirty minutes each day.
- Eat one more vegetable or fruit each day.
- Remove refined sugar from your diet.

And so on. What is your small yet meaningful change?

As you can see, these are not earth-shattering changes to get started. That's the point. The idea is to begin with one small yet meaningful change, and gain confidence in your ability to make a change.

If you miss a day, don't beat yourself up. In fact, being unkind to yourself is the worst thing you can do. It's like beating a dog for misbehavior, the animal becomes afraid and tentative and second-guesses itself. If you don't complete your small yet meaningful change commitment to yourself for one day, evaluate what happened, ask yourself what you can learn from the experience, and start again the next day.

Making this small but meaningful change is about making a commitment to yourself and not self-sabotaging, giving up on yourself, or talking yourself out of this change. Then, once you build confidence and competence after twenty-one days of implementing this small yet meaningful change, you can begin to stack additional behaviors on top of this initial commitment. The next small and meaningful investments are rituals.

RESILIENT RITUALS

Rituals are not about adding work to your daily routine or checking items off a to-do list. Rituals are about honoring yourself and your place in the world by taking time to focus your energy, feel into your body, calm your nervous system, and focus on being present. We spend a great deal of time in our head, and not in our heart, rehashing the past or worrying about the future, but not in the present.

Rituals take us on the longest journey, traveling the eighteen inches from our head down into our heart. Rituals get us out of our analytical mind and into our feeling mind, out of the past and future to ground us in the present. This is the only place where we can effect change.

Engaging in rituals enhances our resilience, increases our mental presence, amplifies our intentionality, and allows us to tap into our inner feeling and knowing. Rituals allow us to be more mindful, attuned to ourselves and our surroundings, and more open to the experiences that unfold in the present moment.

MORNING MEDICINE

Morning is a time when we feel mentally fresh and ready to create without the residue that collects in our minds by the end of each day. Ancient Indian texts refer to the hour and thirty-six minutes before dawn as the *Brahma muhurta*, the creator's hour.

Morning routines are powerful because they set the tone for your entire day ahead. I've never had a consistent morning routine, due to corporate work hours, daycare, and school drop-off, while sometimes squeezing in exercise. The one aspect of my morning routine that is consistent: I focus on an important aspect of my day and envision the best possible outcome.

If I am meeting a new client, I imagine them signing a partnership that will enhance their workforce and their organization while energizing and exciting me about sharing my expertise with them.

If I am coaching a client, I imagine the gains, strides, and positive impact our coaching conversation will have on both of us. If I have a particularly busy day ahead, I may take a moment to envision myself in the eye of the hurricane, everything swirling around me, and feeling the peace and calm of being centered within myself. This visualization reminds me of my power to control how I respond to storms around me.

To enhance your morning medicine ritual, ask yourself:

- *What "medicine" would you like in the morning to feel strong, centered, and balanced for the day ahead?* Perhaps you listen to the same song that pumps you up for three to four minutes before walking into the office or sitting down at your laptop.
- *Where do you want to focus your attention?* Before diving into your phone, emails, the news, and to-do list, can you take time to say a mantra or get focused on how you would like your day to unfold?
- *What is your eye of the storm?* What will support you in beginning your day with peace, enthusiasm, and energy? Is it taking your vitamins? Doing a morning meditation? Listening to a short inspirational message you recorded for yourself the evening before?

DARING TO DREAM

Setting aside time to dream about your future and envision what is possible is a powerful ritual. I have found that experiences, opportunities, and people I have taken the time to dream about coming into my life often arrive when I focus my mental energy on creating a future.

Daring to dream is like taking the time to plant the seed for your future and each time you review your dreams, you are watering the seeds you have planted. If you find yourself daring to dream, yet nothing is happening, don't be discouraged. Just like the seeds of plants in real life, the seeds of your dreams need time to germinate in fertile soil to sprout their first tender stems and leaves.

To engage in your dare-to-dream ritual:

- *Start with visualizing your dreams.* Nothing is too large or too small. Write down your dreams on a piece of paper and post it in a prominent place or look at the paper often.

- *Create a vision board.* Collect images of your dreams, inspirational quotes, and reminders of the life you love today and what you'd like to build for yourself (and your family) for the future.
- *Remind yourself of your progress.* Honor and celebrate even the smallest steps toward your goals to stay engaged and continue to maintain momentum.
- *Share your dreams with another person.* By sharing your hopes and desires with trusted friends and family members, you are more likely to achieve these goals because you've said them out loud and you've recruited the support of another person to help you stay on track.
- *Be patient with the process.* The Practice of Productive Perseverance talks about knowing when to stay, when to go, when to surrender, and how to trust the process. The most important thing you can do as you continue to believe in your dreams is to stay patient and positive. There may be no reason to believe your dreams come true. But then again, there is no reason to believe they won't.

A RITUAL TO REFLECT, RENEW, AND RESET

As you practice new behaviors and ways of being in the world through The Five Practices of Highly Resilient People, holding a ritual for yourself to create a fresh start can feel cleansing and set the tone for your next chapter of life. As you set intentions for your next phase of life, you create a new beginning for yourself. You are making space to create change within, and then, to create change in your work, relationships, and interactions with others.

To engage in a ritual to reflect, renew, and reset:

- *Choose a day to hold this ritual.* Rituals for reflection, renewal, and reset are best held at the start of the year, month, lunar cycle, or week.

- *Reflect.* As you plan for this ritual, first reflect on your life recently. On a piece of paper, draw a line down the center and make two columns with the headings "Keep" and "Let Go." Then, review the various aspects of your life, such as: How do you feel about yourself? Your body image? Your confidence? Your relationships? Your work? Your energy? Write in each column what you'd like to keep doing, experiencing, and feeling, and in the other column, write down what you'd like to change or let go of.
- *Renew.* With your reflection assessment complete, on a separate piece of paper entitled "Renew," write down what energy, experiences, feelings, opportunities, etc., you want to keep and what elements you would like to create for yourself going forward? It is important to phrase these elements positively, so you know what you are creating. For example, instead of writing, "I want to feel less alone," write, "I want to feel surrounded with an abundance of friends and family members." I would suggest you limit this to one or two new areas, beyond the items on your keep list, so you are not overwhelmed by trying to create too much change at once.
- *Reset.* Now, it's time to hold your ritual. Choose a day when you can spend time reflecting on what you are creating and renewing in this next cycle. You can mark this special day by reviewing what you wrote about renewing yourself. Then, you can light a candle and sit quietly for a few minutes, envisioning how you will renew. You can meditate, go for a hike, and keep your areas of renewed focus in your mind.
- *Reassess.* Then, set a date for the next ritual to check in on your renew items. Perhaps the beginning of each day, week, or month you can plan to do a check-in with yourself to see how it's going and continue to reassess from there.

There is no right way to conduct rituals that enhance your resilience. Simply through the practice of engaging in rituals, you bring greater focus and intention to yourself, life, feelings, and experience. Rituals effectively turn off autopilot mode, and even if you don't see as much progress or change as you would like, the act of continuing to focus on yourself and how you would like to evolve will continue to make a difference for you, and by extension the people around you over time.

There is no right or wrong way to create change and growth in your life. These rituals are suggestions for incorporating practices into your life to enhance your resilience, yet you are welcome to adjust these rituals as you see fit or create your own.

13
It's Time to Flourish

It was always only, ever, you.

Read that again.

You can be the change you want to see in yourself, and by extension, the world.

IT ALL STARTS AND ENDS WITH YOU

My twenties were about unraveling and understanding the experiences that formed me in childhood and early adulthood. My thirties were about taking responsibility for myself. My forties and beyond have been about healing and growing more into the person I want to become and creating relationships and a life that bring me joy and fulfillment.

In the beginning of this book, I shared that my own resilience has been tested and strengthened because of my lifelong challenges with severe dyslexia and the PTSD from my terrifying stalker experiences.

The dyslexia has never diminished, and has probably affected me in ways that I am not aware of because, early on, my brain found ways to work around it. It first manifested around the second grade. When talking with my parents, my teachers had praised my intelligence and leadership, but my grades did not reflect that in the second grade when I scored the lowest in my reading age group.

I had difficulty distinguishing similar words like *hoped* and *hopped*. Spelling was also a challenge. Learning to read was also difficult. This frustrated my parents. I was frustrated too. I remember thinking many times, *I'm smarter than this.* In the third grade, I was determined to score higher in reading tests. I spent hours at home, working alone to figure out spellings and word sounds and, eventually, I came up with my own mnemonic and phonetic methods to work around my dyslexia. Thank you, resilient brain wiring!

This helped my reading and writing and my academic performance, but I still find myself walking through airports and wondering about the Wood Fried Pizza advertised at a restaurant—only to realize my dyslexia had transformed "fired" into "fried." (If you ask the editors of this book, they will tell you I'm still doing that now and then in my writing too.)

Directions are still a problem for me, even with a good GPS in the car's navigation system, or the Waze app. I'll arrive home and if you ask me the route I took, I can't tell you. Another strange dyslexia symptom for me is the fact that I cannot, for the life of me, hear music in my head. You know how sometimes you will have a song stuck in your head after hearing it? I've never had that happen. But I'm not sure if that is a curse or a blessing. I guess it depends on the song, right?

So, dyslexia tested my resilience, and I passed for the most part. Like many others who have this disability, I found creative ways to work around it and did not let it limit my education or my ability to act upon career opportunities. I take no little pride in that. Meeting this challenge has made me stronger and more self-confident.

I can say the same about my PTSD from the stalker encounters, but I'm not ashamed to admit that this challenge has been the most difficult and enduring test of my resilience. Just when it seems to have subsided thanks to counseling, medications, or other means, the PTSD jabs me on the shoulder and says, "Nope, still here, kid!"

Working on this book has been cathartic in many ways, but in writing about my stalker experiences and sharing my emotions about them, I triggered my PTSD. This upset me at first, particularly because I'd told one of my editors that it didn't bother me to talk about it. Well, I was wrong.

My resilience muscles were tested again when I found myself asking why my parents hadn't done more to protect me after the first, and, especially, the second and third encounters with this lunatic. Those reflections gave rise to sadness and anger.

The other PTSD symptoms that reappeared as I wrote the book included:

- Difficulty or inability to concentrate
- Increased emotional distress and reactions when I felt threatened
- Reemerging negative thoughts about myself
- Feeling worthless, sad, listless, unvalued, and hopeless
- Volatility and short-fused anger
- Difficulty feeling positive, happy, or joyful

POST-TRAUMATIC GROWTH

When we face our challenges, it provides an opportunity to strengthen our resilience, to learn, and to grow. Although symptoms still reappear from time to time, I no longer meet the criteria for a PTSD diagnosis and haven't for many years now. By applying The Five Practices and many other strategies outlined in this book—as well as other modalities for healing that I'm exploring, perhaps for my next book—I can see the good that has come from facing my challenges.

While I wouldn't have chosen to experience traumatic events, I understand the good that has come from facing them. I am a stronger, more empathetic person. I understand fear and anxiety, which helps me in my work as an executive coach, keynote speaker, and facilitator. I know how to support people on their resilience journeys.

Having the courage to share my resilience story helped me understand the faulty nature of The Vulnerability Bias personally. It also has helped me solidify my own healing, and guide others in their healing.

I encourage everyone to share their stories, and not to be afraid of embarrassment or criticism. Talking about our mental health is critical to our well-being. I believe we have overindexed on the "disorder" aspect of PTSD. This diagnosis is not a disorder. It is a normal and natural way that our human body responds to traumatic experiences. I want more emphasis to be placed on the growth that can occur after a PTSD diagnosis.

I hope my story helps shine more light on the importance of destigmatizing mental-health issues. I want my trauma to be alchemized for good. I want to give voice to the growth and development that often follow experiences of trauma.

My challenges with dyslexia are less of an issue in the real world than they were in my school years. As a neuroatypical person, I manage my dyslexia, asking for help when I need it, and working around this learning disability. Now, my challenges are mostly about sequencing events, letters, and so on, and less about spelling and directions. I still cannot hear music in my head, and thankfully, I never again will be asked to do a geometry proof.

I learned to go with my strengths and use them to overcome my "weaknesses," which is a philosophy I share with Daymond John, the founder of FUBU clothing line who has become a television personality on the hit show *Shark Tank*. He has written and spoken extensively about his own challenges with dyslexia. His reading and spelling levels were so poor that he received low grades in language arts even though he excelled in math and science during his school years.

His father became so frustrated that he would yell at Daymond, and even after a professional therapist diagnosed him with a learning and behavioral issue, his mother refused to believe it. She told the therapist her son was brilliant but wasn't applying himself.

Like me and most other dyslexics who grow up without being diagnosed or given special help in school, Daymond used his resilience to overcome its challenges. He refused to let this one area of weakness define him. In high school, he opted for a co-op work-study program, which required less reading and writing and more practical experience in the real world. That experience launched him on his successful career as an entrepreneur.

He told an interviewer for the Yale Center for Dyslexia & Creativity: "I have this attitude about any challenges you have in life," Daymond says. "You highlight it, address it, and then find out how to work around it. Figure out how to live with it."

I agree with Daymond John. I have found that with enough resilience, I've been able to find success despite having both PTSD and dyslexia. I would not wish either of those challenges on anyone, but I wouldn't give up the unique way I've come to see the world and manage my way in it.

I love the opportunity of turning my challenges into advantages. I relate to the actress Jane Fonda, who spoke about this in a *Harvard Business Review* magazine article in 2018. Most younger people today know this iconic entertainer mostly for her role in the hit Netflix comedy *Grace and Frankie*, but she has shown great resilience over her long career. She has been celebrated for her acting, her beauty, and her courage in taking stands on the Vietnam War and societal issues. Yet, she has also been a controversial figure criticized for her political stances and lifestyle choices. So, when I read that she said there isn't a single person who hasn't experienced loss, hurt, pain, and trauma, I knew she was speaking from experience:

"During my childhood, I could have gone down a dark hole, but my resilience was like radar constantly scanning the horizon, picking up on heat from anybody who could give me love or teach me something. Resilient people can turn their wounds into swords and ploughshares. They can become the strongest and most powerful warriors for good. God comes to us through our scars and our wounds, not our awards and our acclamations."

Yes, you can turn your wounds into swords and ploughshares. Embrace the reality that you always have been and always will be the author of your own life, then you can stop pointing out all the reasons why you can't do what you desire, and you finally see clearly that it was always, only, ever, you anyway.

There's no one else who can heal, develop, learn, actualize, forgive, and grow for you. It was always only ever you. This work is your work and your work alone. It's the universal journey we all take into the unique constellation of experiences that have formed us.

RESILIENCE IS WITHIN YOUR CONTROL

If you lose your job, or incur an injury—any time you are faced with a challenge, you need to know that you have the strength and determination to handle it and move forward to flourish.

While circumstances may be beyond your control, your resilience is absolutely within your control. The Kauai Longitudinal Study is the only study to date that has examined development from birth to midlife (until the age of forty). The study looked at the impact of biological and psychosocial risk factors, stressful life events, and protective factors on a multiracial group of 698 children born in 1955 on the Hawaiian island of Kauai, which is the westernmost county in the United States. The researchers found that, while much of the children's circumstances were outside of their control, their response to those circumstances were not.

While resilient thinking is valuable, when you face challenge, you want to know what to *do*. The Five Practices of Highly Resilient People provides you with an action plan, no matter what action is required. The Five Practices promote resilience. Given that we live in a time marked by both increasing and significant challenges, resilient "doing" is even more important than resilient thinking.

THE SIMPLE POWER OF CHOICE

When you understand that you have a choice in your response, you are free to not simply default to what you have done in the past, or to the role modeling you have internalized from others, but instead, to be the active author of your life.

You always have a choice. Always. Even when your options are not good.

I often hear people say, "Well, I didn't have a choice, so..."

Nope. Stop right there. You can pursue cancer treatment or not. You can stay in the dead-end job or not. You can continue in the relationship or not. There are always at least two doors you can open and walk through.

You tap into your ability to control your environment and your future by exercising your power of choice. Not making a choice is also a decision. Lack of action is passive. You decide even when you do not make a choice.

As adults, our selections are not the responsibility of others, and cannot be ceded to others. Once we recognize we have at least one decision at our fingertips, the next step is determining what to select. When faced with each of these experiences, we may feel overwhelmed, scared, or anxious in the face of choice. These emotions may make it appear as though our array of options is more limited.

When we give up the fight for control, we allow ourselves to accept what is. When we can't control what's happening, we need to challenge ourselves to control the way we respond to what's happening. This is where the real power is. To have faith is to live without being wedded to a particular outcome. It is the ability to cocreate our experience with the forces of life greater than ourselves, rather than strong-arming fate with the brute force of our free will.

THE CHOICE IS YOURS

What we do have control over is our choices. Specifically, we have a choice about our behaviors every single time we face a challenge. Therefore, resilience is not outside of our control. Resilience begins with a choice. Resilience begins with us.

We can engage in behaviors that foster even greater resilience. The Five Practices are the behaviors that serve as spiritual scaffolding—a framework that supports us in choosing the most productive and positive behaviors when we face difficult times. The Five Practices promise to support our navigation through the most complex time in human history.

Instead of allowing complexity, digital impressions, and the amount of change and challenge to overrun our psyche, The Five Practices are an accessible way for us to access greater resilience. They empower us to change our behavior, so that over time, like the airplane charting its destination through incremental choices and subtle course corrections, the aggregate of our decisions leads to resilience that brings forth new and greater opportunities.

Our energy may be unlimited, but our time is not. That means that by choosing a resilient behavior in the face of challenge, we are making a trade-off decision to not choose another, less resilient behavior. Our time is limited in that we do not have the luxury of trying out an array of responses. Our choices of what resilient behavior to exhibit mean we can determine whether we ultimately stumble or soar. We are the authors of whether a given experience makes us better or makes us bitter.

By way of choosing The Five Practices, we choose behavior that effectively addresses the hardships that life inevitably sends our way. Oftentimes, when challenge shows up in our lives, we believe the only options we have are flight, fight, or freeze. The Five Practices expand our choices. They provide an evidence-based framework, based on two decades of research, for making choices that create a more positive and productive outcome whenever we face adversities.

THE SECOND SUMMIT

Many of us are on a journey to what I call the first summit. Climbing the first summit is the pursuit of financial solvency and stability. It can include finding a way to support our family, pay our bills, afford a vacation or a new car, and save for retirement. Getting to the first summit takes many people an entire lifetime. Many struggle to achieve financial security. Just making ends meet is difficult enough. For those still climbing the first summit, The Five Practices can help them address challenges. If they reach financial stability, then the second summit I have identified is finding purpose, the place where their professional and personal goals align in a powerful synergy. Some find their purpose outside of their work entirely, maybe as volunteers serving others with their time and talents, for example.

For those climbing the second summit, The Five Practices are focused on providing guidance, meaning, and the tools to keep striving to find a life of deeper purpose beyond the pursuit of profit. I have worked with many entrepreneurs who have left the companies they have founded, and successful people who have achieved financial stability and are still on the journey toward identifying and living their purpose.

Those who have built wealth often feel more unease or even lost on their journey to the second summit because they had thought their wealth would make them feel fulfilled, but it has not. Once we have enough financial resources to meet our regular needs, to pay our mortgage or rent, utilities, for our cars, cell phones, clothing, and groceries, more financial resources don't make us exponentially happier. Many people climbing the second summit often are confused by that.

When the "shoulds" show up, they wonder why they are not happier and more at ease. Instead, they feel worse for not feeling the way they believe they should. This separation between what is and the way they believe they should feel creates feelings of depression, anxiety, shame, disappointment, imposter syndrome, frustration, isolation, and anger, to name a few.

For some people who have reached the top of the first summit, they may not even realize there is a second, more fulfilling summit, the journey from profit to purpose. If you feel as though you've reached your financial goals, but still don't feel fulfilled, you are likely embarking on your second summit. You are probably on that journey if you have said to yourself, "There has to be something more."

Whether you are climbing your first or second summit, whether you're providing for the essentials or looking to give back, while there will continue to be adversities to deal with, there is opportunity to give back.

If your questions and pursuits are more focused on the existential than the financial, The Five Practices will help you look more deeply into the life you've created, whether you're en route to the first or second summit, and help you explore how to fulfill your life's purpose on your journey.

CHALLENGE CATALYZES

Challenges and adversities create fundamental and forever changes that can serve as opportunities to move forward. In those daunting moments, you can shed old ways that were unproductive and move on to greater opportunities for growth. So, when facing challenges, welcome them as progressive steps up a staircase that will elevate your life.

A TALE OF TWO CITIES

The Three C's are the fabric of our human experience, and these encounters, for each of us, weave a rich tapestry of growth and development. We're never done with our formation. There will be moments in our lives that are the best of times, and there will be moments in our lives that are the worst of times. Here is a tale of two cities:

A former executive colleague living in Rancho Cucamonga, California, in addition to his successful career, also dreamed of being a country music songwriter. Inspired to explore his dreams after hearing my keynote on resilience, he went to Nashville to pursue the yearning he felt deeply within himself to write country songs. While still maintaining his "day job," and to his great surprise, within just two years, a short period of time in the world of country music songwriting, one of his songs was released by a prominent country singer as a single and performed at the Grand Ole Opry, perhaps the most prestigious country music concert stage in the world. This was an entirely unexpected high-high. He described the moment as being "a need-the-jaws-of-life-to-get-my-head-out-of-the-ceiling moment."

So, then, he was a successful executive leading an innovative team, living out his dream as a country music songwriter, with an adoring wife, two adult children, and a beloved dog.

Life was good. But then, his circumstances changed dramatically.

His executive position was eliminated; his mother and his dog died within a month of each other. His father was having heart problems and his father-in-law was placed in hospice. At the same time, his stepson and wife were having severe marital problems that were impacting their two sweet daughters.

When I asked him how he was doing considering the magnitude of challenges he faced, the former colleague said, "I hope it's okay to cry a lot and still be resilient."

I told him it was okay to cry, without a doubt.

He then told me that his life had become a living, breathing country song.

I had another colleague from nearby Calabasas, California, who impressed me with her savvy, intelligence, and incredible talent. She had just taken her "dream job," only to discover after a short time that the job wasn't what she'd hoped it would be.

She received little training and was being asked to do work that was outside the scope of her role and beyond her expertise. Her manager canceled their one-on-one meetings, and she had difficulty getting him to respond to her questions. He refused to give her directions or coaching in her new position.

As she described the landscape of her company to me, I noted several red flags about her job security and advised her to begin looking for a new position.

A week later, she was let go. She was hurt and confused, which is understandable because her confidence had taken a hit. She felt adrift. I encouraged her to look for other opportunities.

Less than ninety days later, she told me she'd found a new high-ranking job with a wonderful company doing work she loved. She also was working on a new music album, and her children and husband were thriving.

She was feeling fit thanks to a new workout routine, and she had been chosen for a national award for service to her sorority.

Just like my friend living in Rancho Cucamonga, she had faced a challenge, but she had been resilient and bounced forward. I encouraged her to soak in every ounce of the joy and goodness.

This tale of two cities demonstrates that for some of us, it is the best of times, and for others, the worst of times, and our fortunes and experiences are always shifting. We will inevitably face the summits of high highs and the valleys of the low lows. None of it is permanent.

One minute, you may be living the dream, and the next, you may be picking up the pieces of a life torn apart by circumstances beyond your control. Resilience allows you to find your way through the rubble to a better existence.

DREAMS ARE DEMANDING

As I finish this book, I am in the thick of it right now. In the thick of writing, yes, but more so exhaustion. On Mother's Day, my younger son gave me a card that said, "I hope you finish the book." Two months later, working nearly every weekend day for ten to twelve hours, it was July Fourth weekend. Once again, I missed out on just about everything: swimming, the amusement park, movies, catching lightning bugs, reading nighttime stories, and bedtime snuggles. I watch on social media as friends go to barbecues and the beach, while I sit, feeling handcuffed to my desk. Here I am, I think, writing, working, while everyone else has fun. It's a privilege to write a book. Yes, yes, it is. I remind myself that this was and still is my dream. This is a dream I waited patiently, and sometimes not so patiently, for over three years to realize, until I found just the right publisher. For a long time, I didn't know if this book would become a reality. I didn't know if I would get to have the feeling and experience of becoming an author. Signing with a top publisher has been a long-held dream, and I am immensely grateful.

The other side of the coin is feeling disgruntled. What I am realizing is that dreams can be demanding. I share this with you right now to give you a peek into my vulnerability. Writing this book has me calling in just about every resilient fiber of my being. It might sound silly, but these last few months, I have felt like a mess. I am worn out, exhausted, and on edge from hours and hours of writing on many nights and almost every weekend. During the week, I run my own consulting and coaching practice, so each work week flows into the next without a break. I'm still committed and excited about publishing this shiny new book for all of you, and it's been a slog. I've been worrying a lot when I write too. Worry that this book won't become what I hope it will be. That you won't like this book. I worry I am missing too much of my children's lives, watching them play and laugh from the window of my office. I am missing moments I can never get back, I think to myself. This feels awful.

I don't have any easy answers or pithy outcomes to share yet. Right now, I am in the mess, the middle of creating something without knowing the outcome, leaning on hope and my willingness to dream into reality the book I have always desired to create. I don't know how it'll turn out. If it'll all be worth it. I promise to tell you what I've learned since and how it turned out on the book tour, okay?

WHY WE NEED RESILIENCE MORE THAN EVER

Some people have shared with me that they are tired of resilience. They dream of never being called resilient again. They are exhausted by being strong and holding it all together. When I hear these comments, I remind people of two important truths:

1. Resilience is not about being strong and holding it all together, as we have learned.
2. We are not exhausted by resilience; we are exhausted and overwhelmed by the unprecedented magnitude and volume of The Three C's we have faced in these recent times.

Most of us, at any given time, are facing more than one challenge. When more than one challenge arrives in our lives, The Five Practices become even more important because the greater the magnitude and volume of challenges we face, without resilience, the greater the likelihood that we will experience an adverse impact from these challenges.

YOUR RESILIENCE MOVEMENT

The moment you choose resilience is the moment you create momentum for change in your life. This momentum creates a movement. This is now your resilience movement. You are the author of your life, the architect of your experiences.

So, what do you do now? Will you continue to pursue being one of the 5 percent? If the answer is yes, you have at your fingertips The Five Practices along with practical tips for implementing changes that will create even more resilience in your life, allowing you to continue to flourish, instead of fold.

WHAT GOT YOU HERE WON'T GET YOU THERE

I belong to a top 100 coaches organization created by one of my mentors, Marshall Goldsmith, who is credited with creating the 360-degree feedback tool. In his book *What Got You Here Won't Get You There*, he wrote that we can change our behavior and thinking each time we take our lives or careers to the next level.

What worked for someone as a director-level employee will likely need to evolve as that person ascends to the senior director and vice president levels. What worked for a woman as a single person won't be acceptable when she is in a committed relationship, and the way parents conducted their lives prior to children will need to change once the responsibility of parenting is upon them.

Similarly, what worked for you before you read this book, your thinking, choices, and actions, are now ripe for a radical upgrade with this new information and the framework of The Five Practices.

All of us desire to experience new achievements, and the manifestation of our dreams. If you continue to do what you always did, you'll get what you always got.

With the new learning from this book, you have an opportunity to do many things in your life differently and experience entirely new outcomes. Many of these changes will feel exciting, invigorating, and energizing. Other changes you make will feel frightening at first. Remember, when you feel afraid, the presence of fear is not a reason to avoid trying something different, fresh, and new; instead, fear is often a marker that, within what makes us feel scared, our most sacred development experience awaits. Making change means you'll continue to hone the behaviors that will support you in creating more positive and productive outcomes. However, The Five Practices will not keep you from facing challenge, they will not inoculate you from pain or loss.

PAIN

The changes you imagine making may be letting go of old ways of being, old ways of believing, and former relationships that no longer serve you. Anytime we decide that an aspect of our lives has come to an end, there can be grief, loss, and pain associated with leaving behind elements of ourselves that no longer serve our best selves and the person we are becoming.

Development and growth are inviting; they can also be painful, just like growing pains we experienced as children, when our joints ached, as our body continued to grow into a more evolved form. While it is human to attempt to avoid pain and seek pleasure, pain is a powerful agent in our formation.

In my experience, God doesn't waste a drop of pain in our formation, and even though it may not be apparent in the moment, or long after the pain has passed, each drop of pain we experience has purpose.

As we part ways and this book comes to an end, I would like to leave you with a poem that I wrote about loss and letting go, whether it is our choice or not, and allowing the river of life to carry us toward our growth. Even if, in the moment, we don't understand the "why" of something happening to us, we can evoke our empowerment circle and take ownership of what is in our control, make choices about how to demonstrate resilience through The Five Practices, while we surrender to what is and trust the process.

NECESSARY LOSSES

Losses are often an inevitable part of growth. Yet, know that loss, like the crowd of sorrows that sweep your figurative house clean of all its furniture, doesn't mean the experience of being cleaned out is any less painful.

I believe in God and a divine plan that is bigger than me and the free will I exert during this life. My faith supports me when I face losses that are unexpected, don't make sense, and are deeply painful.

One of the least helpful phrases often said to those who have experienced loss is "Everything happens for a reason." This phrase orients us to search for a reason why that exists outside of ourselves. Instead, I believe we have the answers we need within ourselves.

I've asked "Why?" countless times, searching for a reason, but when I looked within myself and asked "Why?" I realized I was the only one who could answer that question. Rather than telling people that "Everything happens for a reason," I suggest we offer, "My hope for you is that one day this will all make sense."

When I experienced an untimely loss, I wrote the following poem:

ONE DAY IT WILL ALL MAKE SENSE

One day it will all make sense.
Every bit of it.
We'll see this journey as one long blessed road leading us home,

back to our true selves and our higher purpose.
We'll understand that every drop of pain, anguish, and fear was necessary.
We'll see that none of it will be wasted, and
we'll see that the pain was a gift that brought us greater joy and meaning.
Until then, we breathe.
We show up.
We do our best.
We learn.
We listen.
We tell the truth.
We respond gently, lovingly, and honorably to the highest extent.
We allow all of this to be, to form us, and to guide our path, trusting the process, into the great unknown.
Trust in the wisdom of your journey, trust in the alchemy of your healing, trust in the process, trust in the timing, trust your ability to face this, and trust your magic.
If you asked me the one thing, I would tell you to:
Trust yourself.
Trust your intuition.
Trust your knowing.

We get all fouled up when we listen to others, when we think others know better, when we go against our truest truth, when we don't believe our own eyes, ears, and gut. Trust in your beliefs and experience, and your internal compass will not lead you astray.

STUMBLING TOWARD RESILIENCE

You will fall. It's not *if* you fall, it's when. Take stock of what made you stumble. Then, with the greatest dignity and grace you can muster, stand up again.

Do not judge yourself by how many times you stumble or fall, but by how many times you have the courage and fortitude to stand up again.

Our resilience stories change us. Each challenge faced, battle won, or adversity endured leaves its mark.

But at the end of the day, you are NOT what happens to you.

You are not defined by your mistakes, and you are not defined by your successes.

You are defined by how you rise to meet each moment.

With resilience, vulnerability, hope, and courage.

YOU MATTER

Last thing: You matter. Shush. Don't argue.

You matter.

There has never been a person on this planet exactly like you, and there never will be again. That means that the unique elements of who you are, your strengths and talents, have never graced the surface of this planet, and after you're gone, we'll never ever have anyone like you again.

While you're here, I hope you make your presence matter.

You do that by being the best version of yourself you can possibly be so that those you touch directly and those you touch indirectly get the very best of what you uniquely have to offer.

Why did you pick up this book? Were you looking for a permission slip? A way out? A way to make sense of what is happening in your life? To change your life? To be more resilient?

Have you found what you were looking for? I hope so. What I can tell you is, you have everything within you to tackle the hell outta the life in front of you. If you've already started making changes, congratulations! If you haven't started, start now. Remember, someday is not a day.

Remember that you are both a masterpiece and a work in progress. You are perfect, just as you are in this moment, a true masterpiece. As a work in progress, you are also constantly shifting, changing, and growing. Take comfort in knowing that you are perfectly and wonderfully made and that you have the capacity for development and expansion. Just as resilience isn't a once-and-for-all destination—it is taking one step at a time and tackling adversity—your evolution as a person will never be complete. You get to be reminded that you are both a masterpiece and a work in progress and navigate the dichotomy of being wonderful just as you are while also being on a journey in which you are continually transforming.

Remember that you were already resilient. Now, you know how to recognize, harness, and expand your resilience. I'll be right here by your side as you step out of your comfort zone and get into your performance zone to grow, heal, and develop. Remember the movie *Dumbo*, about the flying elephant, when the crows convinced Dumbo that he needed a magic feather to fly? You are your own magic feather. You have always had within you everything you need to face challenge, demonstrate resilience, and live an amazing life.

When we align the way we live with our deepest truth and truest purpose, our lives align with us. Very few things, including The Three C's, last forever.

Say yes to the adventure because (almost) nothing lasts forever.

Saying yes to being more resilient is saying yes to the adventure that resilience has to offer. Remember, when you face adversity, The Five Practices of Highly Resilient People will ensure that you will always bounce forward, not back. That you have the skills and tools to flourish, even when others may fold.

Thank you for being here on this journey with me and for reading this book. I am grateful to have you as one of the hearts, minds, and voices that are creating our resilient movement. The best is yet to come.

—With gratitude, Dr. Taryn Marie

ACKNOWLEDGMENTS AND GRATITUDE

First and foremost, for Samson and Sawyer: you have taught me the meaning of unconditional love, friendship, how to be a resilient parent, and what it means for my heart to walk around outside of my body. I've loved you since before you were born, and I will love you for eternity.

For every challenge, change, and complexity (The Three C's) that has arrived on the doorstep of my life. I have been your unwitting student, and you have been my teacher. For every rejection, you have been a redirection. For every setback, you have been a well-disguised setup for the next great opportunity.

For my literary agent, Shannon Marven, for believing in me and my work on resilience, for seeing the possibility, and for being both an incredible guide and a student of this work. I am endlessly grateful for your empathy, intelligence, and dedication to your craft.

For the Collideoscope team, for introducing me to Shannon Marven. I will be forever grateful!

For my brilliant editor, Lauren Marino, and the entire Hachette team.

For Gene Rapisardi, for offering to carry my books on my book tour since before there was a book or a tour.

For Palak Patel, my dear friend, unicorn, accomplice in adventure, the little sister I always wanted, and the best vegan chef.

For Mona Patel: you always inspire and uplift me. You are bringing my average way up by being in your presence.

For Hayley Hughes, who spent countless hours helping me review the empirical literature for this book and ensured that I was up to date on the resilience literature. I am deeply grateful for your investment in bringing this book to life.

For Jane Fish, who has been with me from the beginning and created all the beautiful graphics you see in this book. You have allowed me and so many others to "see" the visual representations of resilience that I have only been able to describe in words. I am eternally grateful that you share your tremendous talents with me and RLI!

For Kseniya Berson, who has been my go-to person for photography for forever and shot the photo of me for this book cover. You're hilarious and driven, funny and kind, and beautiful and humble. Your presence raises the bar for everyone you meet, in all the best ways.

Dr. Bonnie Braun, for the opportunity to look deeply into the experience of women from low-income rural families, to read their personal and poignant interviews, and to bring their stories to light. To the women who participated in this study, as part of the University of Maryland's extension program, I honor your journey, admire your strength and candor, and thank you for teaching me about resilience. Also, to Joanna, formerly Waldman, along with Dr. Braun, for being my coauthor on "Hidden Hurdles to Resiliency." I knew this was my first paper on resilience, at the time. I didn't know then that it would be the first of many!

For every person who has sustained a neurological injury and your family members with whom I have met or corresponded, a heartfelt thank-you to you for sharing the most personal and profoundly vulnerable elements of your journey with me. Thank you for your candor and authenticity; you have taught me about the meaning of resilience and inspired me to appreciate the power of resilience to a much greater degree through your stories and lived experience.

For all of my *Flourish or Fold: Stories of Resilience* podcast guests, who generously share your "behind the scenes" stories with the world, thank you for demonstrating that The Three C's are inherent in everyone's lives and accompany every accomplishment, no matter how seamless it may appear from the outside. To all our *Flourish or Fold* listeners, thank you for being a part of this beautiful show we have created and for your faithful investment of your time in these conversations.

To every person alive, as well as those that have passed on, for generously allowing me to share their stories for the purpose of underscoring the power and potency of resilience in our lives. In the spirit of The Resilient Practice of Grati-osity, I am filled with gratitude for your generosity.

NOTES

Introduction: Resilience—The Essence of Being Human

Jon Clifton, *Blindspot: The Rise of Unhappiness and How Leaders Missed It* (Washington, DC: Gallup Press, 2022).

"Resilience in an Age of Uncertainty" (white paper), BetterUp, https://grow.betterup.com/resources/resilience-in-an-age-of-uncertainty.

T. M. Dezfulian, J. Waldman, and B. Braun, "Hidden Hurdles to Resiliency," *Family Focus* 50 (2005): 3, 12.

J. C. Arrango-Lasprilla et al., "Traumatic Brain Injury and Functional Outcomes," *Journal of Head Trauma Rehabilitation* 21, no. 5 (2005): 422–423, https://pubmed.ncbi.nlm.nih.gov/17653944/.

Chapter One: Challenge Cultivates Resilience

Elizabeth Gilbert, *Big Magic: Creative Living Beyond Fear* (New York: Riverhead Books, 2015).

Chapter Two: The Five Myths and Truths of Resilient People

Diane Contu, "How Resilience Works," *Harvard Business Review*, May 2002, https://hbr.org/2002/05/how-resilience-works.

Daniel Honan, "The Stockdale Paradox: How Optimism Creates Resilience," Big Think, November 9, 2012, https://bigthink.com/articles/the-stockdale-paradox-how-optimism-creates-resilience.

Chapter Four: The Practice of Vulnerability

Margery Williams, *The Velveteen Rabbit* (New York: Doubleday, 1922).

"Air Jordan III: The Shocking Story of the Greatest Shoe Michael Jordan Never Wanted," Mental Floss, July 31, 2015, https://www.mentalfloss.com/article/584677/air-jordan-iii-shocking-story-greatest-shoe-michael-jordan-never-wanted.

Chapter Five: The Practice of Productive Perseverance

Angela Duckworth. *Grit: The Power of Passion and Perseverance* (New York: Scribner, 2016).

Arianna Huffington, "Resilience+: My Word of the Year," Thrive Global, https://thriveglobal.com/stories/arianna-huffington-resilience-plus-word-of-year-2022/.

Flourish or Fold: Stories of Resilience podcast with Terrill Haigler, https://www.resilience-leadership.com/flourish-or-fold-stories-of-resilience.

Tyra Banks, "Personal Brand Power," *Masters of Scale* podcast #82, https://mastersofscale.com/tyra-banks.

"Valedictorian Shares Important Life Lesson | Kyle Martin Speech," *Goalcast*, February 25, 2020, https://www.youtube.com/watch?v=vJNh_A-LlvA.

Bonnie Ware, *Top Five Regrets Expressed by the Dying: A Life Transformed by the Dearly Departing* (Carlsbad, CA: Hay House, 2019).

Flourish or Fold: Stories of Resilience podcast with Heidi Powell, https://www.resilience-leadership.com/flourish-or-fold-stories-of-resilience.

Flourish or Fold: Stories of Resilience podcast with Amberly Lago, https://www.resilience-leadership.com/flourish-or-fold-stories-of-resilience.

Chapter Six: The Practice of Connection

"Ben Nemtin: From Crippling Depression to Playing Hoops with Obama" podcast, *Ideas Elevated*, Comcast NBCUniversal LIFT Labs, December 11, 2019, https://lift.comcast.com/podcasts/ben-nemtin.

Flourish or Fold: Stories of Resilience podcast with Chase Bell, https://www.resilience-leadership.com/flourish-or-fold-stories-of-resilience.

Flourish or Fold: Stories of Resilience podcast with Seth Joyner, https://www.resilience-leadership.com/flourish-or-fold-stories-of-resilience.

Elizabeth Edwards, *Resilience: Reflections on the Burdens and Gifts of Facing Life's Adversities* (New York: Crown Archetype, 2009).

Cigna, *Loneliness and the Workplace: 2020 U.S. Report*, https://www.cigna.com/static/www-cigna-com/docs/about-us/newsroom/studies-and-reports/combatting-loneliness/cigna-2020-loneliness-report.pdf.

Amanda Palmer, *The Art of Asking*, TED Talk, March 1, 2103, https://www.ted.com/talks/amanda_palmer_the_art_of_asking?language=en.

Flourish or Fold: Stories of Resilience podcast with Natalie Egan, https://www.resilience-leadership.com/flourish-or-fold-stories-of-resilience.

R. Graber, R. Turner, and A. Madill, "Best Friends and Better Coping: Facilitating Psychological Resilience Through Boys' and Girls' Closest Friendships," *British Journal of Psychology* 107, no. 2 (2016): 338–358, https://pubmed.ncbi.nlm.nih.gov/26110231.

Aimee Groth, "You're the Average of the Five People You Spend the Most Time With," *Business Insider*, July 24, 2012, https://www.businessinsider.com/jim-rohn-youre-the-average-of-the-five-people-you-spend-the-most-time-with-2012-7.

Chapter Seven: The Practice of Grati-osity

Robert Emmons and Anjli Mishra, "Why Gratitude Enhances Wellbeing. What We Know. What We Need to Know," chap. 16 in *Designing Positive Psychology: Taking Stock and Moving Forward*, ed. Kennon M. Sheldon, Todd B. Kashdan, and Michael F. Steger (New York: Oxford University Press, 2011).

Robert A. Emmons, *Gratitude Works! A 21-Day Program for Creating Emotional Prosperity* (San Francisco: Jossey-Bass, 2013).

"The Science of Gratitude & How to Build a Gratitude Practice," *Huberman Lab* podcast #47, November 22, 2021, https://www.youtube.com/watch?v=KVjfFN89qvQ; Andrew Huberman's notes for same, November 25, 2021, https://podcastnotes.org/huberman-lab/episode-47-the-science-of-gratitude-how-to-build-gratitude-practice-huberman-lab/.

Stephen Covey. *The Seven Habits of Highly Effective People: Powerful Lessons in Personal Change* (New York: Fireside, 1990).

Evan Walker, Elizabeth Bruns, and Gurpreet Dhaliwal, "The VA My Life My Story Project: Keeping Medical Students and Veterans Socially Connected While Physically Distanced," *Federal Practitioner* 38, no. 12 (2021): 568–573, https://pubmed.ncbi.nlm.nih.gov/35177886/.

Chapter Eight: The Practice of Possibility

"Journey Finds Replacement Singer on YouTube," Wired, December 5, 2007, https://www.wired.com/2007/12/journeys-replac/.

"Meet Journey's New Singer—Arnel Pineda," People YouTube, June 26, 2008, https://www.youtube.com/watch?v=VccPl_uLpWA.

P. O'Connor, "Tolerance of Ambiguity: A Critical Future Fit Skill for the Evolved World of Work," *HR Future*, October 26, 2021, https://www.hrfuture.net/future-of-work/trending/tolerance-of-ambiguity-a-critical-future-fit-skill-for-the-evolved-world-of-work.

Chapter Nine: Resilient Parenting

Glennon Doyle, *Love Warrior: A Memoir* (New York: Flatiron Books, 2017).

Marshall B. Rosenberg, *Nonviolent Communication: A Language of Life* (Encinitas, CA: PuddleDancer Press, 2015).

Flourish or Fold: Stories of Resilience podcast with Heidi Powell, https://www.resilience-leadership.com/flourish-or-fold-stories-of-resilience.

Chapter Ten: Resilient Leaders, Teams, and Organizations

"The Resilience Imperative: Succeeding in Uncertain Times," McKinsey, May 17, 2021, https://www.mckinsey.com/business-functions/risk-and-resilience/our-insights/the-resilience-imperative-succeeding-in-uncertain-times.

Tim Cook, "This Is Tim: Apple's Q4 2020 Call with Analysts" (transcript), Six Colors, October 2020, https://sixcolors.com/post/2020/10/this-is-tim-apples-q4-2020-call-with-analysts-transcribed.

Keith Ferrazzi. "Resilience Is a Team Sport." *Forbes*. July 16, 2020, https://www.forbes.com/sites/keithferrazzi/2020/07/16/resilience-is-a-team-sport/?sh=57115c94fbf4.

Keith Ferrazzi, Kian Gohar, and Noel Weyrich, *Competing in the New World of Work: How Radical Adaptability Separates the Best from the Rest* (Boston: Harvard Business Review Press, 2022).

Charles Duhigg, "What Google Learned from Its Quest to Build the Perfect Team," *New York Times Magazine*, February 25, 2016, https://www.nytimes.com/2016/02/28/magazine/what-google-learned-from-its-quest-to-build-the-perfect-team.html.

Cigna, *Loneliness and the Workplace: 2020 U.S. Report*, https://www.cigna.com/static/www-cigna-com/docs/about-us/newsroom/studies-and-reports/combatting-loneliness/cigna-2020-loneliness-report.pdf.

Chapter Thirteen: It's Time to Flourish

Gabriel Joseph-Dezaize, "Life's Work: An Interview with Jane Fonda," *Harvard Business Review*, March–April 2018, https://hbr.org/search?term=gabriel%20joseph-dezaize.

E. E. Werner, "Risk, Resilience, and Recovery: Perspectives from the Kauai Longitudinal Study," *Development and Psychopathology* 5 (1993): 503–515.

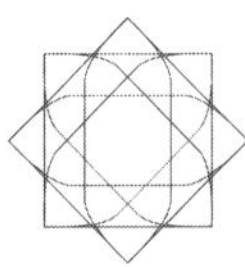

DR. TARYN MARIE

RESILIENCE LEADERSHIP INSTITUTE

Unlock Your Potential to Harness Resilience, Mental Health, and Well-being

---

You can learn more about Dr. Taryn Marie Stejskal and how she can help you and your organization on her website. **Scan the QR Code.**